# BRACERO RAILROADERS

# BRACERO RAILROADERS

## THE FORGOTTEN WORLD WAR II STORY OF MEXICAN WORKERS IN THE U.S. WEST

## Erasmo Gamboa

University of Washington Press

Seattle • London

© 2016 by the University of Washington Press
Printed and bound in the United States of America
Design: Dustin Kilgore
Typeset in Cassia, designed by Dietrich Hofrichter
20   19   18   17   16      5   4   3   2   1

**University of Washington Press**
*www.washington.edu/uwpress*

Library of Congress Cataloging-in-Publication Data
Names: Gamboa, Erasmo, author.
Title: Bracero railroaders : the forgotten World War II story of Mexican
    workers in the U.S. West / Erasmo Gamboa.
Other titles: Forgotten World War II story of Mexican workers in the U.S. West
Description: 1st edition. | Seattle : University of Washington Press, [2016] |
    Includes bibliographical references and index.
Identifiers: LCCN 2016007087 | ISBN 9780295998329 (hardcover : alk. paper)
Subjects: LCSH: Foreign workers, Mexican—United States—History—20th
    century. | Railroads—United States—Employees—History—20th century.
    | World War, 1939–1945—Manpower—United States. | World War,
    1939–1945—War work—United States. | Railroads—United States—
    History—20th century. | United States—Emigration and immigration—
    Government policy—History—20th century. | Mexico—Emigration and
    immigration—Government policy—History—20th century. | World War,
    1939–1945—Participation, Mexican American. | World War, 1939–1945—
    Economic aspects—United States. | Railroads—West (U.S.)—History—20th
    century.
Classification: LCC HD8039.R12 U634 2016 | DDC 331.6/2687207809044—
    dc23
LC record available at http://lccn.loc.gov/2016007087

*For Adriana Cristina,*
*Andrea Elena, and Carole*

# Contents

*Illustrations follow page 94*

# Preface and Acknowledgments

**W**hen the final story of the American railroads has been written, a chapter of interest and significance will record the substantial part that Mexicans played in helping to maintain thousands of miles of war-burdened tracks at a time when, without this labor, these tracks would surely have been seriously weakened, with unquestionably adverse effect upon the war effort. It was a fortunate day back in May 1943 when the state departments of the two countries, in conjunction with the War Manpower Commission and immigration officers, negotiated agreements permitting the entry of six thousand Mexican citizens into the United States for unskilled labor on the railroads, a number that was increased to twenty thousand in June of that year, to forty thousand in March 1944, to fifty thousand the following July, and, early March 1945, to a new ceiling of seventy-five thousand.[1]

## ACKNOWLEDGMENTS

Several early influences inspired this book on the World War II bracero railroad workers. I grew up in rural Washington State, where trains and railroad tracks intersected with everyone's daily lives. My father, Gumecindo Gamboa, shared his memories with me about working on the railroad during the 1920s. The railroad had taken him and his friends far away from Edinburg, Texas, to Ohio and West Virginia. The omnipresent trains of my youth, coupled with my father's railroad history, led to a personal interest in learning more about Mexican track laborers. As a historian, I had written about bracero agricultural workers in the Pacific Northwest during World War II. I realized that I had overlooked the important experiences of the wartime bracero railroad workers. This omission motivated me to write the forgotten story of more than one hundred thousand Mexican braceros employed in the U.S., maintaining the all-important network of railroad tracks during World War II.

Later, in 2000, I worked on a lawsuit to recover decades-old unpaid wage deductions owed to the wartime generation of agricultural and railroad braceros. My association with the lawsuit provided an opportunity to gather much archival information and to develop a deep awareness and empathy for braceros' wide range of harsh experiences. I collected rich and detailed first-person narratives from former bracero and Mexican American railroaders. Workers' reflections were also found in historical documents or shared by their spouses and descendants. To be sure, I would not be as informed had I not worked on this lawsuit. I owe a great debt of thanks to Enrique Martínez for his confidence in asking me to work on the lawsuit and help bring redress to this generation of Mexican workers.

Numerous other people have made equally important contributions to this book. I am particularly indebted to Andrea E. Gamboa, who shares my passion for social history. She became an active and encouraging participant in the research by helping to uncover records of the bracero railroad workers in archival collections in México and the United States. Felipe M. Méndez carefully read and edited early drafts of the manuscript, offered helpful feedback, and asked questions that greatly enhanced the story. Ana Davenport and Ellen Palms offered valuable help preparing the manuscript.

The pursuit of knowledge about the railroad braceros took me in many directions and brought me in contact with people whom I would never have met otherwise. Vicky Sierra, Eulalio Partida, Mike Rivera, and Fernando Barba González are among the many women and men who graciously welcomed me into their homes and responded to my inquiries about their experiences. Now elderly, much time has passed since working on the railroads; recalling some of their experiences brought back unpleasant memories. Still, they shared my desire to tell their stories, and I am very appreciative. Of course, the braceros and their families whom I never met (but whose names and voices of distress appear in the archival records) are just as indispensable to the book.

I wish to acknowledge Ranjit D. Arab, at the University of Washington Press, for his enthusiasm and stress-free way of facilitating publication of the book. I am grateful for his exuberant commitment to the project. I am also indebted to Deborah Barker at the Franklin County, Kansas, Historical Society; and Cara J. Randall at the California State Railroad Museum for assisting with the illustrations. The indispensable support and encouragement of all these and other unnamed persons made this a most rewarding endeavor.

# Abbreviations

| | |
|---|---|
| AAR | Association of American Railroads |
| AFL | American Federation of Labor |
| AT&SF | Atchison, Topeka & and Santa Fe Railway |
| BMWE | Brotherhood of Maintenance of Way Employees |
| CB&Q | Chicago, Burlington and Quincy Railroad |
| CMStP&P | Chicago, Milwaukee, St. Paul and Pacific Railroad |
| CNW | Chicago and North Western Railway Company |
| CTM | Confederación de Trabajadores de México (Confederation of Mexican Workers) |
| FEPC | Fair Employment Practices Committee |
| GN | Great Northern Railway |
| LULAC | League of United Latin American Citizens |
| NP | Northern Pacific Railway |
| OPA | Office of Price Administration |
| PFE | Pacific Fruit Express |
| RRB | Railroad Retirement Board |
| SP | Southern Pacific Railroad |
| UP | Union Pacific Railroad |
| USES | U.S. Employment Service |
| WARE | Western Association of Railroad Executives |
| WMC | War Manpower Commission |
| WP | Western Pacific Railroad |

# BRACERO
# RAILROADERS

# Introduction

Several interconnected interests and questions led to the writing of this book. My roots are in a small farming community in eastern Washington's Yakima Valley. Framed by two ranges of low hills, this area of the Pacific Northwest is nothing short of a farmer's paradise. With sufficient irrigation, agricultural production is limited only by the relatively short six-month growing season. Even so, the valley supplies the nation and global markets with an abundance of fruits, vegetables, and other agricultural products. Since the early twentieth century, industrial agriculture, the mainspring of life in the valley, has relied on a plentiful supply of laborers to work the land. Over time, commercial agriculture has extracted the human energy of generations of Native American, Asian and Asian American, and white as well as Mexican and Mexican American laborers.

A cost-effective and efficient railroad system to transport the valley's extraordinary volume of farm produce to market has been just as essential to the area's economy. This industry, too, required an ample supply of workers, at least until the 1960s, when many of the railroad depots and loading platforms began to close in the face of competition from the trucking industry. Thereafter, the railroad required fewer and fewer workers, and today, the distinctive and once-constant sound of moving freight and passenger trains along the floor of the Yakima Valley has faded. The trains have given way to convoys of long-haul diesel trucks that now carry most of the freight to and from the area. There is little question that the railroad is still key to the valley's economy, but the golden age of trains is clearly in the past.

There is another, more personal, side to my interest in the intersection of agriculture and the railroads. Like so many others before him, my father worked the soil of Yakima farms until old age impaired his physical ability. Over the course of many conversations after he ceased agricultural labor, I gradually began to learn more about his life experiences. Born in México at the turn of the twentieth century, he immigrated to the United States at the age of sixteen. He spent much of his life as a seasonal farmworker in Yakima, but before that he had been a track worker with the Baltimore and Ohio Railroad, one of the nation's oldest railroads. In the 1920s, in the company of other Mexican track workers, my father repaired rail lines and flagged trains in Ohio and farther east into Maryland and West Virginia, close to the nation's capital. His generation delineated the beginning of what became a sustained passage of railroad labor from México to the United States.

Some years ago, at a signing event for my book *Mexican Labor and World War II: Braceros in the Pacific Northwest, 1942–1947*, a woman approached to say that although she appreciated this book on the region's history of Mexican agricultural labor, I had omitted a key component of wartime bracero labor. Her husband had been a bracero during World War II, but not as a farmworker. The U.S. government had contracted him to work on the nation's railroads. My book, she told me, said nothing about the braceros who came from México to help keep the war trains moving. She was correct: I had overlooked the Mexican railroad workers of that period. Not a criticism, but pointing me to another facet of the bracero program.

I set out to correct this oversight and write the history of Mexican railroad workers like those of my father's generation and, more to the point, like this woman's husband. In the process, I learned that the agricultural and railroad industries of the West were inextricably linked. At different times they were closely interdependent on each other to develop and thrive. Farmers relied on trains to transport produce and bring supplies, and the railroads needed farm produce to load their cars. Just as important, beginning in the early 1900s, both industries grew increasingly reliant on, and developed an identical interest in, an endless supply of Mexican laborers to take on the most physically demanding and lowest-paid tasks. Beginning with the Immigration Act of 1924, and except for the 1930s, when the Great Depression hit the railroads hard, Mexican immigrants gradually replaced other ethnic and racial communities of railroad workers to become the preferred choice of labor on most western tracks.

The advent of World War II brought an unprecedented and robust full-employment economy, until railroads and farms with low-wage jobs found themselves unable to compete with other industries for workers. In response, the U.S. government turned to México to ensure that the economy's privately owned railroad and agricultural sectors had sufficient supplies of labor. For the duration of the war, U.S. and Mexican federal officials managed the movement of transnational agricultural and railroad workers under the terms of a binational administrative agreement.[1] This book centers on the history of Mexican railroad workers who participated in that war-time labor compact between México and the United States. Although the labor agreement, officially called the Temporary Migration of Mexican Non-agricultural Workers, is generally understood as an expedient transborder transfer of human social capital in times of a national emergency, it represents much more. That is, by World War II the racial inferiority of Mexicans had been firmly established among railroad companies and the general public. The wartime labor agreement simply built on existing fixed racially constructed labor practices to transport braceros to perform low-paid, dangerous railroad jobs. In the face of serious wartime worker shortages in low-wage occupations, it is not difficult to understand why Mexican contract workers were necessary to U.S. farm production. However, the importation of industrial railroad labor raises other issues.

Dating back to the early 1900s, railroad employees, including track workers, successfully organized trade unions to safeguard their jobs from competition particularly among immigrant labor. So how did the railroad industry manage to win approval from the Brotherhood of Maintenance of Way Employees (BMWE) to import low-wage Mexican workers during World War II? What do the experiences of these temporary, nonunion contracted laborers reveal about the work culture of the railroads, the braceros themselves, and U.S.–México relations? In addition, if the blueprint for the World War II bracero railroad program developed well before 1941, how does the experience of my father's generation with the Baltimore and Ohio Railroad help frame our understanding of the generation of Mexican industrial workers who came north to keep the trains running and help the nation win the Great War?

As a result of extensively researching this topic, I have learned to appreciate the enormous human and technological energy expended to generate and transport record levels of farm, forest, and factory production during World War II. Because the wartime generation of Mexican railroaders entered the United States at a most critical period, where do the experiences of these men fit in the historical record of the global war? Where does México itself fit into this discussion? Relations between México and the U.S. were gravely strained in the years leading to World War II. Clearly, México was also conscious of the racism experienced by U.S. residents of Mexican descent, yet the government agreed to permit more than three hundred thousand of its citizens to enter the U.S. as contract workers during the war years. What did México expect to gain, and were these goals realized? This book attempts to answer these questions and generate other important inquiries.

Finally, and purely for intellectual reasons, this book draws particular attention to Pacific Northwest social and labor history. From the viewpoint of Mexican American and Chicano history, the Pacific Northwest remains one of the least studied regions of the United States.

Just how and under what circumstances thousands of Mexicans immigrated to the U.S., and subsequently to the Pacific Northwest, is only now beginning to be understood. In most cases, the recurrent interpretation of Mexican American migration to and settlement in the Pacific Northwest begins with the postwar arrival of migratory farmworkers of Mexican descent. This interpretation is so ubiquitous that the term "Mexican" has nearly become synonymous with "migrant worker."

Despite mass worker immigration in the twentieth century from México and transregional migration to the Pacific Northwest, the history of industrial workers to the region is largely absent. This failure to visualize the historical importance of nonfarm Mexican labor in facilitating the development and sustaining the growth of the Pacific Northwest (and the larger American West) economy has worked to obscure and marginalize Mexican Americans. This may have been the precise concern raised by the woman at my book signing years ago. Although it has taken several years to address her criticism, this volume is a partial response. In the first chapters of the book I examine the development of the railroad industry and the employment of Mexican labor in the Pacific Northwest during the first half of the twentieth century. This focus is instructive because it serves as a useful contrast to other regions where the railroads also relied on a similar ethnic Mexican workforce. Moreover, the Pacific Northwest occupies a particular space that is peripheral and distant from the Southwest—the customary points of entry and observation for Mexican immigrant labor.

Until the unprecedented economic collapse of the 1930s hit the railroad industry, a handful of companies had expanded to monopolize America's transportation capacity. These years of contraction serve to lay out some of the immediate problems railroads faced when the nation entered war. The industry faced having to retool equipment and rebuild infrastructure rapidly. But that was the least of the concerns. Restarting the flow of Mexican labor that had been cut off by the Depression surfaced as well. Across the railroad industry, the want of track workers threatened the railroad's capacity to the point that the crisis drew the attention of government officials. The government's emergency war plan to contract Mexican railroaders in México and transport them to the United States went into effect.

The second half of the book covers the day-to-day administration and the failures of the bracero railroad program as well as the experiences of the men themselves. At times, straightforward problems, such as the recruitment of labor, are often the most difficult to sort out. As clear-cut as it seemed, a coalition of railroad executives and government officials could not simply enlist Mexican laborers for employment in the United States. Labor shortages notwithstanding, any suggestion to authorize the federal government to contract workers in México also had to address highly sensitive immigration issues, the concerns of the BMWE, opposition from an ingrained race-sensitive railroad work culture, as well as political opposition. I examine these and other issues from different perspectives in the U.S. and México. Consider, for example, how Mexican Americans and Mexicans greeted the news about the bracero program. As Ana Elizabeth Rosas has written, many of the repatriates held vivid memories of the lingering anti-Mexican sentiment that underscored the Depression-era deportation of more than six hundred thousand.[2] Now the United States was asking México to send its citizen workers back to the U.S.?

No sooner did the Mexican braceros arrive at the work sites when U.S. officials, in their role as administrators and employers, began to lose sight of the guarantees and rights that had been promised the laborers. Looking at the harsh daily reality of these workers exposes the folly of obligating non-English-speaking Mexican laborers to a contract in an alien social and work environment. The conditions were outlined in individual work contracts, but the braceros had no voice in the negotiations of the agreement. Building on Kitty Calavita's analysis of the function of the state in labor procurement, this book explores the contradictory role played by Mexican and U.S. government agencies that determined the difficult experiences many men endured working the railroads.[3] Mexican officials were equally if not more complicit in the hardships of the braceros; their pattern of general unresponsiveness to their own citizens cannot be exaggerated.

Despite the unintended results of the labor program, the overall experience of the Mexican railroaders offers some instructive lessons. The men, regardless of their limitations, did not always despair; nor did they resign themselves to the unfortunate circumstances that came at the hands of their employers and the indifference of U.S. and Mexican governments. In the United States, some braceros retaliated by walking away from their employers in protest; others were even more defiant and organized effective local work strikes to seek relief. In this manner, they shattered the employers' ex-

pectation that fixing workers to a legal instrument would result in an ac-
quiescent labor force. The Mexican women closely related to these braceros
were not passive either. Where other studies on bracero families state that
women "did not bring up the continued deterioration of their quality and
standard of living," this book finds otherwise.[4] In fact, wives, mothers, and
other relatives tried to intercede on behalf of the bracero men by appealing
directly to México's president, Manuel Ávila Camacho. Of course, the departure of the workers also served to disrupt families and burden the women
with added responsibilities back in México.

The allied victory in the fall of 1945 signaled the beginning of the final
stages of the bracero railroad program. By the following year, the government had officially repatriated most of the railroaders to México. However,
some of the men deserted from their railroad employers and chose to remain in the United States, an unintended consequence of the program. In
other cases, no sooner did repatriated men arrive home than they began
preparing to return to the U.S. as free wage earners or by reenlisting in the
ongoing U.S.-México bracero farmworker program. After the war, undocumented immigrant labor flows escalated tremendously alongside an increasing number of braceros contracted to work on U.S. farms. This immediate post–World War II spike in immigration underscores a demographic
phenomenon started by the wartime bracero programs that continued
largely unaffected by numerous deterrence measures until the end of the
twentieth century.

Several other issues remained unresolved after the end of World War II.
One issue that continues to occupy the minds of many surviving braceros
and implicates both México and the United States, is the return of all wages
that had been deducted from the bracero workers, both railroad and agricultural workers. From 1942 until 1947, employers withheld a percentage of all
wages earned for deposit in an obligatory "savings plan" account in México.
Because the banks never paid many of the men, the deductions were a form
of wage theft. Decades have gone by and despite petitions, lawsuits, and political promises to pay back all of these earnings, the elderly workers and
their descendants, residing in both México and the United States, are met
with a circle of denials and continue to wait for their earned income.

* * *

The bracero railroad program and its counterpart in agriculture did not originate entirely from the exigencies of World War II. Its roots lay in the experiences of my father and the generations of thousands of other Mexican laborers who emigrated from México beginning in the early 1900s. Largely unrestricted from migrating north during these years, they came to occupy the vacancy left by other immigrant workers no longer permitted to immigrate by legal means to the United States or who were fortunate to move out of low-wage railroad jobs. In the place of controlled Mexican immigration, the bracero program acted to beckon countless emigrants, legal or not, north to the United States. The government-sanctioned labor programs of World War II served as the architect for generating vast postwar transnational Mexican immigration. In many ways the World War II bracero programs served to engineer the racialized postwar transnational labor flows across the U.S.-Mexican border. I agree with Natalia Molina, whose work demonstrates how racial categories once constructed carry forward to function just as effectively in different spaces and time.[5] The racial categorization of Mexican labor in the decades before World War II was just as important a factor in the harsh treatment of the men as was the empty promises of the workers' contracts.

Despite lessons learned from the World War II bracero railroad program, the idea of another state-managed bracero-like labor program (disguised as H2A visas for workers or using such euphemistic terms as "guest workers") prevails today among some employers and government officials. By stepping back to the past, this book urges caution about implementing such ideas. I tell the story of the World War II Mexican railroaders in the U.S. by grounding their experience in history, in a straightforward manner, from the bottom up. My intent is to give the Mexican men and women their voice. They were, after all, no different from other ordinary individuals who walked across the stage of history, except their voices are absent in most World War II narratives. Throughout this book, in certain places, I left their names and accounts as they themselves wrote them; the braceros' limited written-language skills discloses much about their lives. For the most part, they were common men who answered the call to serve on the domestic front of a foreign nation at war. While historians have told the story of World War II from many perspectives, the history of the Mexican railroad braceros remains largely obscured.[6] With the publication of *Bracero Railroaders*, this generation of men and women now find a place in the pages of history.

# Chapter 1

# Labor and the Railroad Industry before World War II

In the early decades of the twentieth century, restrictive immigration legislation in the United States forced railroad companies long accustomed to an open source of foreign-born Asian and European laborers to gradually turn to Mexican immigrant and Mexican American workers. They were judged to be similar to other immigrants for their willingness to work for low pay, learn the necessary job skills, and accept arduous work conditions. Railroad companies reconfigured their workforces with scores of Spanish-speaking workers.

In the Pacific Northwest the railroad industry faced an added problem: a sparse population from which to draw its workforce. Consequently, railroad employers were more dependent on labor supply companies as to satisfy their labor needs. Railroad construction in the Pacific Northwest commenced after Congress authorized in 1883 a second transcontinental rail line across the northern half of the country. In similar fashion to other parts of the western United States, the railroad became the most practical way of linking the region's resources to eastern urban and industrial centers, as well as to larger global markets. The ever expanding network of rail lines stretched across the rugged terrain of the Pacific Northwest, indiscriminately consuming generations of immigrants and migrants as it grew. Resembling a choreographed sequence of European, Asian, Mexican, and American ethnic groups, these communities mirrored the systemic migration patterns already familiar in the Southwest and the East. Often overlapping with one another, these working-class communities of track laborers were crucial to the area's burgeoning railroad industry and larger corresponding agricultural and industrial economies.

Before the Immigration Act of 1924, which instituted quotas limiting the arrival of immigrants from particular countries, Pacific Northwest railroad companies could choose laborers freely from among a vast array of ethnic groups. Although the number of immigrants arriving in Washington State was never sufficient to match population growth in other parts of the country, the number is telling. In the first decade of the twentieth century, foreign-born immigrants from other parts of the nation increased Washington State's population six times faster than the national rate of immigration. At the time, just two out of every ten Washington residents had been born in the state; the rest had migrated from other parts of the country.[1] Given the relatively small Native American population, railroad companies benefited immensely from the influx of newcomers in order to fill low-wage track jobs. Population gains pushed the railroads to expand to meet the increasing demand of rail service brought about by overall regional economic growth.

In the years between the dawn of the twentieth century and the beginning of World War I, the Pacific Northwest entered its second period of robust railroad expansion. New and improved stations, repair plants, and equipment characterized this phase. In addition to new yard and building construction, railroad companies upgraded existing lines and laid thousands of additional miles of new track. In so doing, the railroads connected every corner of the Pacific Northwest to one another, integrating the region's internal economy and linking it with national markets. The railroads were particularly effective in encouraging a phenomenal expansion in the quality and quantity of agricultural production. They stimulated agriculture in ways previously unimagined by producers through faster, more direct, and therefore more efficient delivery of commodities to markets.

In Oregon the Klamath Basin, Willamette Valley, Hood River, Rogue River, and Treasure Valley areas matured into important geographic hubs for agricultural shipments of fruits and vegetables destined for the principal eastern and southern markets. Similar to Oregon, Washington's Yakima and Skagit Valleys, along with farms in the upper Columbia Basin, shipped increasing freight car loads of high-market-value fruits and vegetables. In Idaho the state's crop-producing areas grew into a belt of rich farming communities connected by rail lines from Nampa to Idaho Falls. By the 1920s the Pacific Northwest had a solid national reputation for good-value, high-quality agricultural production.

As railroad companies worked to link regional key farming centers, they established various service facilities to maintain and repair their freight equipment. For instance, when the Pacific Fruit Express began to transport large shipments of fruits and vegetables in ice-cooled wooden cars, the company established a complete repair shop in Nampa and a light repair facility in Pocatello, Idaho.[2] These plants provided scheduled maintenance and repairs essential to ensuring that heavily loaded freight cars originating in the Pacific Northwest reached their destination in the east. Similarly, the Southern Pacific (SP) maintained yards, repair shops, and roundhouses in Eugene and Portland for its operations in Oregon. The Northern Pacific and Great Northern improved their repair and shipping facilities as well. Throughout the region railroads became an essential sector in the economy of large and small farming centers.

The enlarging network of railroad lines did not converge solely at farming areas. Portland, Seattle, and Spokane—already well-established centers of rail activity by the 1900s—improved their railroad service despite the promotion and prominence of electric-powered railcars, automobiles, and trucks. Many years would pass before these new contrivances in urban transportation could challenge and disrupt the large railroad carriers' monopoly of heavy and long-distance freight and passenger service. Track construction and maintenance alone, with its high turnover rate, required an enormous number of both permanent and temporary workers. Once the rail was set, the job of maintaining the line in good operating condition required approximately 155 maintenance-of-way workers per one thousand miles of track.[3] The railroad companies also required low-skilled workers in the train yards and car repair and engine shops.

Some occupations in the railroad industry required highly skilled workers rather than ordinary laborers, so the railroad industry organized workers in a hierarchical structure based on craft, trade skills, and seniority. In this highly stratified workforce, maintenance-of-way jobs ranked lowest as a result of the elementary skill level and seasonal and transient natures of the job; as a means to ensure sufficient worker labor pools, railroad companies sought out vulnerable, newly arrived, unskilled immigrants for this kind of work. Maintenance-of-way work became associated with recent immigrants and nonwhite ethnic laborers. To avoid the stigma, many domestic workers and some European immigrant workers shunned these jobs. Consequently, maintenance-of-way track laborers, among all railroad positions, were the most challenging for railroad companies to recruit and keep on the job.

When the mainline of the Northern Pacific (NP) railroad neared the Pacific Northwest region in the 1880s, the company began to tap a large pool of

Chinese immigrant labor that had entered the country ahead of the Chinese Exclusion Act of 1882. Following the pattern in California, Chinese laborers gravitated from the gold-mining districts of Oregon and Idaho to railroad jobs. They proved to be excellent workers. Following the lead of companies like the SP, which relied on Chinese labor to extend its lines from California into Oregon, the NP employed nearly fifteen thousand Chinese men in track construction.[4] By the 1890s, however, the era of the Chinese workers in railroad construction began to wane, as fears of a mounting "yellow peril" led to immigration restrictions and increasingly violent anti-Chinese agitation.

Following the initial construction of the main lines, railroad companies were content to hire local track workers where available and supplement them with immigrants from northern and western Europe. The nationwide Pullman Strike of 1894—together with pledges of support from the American Federation of Labor, the Industrial Workers of the World, and the United Brotherhood of Railway Employees—galvanized unskilled workers and worried the railroad officials sufficiently enough to institute changes in employment practices, such as increased wages and better working conditions. To circumvent potential union agitation and worker solidarity, the railroad companies segregated track crews along racial and ethnic lines. To discourage workers uniting against employers, railroads turned to labor contractors to obtain their workers. The railroad companies rendered union organizers ineffective by manipulating labor disputes to appear as divisive ethnic differences among workers or disagreements between contractor and laborer, rather than as legitimate issues thwarting labor organization.

A perfect example is the way Japanese immigrant labor was used by the industry to polarize its workforce, pitting workers against each other. By 1908, when the Gentleman's Agreement placed limited restrictions on emigration from Japan, approximately 55,000 Japanese immigrants came to the U.S. mainland and another 150,000 to Hawaii.[5] Despite limitations on migration between Hawaii and the mainland, the Japanese immigrant population grew substantially, surpassing the Chinese in the West and the Pacific Northwestern states. By 1890, 12,177 Japanese immigrants resided in Washington State, a 200 percent increase from the previous decade.[6] This community, drawn by economic opportunities, continued to grow until 1908 and in doing so became an alternative and highly desirable source of labor for the railroads. Employers promoted Japanese immigration to the Pacific Northwest by encouraging their workers to write to friends and relatives in Japan urging them to emigrate. Moreover, labor agents traveled to Japanese port cities on behalf of the railroads to recruit potential workers. In Japan these agents readily advanced the cost of passage to the U.S. plus thirty dollars, to qualify workers under the destitute person provision of the Foran Act.

By appropriating the prevailing social attitudes that led to the Gentlemen's Agreement, the railroads intensified racial and ethnic distinctions, creating animosities among its diverse workforce. Accordingly, supervisors with the Great Northern, Northern Pacific, Southern Pacific, and Union Pacific railroad companies openly lauded the Japanese as extremely reliable, competent workers, and much superior to employing white immigrant ethnics for the track work. Not surprisingly, the companies' favoritism toward Japanese workers did not transcend outside track employment. In the higher-wage positions in roundhouses, stores, and shops, the railroads and the unions brought into play an explicit whites-only policy, relegating Japanese workers almost exclusively to track maintenance.

As rail traffic intensified, a need for labor forced railroad companies to begin to contract with large recruiting firms that specialized in procuring immigrant and ethnic laborers. These highly organized contracting firms had the capacity to tailor their recruiting methods to match successive waves of immigrant railroad workers. The Oriental Trading Company stood as a giant and archetype among railroad labor supply houses. Because of the company's efficacy in recruiting labor from Japan and Hawaii, it eventually became the exclusive supplier of immigrant labor for such major western railroads as the Great Northern, Northern Pacific, Southern Pacific, and Union Pacific. The Oriental Trading Company profited handsomely from its contracts with the railroads. As long as the company consigned enough workers for a flat fee, the railroads tolerated its practice of using any means necessary to extract profits from the workers. Left to its own devices, the supply company aggressively sought to procure workers. More lucrative returns came from the exclusive right to provide personal services to the immigrants, which enabled the Oriental Trading Company to operate its own boarding and supply houses. It skimmed a daily ten-cent commission from workers barely earning $1.10 per day. The workers saw other deductions from their wages, including a $1.00 monthly language-translation charge, medical fees, and a surcharge on any remittances sent back to family members in Japan.[7]

As eastern and southern immigrants arrived in the Pacific Northwest, the ethnic diversity of the railroad labor force swelled. By the turn of the twentieth century, and until the Immigration Act of 1924, increased numbers of

Greek, German, Italians, Bulgarian, and Austrian workers entered the ranks of unskilled railroad employment. Different from earlier European immigrants, they were not second-step or partially assimilated immigrants who had previously lived in other parts of the nation before coming to the Pacific Northwest. Many times, labor agents recruited these immigrants directly after arriving in the United States for railroad work. Similar to Asian ethnic groups, the distinctive southern and central European nationalities and cultures made them outsiders and consequently victims to the catalog of abuses at the hands of labor contractors and railroad companies.

For the most part, labor contractors who specialized in procuring non-English-speaking European immigrants for the railroads never garnered empathy for the workers. In 1914 an inspection of immigrant work crews with the Chicago, Milwaukee, St. Paul and Pacific Railroad found "reprehensible" and "detestable" living and job conditions.[8] Like the Japanese, these workers also paid exorbitant charges and kickbacks to labor contractors for scanty and unsanitary quarters, paltry medical services, transportation, board, and other miscellaneous services. Paid an average of $1.75 to $2.25 per day, European immigrants were hardly better off than their Asian counterparts. At work, supervisors used a "speed up" system to extract the maximum effort from the men until the work environment physically wore them down. The practice of pushing the workers to their limit worked to the advantage of the labor contractors; this system kept them busy bringing in fresh, unbroken labor.

Organized labor did little to protect the rights of European and Asian immigrant workers, as it considered immigration a threat to union solidarity. In Washington the State Federation of Labor viewed southern and eastern European workers with immense disfavor and as a "menace to the American standard of living."[9] The Brotherhood of Maintenance of Way Employees (BMWE) openly characterized white immigrant ethnics as a reprehensible pool of "outcast groups." European immigrants "threatened the nation's social and economic conditions by lowering our living standards," declared A. F. Stout, national legislative representative for the BMWE. If allowed to act, the BMWE intended to prevent further immigrants from entering the United States regardless of the claims of the railroad companies.[10]

Regardless of race or ethnicity, the endless supply of cheap and malleable workers constituted a bonanza for labor contractors and railroad companies alike. This lucrative arrangement ended with the labor shortages of World War I and the passage of the 1921 National Origins Act. The outbreak of the war affected the labor supply in several important ways. First, the robust war economy meant that the railroads and labor contractors faced a dwindling supply of track laborers; this forced them to adopt more efficient ways to obtain workers. Higher wages and better employment conditions pulled workers from lower-salaried railroad jobs. Some immigrants elected to return to their native countries after experiencing the double effect of the pressures to "Americanize" coupled with widespread xenophobia directed against the "unassimilable" aliens. After the war, Congress acted to severely curtail the entry of southern and eastern European emigrants to fewer than 20 percent of all immigration slots allocated to Europe. Railroad companies felt the compound effect of restrictions on Asian and European immigrants as well as the siphoning of workers as a result of the powerful postwar industrial economy.

To offset the dwindling workforce, railroad companies sought alternative sources of track men. World War I had initiated the "great migration" of unprecedented numbers of African Americans from the Southeast to northern industrial cities. Not unpredictably, vehement residential and job segregation effectively confined African American migrants to bottom-rung jobs and undesirable residential areas in Detroit and Chicago's South Side. Faced with stiff competition from manufacturing and organized labor, the railroad companies now turned to these newly arrived African American migrants for low-skilled track and maintenance work. Unlike eastern carriers, however, the western railroad companies lacked a migratory pool of African Americans from which to draw. Railroads like the Great Northern and the Southern Pacific pressured their labor agents in Midwestern cities to sign up African Americans for railroad employment in the West.[11]

Although some did respond to recruiters, the strategy proved largely unsatisfactory, and the numbers were insufficient to offset the huge labor losses. "They don't stay long enough," wrote one railroad official from Sandpoint, Idaho.[12] Not surprisingly, African American job mobility resulted from the same hard racism in many western cities that was prevalent in the South and the Midwest. It went beyond Jim Crow or segregated racial practices. Cognizant of the way the railroad companies often recruited African Americans to break strikes or to depress wages, whites aggressively barred them from receiving public services and accommodations, railroad employment, and union membership.

In the early years of organized labor, nonwhites were not barred altogether. The American Federation of Labor (AFL), for one, did not begin with a color bar limiting African American members. By 1895, however, the AFL began to admit racist unions that discriminated against African American workers. At the turn of the twentieth century, the AFL explicitly limited African American membership to Jim Crow affiliates of larger national unions. The implications of less-than-complete membership translated into little or no voice for African Americans in federal unions. Associate membership below full entitlement assailed the autonomy and strength of African American labor. The BMWE embraced similar exclusionary practices, permitting African Americans to join auxiliary groups that prohibited them from having a voice in collective bargaining or opportunities for job advancement. Such conditional union membership reflected the racism of the times. To do otherwise would have intimated racial equality, that African Americans were on similar footing with whites. As one nonrailroad union expressed, membership simply stated meant: "White Christian males."[13]

Job discrimination against African Americans set the standard for the barring of other nonwhite laborers. As a whole, unions acted against "Orientals," Native Americans, and Mexicans in the same manner as they treated African Americans.[14] The privilege of race became pervasive among union workers that challenges to the culture of discrimination fell flat. Because substantial western migration of African Americans did not take place until World War II, and job and union discrimination limited their opportunities (outside of work in sleeping and dining cars), African Americans did not play a major role in railroad employment in the Pacific Northwest and other western locations. This is not to imply that the railroad industry would not hire them, however. In light of labor shortages and immigration restrictions on Asia and Europe, the industry took anyone willing to work under rigid conditions and not wish to advance or be unionized. A railroad spokesperson put it this way: "We would take the colored men if we could get them, but they are simply not available."[15]

In 1928 the general counsel of the Association of Railway Executives challenged a congressional committee during hearings to curb Mexican immigration. Faced with the dwindling supply of track laborers, the spokesperson asked: "Are you going to cut off this source of supply? . . . What greater calamity . . . could come to a people [the railroad industry] than to find themselves all of a sudden cut off from labor necessary to carry on their enterprises?"[16] Indeed, between the early 1900s and the 1920s, the railroad industry, especially in the Southwest and Midwest, had grown increasingly dependent on Mexican labor for track construction and repair. According to the congressional Dillingham Commission on Immigration, by 1911 railroad companies in California, New Mexico, Arizona, and southern Nevada openly sought out Mexican laborers for new construction in place of other immigrants.[17]

The predilection toward Mexican labor can be explained this way: the Mexican immigrant population, not having the limits and exclusions that had been placed on European and Asian immigrants, had surged. The labor market in the Southwest was saturated. Consequently, whereas companies customarily paid Greek immigrant laborers $1.60 per day, Mexican section hands (railroad workers) hired on at $1.25. The railroad industry seized the opportunity to systemically employ this cheap and expanding source of labor for its track lines in the Southwest and elsewhere. To justify using Mexicans as stand-ins for other laborers, the railroad industry, as well as other employers, constructed a social and racial view of Mexicans as being innately superior workers. When tested in the arid and extreme desertlike southwestern environment, Mexicans proved excellent workers, employers argued. The harsh work environment together with the physical demands and seasonal nature of track work turned other workers away, they insisted, but not Mexicans. A railroad spokesperson explained the industry's partiality toward Mexicans: "We are employing them to have them exercise their strong backs at hard work. We are not employing them because they are of a high type of intellectuality. If we employed them because of their mental attainments, we could not employ either Mexicans or those colored people."[18] In truth, the preference for Mexican track labor had little to do with that group's supremacy over other ethnic workers. Facing the reality of a contracting European and Asian labor market, the railroad industry understood that Mexicans were crossing the border into the United States in larger numbers.

The growing pool of Mexican workers was close to being the ideal solution to the industry's labor needs in the economic boom years after World War I. Their labor was necessary in many areas outside of the border areas, where companies had to constantly replenish track workers because of new line construction and maintenance of existing routes. There was also regular turnover of workers as they left for better jobs in other industries. The railroads systematically pulled Mexican rail workers away from the Southwest to fill labor shortages in other regions of the country. Lured by wages superior to what they could earn in such states as Texas—but still below the

earnings of white workers—Mexican laborers dispersed northward following the rail pathways of the employing companies.

The migration of Mexican immigrant labor northward evolved into a
discernible pattern of geographical mobility. In 1910 the federal census listed
2,645 Mexicans living in Oklahoma. Most of the population worked mainly
as section hands, coal miners, and farm workers. Upon closer inspection,
however, the majority of the Mexican population resided in Oklahoma City,
where 84 percent of the demographic worked for the Santa Fe, Frisco, Rock
Island, and Katy railroads.[19] Over the next twenty years Mexican railroad
communities developed along every major rail juncture in Oklahoma.[20]
Employed by giants of the industry—the Atchison, Topeka and Santa Fe;
the Chicago, Rock Island, and Pacific; Saint Louis–San Francisco; and the
Missouri, Kansas and Texas railroads—Mexican laborers formed the main-
stay of section and extra gang crews. For some companies this immigrant
labor force had become indispensable. Fearing congressional restrictions
on Mexican immigration, the Santa Fe railroad warned it "would be greatly
crippled" without the Mexican workers, as they constituted between 85 to 90
percent of track laborers during the 1920s.[21]

Some Mexican railroad workers followed the tracks farther north to railroad hub cities like Chicago, Detroit, Cleveland, Pittsburgh, Minneapolis,
and other northern and eastern cities. By 1916 in Chicago—a junction where
eastern, western, and southern railroads connected—206 Mexican workers
were employed with the railroads; as a result, a large Mexican railroad box-
car community grew exponentially there until the Great Depression. During
the 1920s, on average, slightly more than five hundred new immigrants arrived annually to join Mexican track crews operating in and out of Chicago.
The pattern seen in Oklahoma repeated itself as Mexican laborers comprised 80 to 100 percent of extra gang crews with some upper Midwestern
carriers.[22] From the Chicago–Great Lakes area, railroad companies such as
the Great Northern and the Chicago, Burlington and Quincy, also gradually
replaced or augmented their track crews on the eastern lines with Mexican
immigrants. Throughout the 1920s Texas-based labor agents regularly recruited Mexican railroad workers for the eastern and midwestern railroads.
As historian Dionicio Nodín Valdez has written, by the advent of the Great
Depression, Mexicans represented nearly one-half of all track and maintenance laborers on the sixteen largest lines in Chicago and in cities from
northwestern Indiana and east to Saginaw.[23]

At the end of World War I, some companies like the New York Central Lines held on to their Mexican workers by persuading skilled employees not to return to México but to remain employed with the rail company. Encouraged that the company regarded them as good employees, some men elected to stay and became permanent residents in the vicinity of Buffalo, New York. Years later, the experience gained by these men would prove essential to the New York Central. During World War II, these men would translate and teach important jobs skills and safe work practices to arriving Mexican bracero railroaders.[24] Mexican rail workers had barely arrived in the Chicago and the surrounding Great Lakes area when, to the dismay of the BMWE, the Great Northern and the Northern Pacific railroad companies began recruiting them for their lines connecting west, toward Montana and the Pacific Northwest coast. Decrying the infiltration of Mexicans, union officials were concerned over the fact that "there is hardly a place where one does not find them."[25]

As the use of Mexican laborers spread westward along the states bordering Canada, southwestern railroad companies moved workers for track work into the Mountain West: Colorado, Wyoming, and southern Idaho. Beginning in 1907, labor contractors judged Mexicans similar to the Japanese and dispatched several thousand Mexican workers out of El Paso for track crews operating in the Rocky Mountain states. As in the Midwest, Mexicans gradually comprised the core of many track crews. In Colorado, by the 1920s, the AT&SF rail company reported divisions with crews that were 85 to 90 percent Mexican.[26] The dispersion of Mexican laborers further away from México's border and in the direction of the Pacific Northwest is illustrated by a June 1942 letter by Charles Soto Sánchez, who had been jailed in Walla Walla by immigration authorities.[27] Sánchez's experience is not atypical of Mexican laborers who sought employment at the time in the nation's western corner. According to his testimony, Sánchez's family left México around 1904, during the final years of the Díaz dictatorship. Once in the United States, Sánchez's father found work with the Santa Fe company, which took the family to Holly, Colorado. Next, the family moved to Garden City, Kansas. A subsequent move relocated the family to Montana for work in an "all Mexican crew" with the Chicago, Milwaukee and St. Paul Railroad. By this time the family, along with several other railroad families, became part of the leading edge of a crescent of Mexican railroad labor that extended up from Texas through Oklahoma, Kansas, Wyoming, and arriving at the Montana-Canadian border. In 1918 the Chicago, Milwaukee and St. Paul Railroad transferred the entire group of Mexican workers from Montana to Tacoma, Washington.[28]

As Mexican immigrant railroaders migrated into the Northwest, they embodied a community of workers fanning away from the Mexican border toward the Great Lakes and eastward as well as west to the Pacific Coast.[29] Mexican labor migrated rapidly and constantly across regions and from place to place. One Chicago steelworker, interviewed by Paul S. Taylor, recounted entering the United States from México in 1915. In ten years he had worked alongside Mexican and Japanese American section crews in Colorado, Idaho, Texas, Utah, and Wyoming. Another former railroad section worker hand emigrated from Guadalajara in 1913 and worked his way north taking jobs with the railroad. In 1923 this worker left the railroad camps and set up his own barber shop in Pocatello, Idaho, catering exclusively to Mexican sugar beet and railroad workers. A few years later, he and other Mexicans shipped out under contract to the Alaska fishing industry. Returning once again to the Pacific Northwest, he opened another barbershop in Portland, Oregon. Finally, in 1925, he settled down employed as a steelworker in Illinois.[30]

A third distinguishable stream of Mexican workers to the Northwest originated in California and flowed north through Oregon and on to the Canadian border. Since the 1880s, California's rail industry had employed Mexicans as well as other immigrant laborers. The contracting source of Asian immigrants at a time of economic expansion obligated the railroad companies to methodically search out Mexican track workers. By 1906 the Southern Pacific had a regularly scheduled carload of Mexican workers arriving weekly from El Paso and Laredo, Texas, to southern California. From there, the company dispatched workers north to its northern California and Oregon divisions. By the start of World War I, the outward ripple of a wave of Mexican railroader workers—coming north from California, others through the Rocky Mountain states, and still more from the Upper Midwest and the East—began to converge in the northwesternmost corner of the country. Taylor's research during the 1930s on Mexican track laborers on nine western railroads attests to this fact. His study revealed that between 1909 and 1929 the Mexican immigrant work force expanded dramatically from 17.1 percent to 59.5 percent. He examined lines in the Pacific Northwest operated by the following companies: Union Pacific, Denver and Rio Grande, Northern Pacific, Oregon Short Line, Oregon Railroad and Navigation, Southern Pacific, and Great Northern.[31]

At first the presence of Mexican immigrants on northwestern track lines was inconspicuous because of the population of other immigrants, but by the onset of the Great Depression, Mexican laborers were commonplace in railroad communities in Idaho, Oregon, and Washington. The spread of Mexican labor astonished and dismayed the Brotherhood of Maintenance of Way Employees. As they saw it, the railroad industry had already demonstrated a clear preference for Mexicans as utility workers throughout much of western half of the United States. According to the BMWE, Mexicans were beginning to saturate the entire industry and as such were no longer "confined to the Southwestern states, as was the case several years ago."[32]

Railroad companies, such as the Southern Pacific, would contract with Mexican workers for a specific length of time, at a specific work location along a company's entire network of tracks. In other cases, however, the workers were in effect free laborers or "step migrants" who ventured north on their own following potential leads for job opportunities away from the Southwest's flooded labor areas. Many left the Southwest to escape the deeply rooted and widespread animosity directed against Mexicans. Sometimes, the immigrants found relief. In Pocatello, Idaho, for example, where labor was scarce, Mexicans stood a chance of getting better and higher-paying jobs in company stores, car shops, and roundhouses. In contrast, because of entrenched racism, Mexican workers in Colorado and Texas had little hope of getting even the most subordinate roundhouse jobs, such as cleaning and washing locomotives.

The opportunity of railroad work in a less discriminatory atmosphere established a chain migration of workers entering the Pacific Northwest. More often than not, the pattern would start when one person found employment, settled, and later wrote to relatives and others to come as well. Thus a social network of extended Mexican families and friends evolved in several railroad centers. Pocatello, Idaho, was such a location. Before World War I, the city already had a reputation as a Mexican railroad community; the immigrants worked for Union Pacific and clustered adjacent to the train yard. A longtime Mexican American resident of Idaho recalled that when they "really wanted to be with a lot of Mexicans we would come here to Pocatello on the train."[33] Mexicans created their own residential space in places like Orchard, Idaho, where they lived in box cars or other types of shelter near roundhouses, yards, and track junctions.[34]

The close ties between the agriculture and railroad industries provides significant insight into Mexican railroad labor migration to such regions

as the Pacific Northwest. Until World War II increased industrial manufacturing, the agricultural economy produced almost all of the freight for the
western region's railroads. The railroad and agricultural industries comple-
mented one another in other ways. By the 1920s both industries drew workers from the same pool of unskilled Mexican immigrants. In some areas the
Mexican workers crossed easily between farm and track jobs, creating an
undifferentiated community of railroad and agricultural laborers. When
Mexicans with the Milwaukee, Chicago, and Saint Paul Railroad Company
lost their jobs in Washington State, some men returned to México while others remained in state to find work on farms. In 1919 some of the ex-railroad
workers who had come from Montana to Tacoma moved to the Yakima Valley, purchased land, and started farming in Wapato.[35] This is not to suggest
that all Mexican track workers became farmers, but many men of Mexican
descent in the Pacific Northwest experienced farm or railroad work at one
time or another.

The primary flow of Mexican track workers developed as the result of
zealous labor agents working to supply to the various railroads. When the
1924 immigration restrictions further crippled the industry's ability to obtain sufficient Asian and European workers, labor agents shifted their attention to recruiting Mexican laborers. Conditions on both sides of the border
made Mexican workers a labor recruiter's dream come true. Wretched social
and economic realities in México resulting from the Mexican Revolution
of 1910, and lasting well into the late 1920s, encouraged scores of Mexicans
to cross to the United States for relief. While difficult, the journey did not
present insurmountable barriers. Until 1922, Mexican immigrants had to
meet few prerequisites, outside of a seldom enforced head tax and literacy
requirement, to enter the United States. In any case, prospective immigrants
arriving at the U.S.-México border found it practically unguarded and easy
to cross.

Successive years of open immigration between the two countries rapidly
transformed the Southwest into a labor supply paradise. One observer of the
swelling pool of laborers in the region dubbed Los Angeles, disparagingly
so, "the great Mexican peon capital of the United States."[36] Other cities, such
as El Paso and San Antonio, Texas, had similar concentrations of Mexican
immigrant labor. From California to Texas, labor recruiters capitalized on
the law of supply and demand and dispatched scores of Mexican workers
to labor short railroads in the Pacific Northwest and elsewhere. Two types of
labor contractors, either commissary companies or individual agents, sup-

plied workers to the railroads. Commissary companies had the most inten-
sive operations by far. The Holmes Supply Company, headquartered in Los
Angeles with additional offices in El Paso, exemplifies this type of provider.

In the 1920s the Holmes Supply Company monopolized all labor pro-
curement for the Santa Fe and Southern Pacific Railroads. With offices in
México, the company subcontracted with agents in Ciudad Juárez, and
other Mexican localities, to enlist and dispatch labor across the line to El
Paso or Los Angeles. Once in the United States, workers were rerouted to the
Great Lakes and Pacific Northwest. Other commissary companies (such as
the Manning Labor Agency located in Tucson, Arizona, and El Paso, and the
Boland Agency and the Peterson Employment Agency of Kansas City) were
in the business of procured Mexicans. Among them all, the Holmes Supply
Company had the most extensive operation, prompting railroad executives
to describe it as a "substantial institution" unequaled in its capacity to acquire Mexican workers.[37]

The commissary companies involved with recruiting Mexican laborers
were thus indispensable to the railroad industry. For their part, the railroad
companies provided free transportation to and from the work site, along
with boarding and kitchen cars, fuel, water, and ice. Theoretically, the railroads did not charge the workers for these services. In practice, however, the
commissary extracted highly inflated payments from the workers for food,
blankets, clothes, and other services. Accordingly, the workers paid for food
whether they ate or not—a practice that returned solid profits for the contractors. The mutual interests between railroad and commissary companies
represented a win-win situation for both entities. Through the commissary
companies, the railroads always had a sufficient labor force at very low
costs and were relieved of the responsibility of boarding and feeding track
crews. The commissaries incurred zero transportation costs for delivering
the workers and had exclusive rights to operate merchandise stores for the
railroad labor force. The incentive for higher profits pressed the commissaries to deliver the maximum number of men anywhere the railroads needed
them.

Individual or independent labor agents worked alongside the commissary companies. Often of Mexican descent, these labor contractors, called
"enganchadores" ("hookers") could not compete on the same level as the
commissary companies. At best, they were ethnic middle men called upon
sporadically to recruit labor for the larger commissary companies or directly for the railroads. At times, *enganchadores* served to quell discontented

workers. Lacking the privileged position enjoyed by the commissary companies, individual labor agents relied on a variety of ploys to derive profit for their services. The most common practice involved collaring unsuspecting workers into signing a work agreement to get employment. Under these circumstances, Eleno Hernández, needing to provide for his wife and five children, signed on to work with the Southern Pacific Railroad in 1930.

At first an official of the U.S. Employment Service in San Antonio explained the terms of employment to Hernández. The job would last six months with free transportation to and from the work site. To get the job, however, he had to go through a labor agent and sign a written work contract. This maneuver became commonplace as labor agents regularly extorted signatures from the largely illiterate Mexican and Mexican American workforce. At other times, the defenseless nature of recent immigrants made them highly vulnerable at the hands of a skilled labor contractor. On the job, Hernández learned that his signature authorized several deductions from his earnings. He paid a onetime surcharge of three dollars to the labor agent for getting the job. In addition, Hernández had to pay a two-dollar monthly fee for medical services and the use of a cooking stove. Within a month, his job ended ("through no fault of my mine, that I know"), leaving him stranded and without the means to return to San Antonio.[38] He did not have "a chance to stay on the job and finish the six-month period. I was told to get back to San Antonio the best way I could." Hernández could stay in the area and ask to be rehired, but he could expect to pay the three-dollar job fee again. Through this scheme of turning over the workforce, labor agents pocketed tidy sums as the same workers got hired and rehired.[39]

\* \* \*

A floating population of single Mexican men could be found in extra gang and section crews in other areas of the Pacific Northwest. These men, nameless and unknown unless mentioned in accident reports, were part of a great dispersion of Mexican railroad labor away from the U.S.-México border and north to the Canadian boundary. As Congress described it in a series of immigration hearings in 1930, Mexican railroad labor by the 1920s embodied "seepage" from the Southwest to the "center stage" of the nation.[40]

# Chapter 2

# The Great Depression, Deportations, and Recovery

Until the onset of the Great Depression, the railroad industry easily controlled the lion's share of the nation's transportation capacity. The economic crisis of the 1930s hit the railroads, just as competition from the trucking industry grew. To adjust to the economic downturn, railroad carriers adopted several strategies to compensate for lagging business. Where possible, they upgraded to more efficient equipment and merged with other carriers to avoid going out of business. Above all, railroad carriers lowered maintenance standards and slashed their labor force, especially track crews, from peak employment in the 1920s to bare bones.

As the railroad industry grew impressively through World War I, so did the trucking industry until it began to challenge the railroads for freight business. In 1916 railroads accounted for 77.2 percent of all freight shipments, while motor, air, and water transport companies combined transported slightly more than 20 percent.[1] However, in 1912 the California state legislature had instructed the California Highway Commission to begin using public expenditures to construct an extensive web of concrete roads. Other states soon followed, creating their own statewide system of modern roads. Four years later, President Woodrow Wilson signed the Federal Aid Road Program, initiating a joint federal- and state-funded program to promote national modern highway construction. Within two years, the first road project completed under the Federal Aid Road Program opened in Contra Costa County, California. Once motorists experienced the advantage of well-engineered paved roads, they lobbied for additional public spending to develop more highways. Enthusiastic public support of modern roads eventually developed into an extremely popular "good roads movement" to increase the number of miles of paved roads across the country.

By the 1920s the federal and state arterials began to connect with each other to create the nation's expansive highway system. Well-engineered roads along with a rapidly growing American automobile and truck industry symbolized the prosperity and new social freedom characteristic of the decade. Paved highways and roads allowed motor carriers, especially private automobiles and light trucks, to continue cutting away at intercity railroad freight and passenger service. Outside of short-distance passenger and light freight hauls, however, railroad carriers still dominated the transport industry.[2] Nonetheless, increasing public expenditures to improve the nation's roads had important ramifications for the railroads.

Until the start of World War I, the federal government had subsidized railroads through land grants and other measures. During the 1920s, Congress gradually began diverting public transportation funds to highway and airport construction in open competition with trains. The railroads went on the defensive, by attempting to paint the "good roads movement" as little more than unwarranted propaganda against the rail industry. They lobbied Congress to consider regulating and taxing commercial trucking companies at both state and federal levels. Because of these pressures, the Interstate Commerce Commission held hearings until 1925 to determine if federal support of motor transportation had any deleterious effects on the railroad industry. The hearings did little to slow the increasing competition between the railroads and motor vehicles. For obvious reasons railroad unions joined the railway companies opposing the trucking industry. In 1932 twenty-one railroad labor organizations pledged their support by calling for more comprehensive regulation of bus and truck transportation. Lobbying before the Federal Interstate Commerce Commission, unions argued: "We know of no reason why forms of transportation competing with the railroads should not be regulated in the same manner."[3] The unions understood their livelihood were at stake, but they stood convinced that railroads could offer comparable service provided the federal government regulated motor vehicles to the same degree as trains.

The railroads faced challenges far more complex than expanding motor transportation. Federal support of air service and pipeline and water transports continued to slice away at the railroad's dominance. President Franklin Roosevelt described the first coast-to-coast highway as a significant twentieth-century accomplishment no less important than the completion of the initial transcontinental railroad in the 1800s. Exhorting the nation stymied in the grip of the Great Depression to move forward, he saw the new highway as an embodiment of American "can-do" and the completion of a journey started a hundred years earlier. Within a year, the president pushed ahead by proposing a nationwide infrastructure of modern integrated superhighways.

While the president's plans and appropriations for a highway system were intended to create jobs and stimulate the nation to economic recovery, the railroad companies saw it as a blatant concession to the trucking and bus businesses. By 1929 the railroad industry had suffered a serious blow as constant improvements to highways carrying nearly twenty-six million private and commercial motor vehicles sliced into their near monopoly of transportation.[4] And the situation only got worse: improvements in road vehicle technology and competition for intercity and rural passenger traffic from such operators as the Greyhound and Trailways bus companies practically eliminated intercity train travel by 1933.[5] The Great Depression plunged the railroad industry to near collapse.

From the onset of the economic slowdown, the industry experienced a sharp reversal in freight and passenger traffic. The railroad workforce stood at approximately 1.6 million throughout the 1920s, but three years into the Depression, the number of workers fell below one million, where it remained until the beginning of World War II.[6] Within a year of the Depression, industry earnings had plummeted to the lowest point since the post–World War I recession of 1921.[7] The number of miles of track in operation gradually fell between 1929 and 1939. With fewer trains running and lighter freight loads, the carriers allowed the maintenance on some divisions of the track system to deteriorate below pre-Depression standards. Between 1936 and 1940, the final years of the Depression, rail companies laid fewer miles of new track or replaced worn rail and crossties compared to 1927–30 levels. All together, the rail industry's hard times were reflected in the reduction of capital expenditures on roadway and railroad infrastructure.[8]

Many track laborers were immediately laid off during the Depression as a result of ethnic and racial discrimination, low-skill job requirements, and the curtailment of line maintenance and construction. Railroad crew foremen began to discharge large numbers of workers, with African Americans hit the hardest. Denied full membership in unions and lacking job security, they were the first to go. Even though African American railroad employees held membership in affiliated unions, they lacked a voice in contesting disproportionate wage rates, seniority issues, and discrimination in promotion. As jobs became scarce, unions renewed their attack on African Americans by using arbitrary seniority rights to deny them the rights purported under union membership.

By 1933 the Brotherhood of Maintenance of Way Employees estimated that railroads had slashed their combined track workforce by nearly 50 percent. Four hundred thousand railroad workers were unemployed by 1931, and twelve months later an additional two hundred thousand track laborers were jobless.[9] In an attempt to offset worsening unemployment, the BMWE accepted a 10 percent industrywide reduction in wages over a twelve-month period beginning in 1932. Despite rolling back pay, however, the railroads continued to lay off workers, forcing the union to consider other measures to mitigate these losses. In some cases, laborers agreed to work fewer days per week so that others could remain employed. Conditions worsened and by 1934 track workers considered themselves extremely fortunate if employers called them to work eight days out of each month. Wages continued to drop until they reached "starvation levels," according to the BMWE. The union accused the railroads of using the Depression to dismiss higher-paid BMWE members in favor of nonunion, often minority, track workers who were willing to accept pay of ten to twelve cents an hour.[10] Indeed, as carriers replaced its regular workforce for stand-in cheaper labor, many railroaders resorted to keeping vegetable gardens, chickens, milk cows, and selling dairy products or firewood to survive.[11]

A measure of how hard the depression impacted labor can be seen in the devastation to Southern Pacific Railroad workers. In 1929, Southern Pacific had 89,304 employees. Two years later, the company had slashed the workforce by over 50 percent to 41,863.[12] This unprecedented drop in jobs set the stage for increased racial and ethnic animosity, pitting white against nonwhite railroaders. As conditions worsened, some public and private individuals and organizations blamed immigrants, particularly noncitizens, for the wearisome and seemingly endless months without employment. In this contentious atmosphere, zealous xenophobes began to target the multiethnic working communities that historically had characterized much of the western railroad labor force.

Japanese Americans and Mexican Americans predominated among nonwhite track laborers in the West at the outset of the Depression. Cutbacks forced many Japanese Americans to leave railroad employment for urban centers or attempt to enter the fresh-market farming economy. Despite the widespread racial animosity and legislation prohibiting landownership, some Japanese Americans were able to become landowners in some farming areas in California, Idaho, Oregon, and Washington. Among those who remained with the railroads, some Japanese Americans used seniority acquired from years of employment to avoid losing their jobs. Until the across-the-board forced removal and internment of Japanese Americans during World War II, those who held positions as foremen or supervisors could sometimes use their authority to partially insulate their brethren and keep them gainfully employed.

The Depression affected Mexican-descent laborers differently. So many Mexican emigrants had arrived in California for railroad and farm work between 1920 and 1930 that the state's Mexican-origin population increased fourfold by the end of the decade, reaching 6.5 percent of the state total.[13] Outside of California, a similar but less vigorous expansion of the Mexican immigrant community developed as well. Because the federal census did not adequately enumerate the Mexican-origin population in the Pacific Northwest until the 1970 census, the degree of migration and immigration flows remains unknown.[14] The 1930 census count of foreign-born Mexicans, exclusive of second- and third-generation children, ranked Washington twenty-ninth in the nation.[15] Next door, in Idaho, the Mexican government's sponsorship of Pocatello's Comisión Honorífica attested to a smaller but growing and thriving Spanish-speaking immigrant community in the state. Interviewed in Pocatello in 1992, Juanita Zazueta Huerta recalled the festive patriotic community celebrations held in commemoration of México's national holidays.[16]

Pocatello became known as the Gate City because eastern, southern, and western railroad lines converged there. Over time, the eastern side of the city resembled an intermingled web of Greek, Italian, African American, and Mexican railroad communities. Residents recalled widespread social discrimination that segregated these same ethnic groups to the rear and left side of the local theaters. The Mexican section grew slowly, but by the time eighteen-year-old Mike Rivera arrived from Colorado in 1935, the community had a vibrant social life. Despite the discrimination, the Pocatello railroad community was very much a part of the city's social citizenry. José M. Ortega, working as a yard clerk for Union Pacific, performed as leader of the Ortega Rhythm Aires Orchestra in dance halls in Pocatello and elsewhere in southern Idaho.[17]

The enormous and rapid scale of recruitment and employment among Mexicans and Mexican Americans in the years before the Depression held this ethnic group from gaining promotion to supervisory positions. Although some worked in the yards and car shops, the vast majority of these workers remained fixed to section crews doing ordinary pick-and-shovel track employment. Caught off-guard by the sudden economic collapse, many communities, organizations, and some employers took steps to provide some measure of relief to laid-off workers. In an attempt to lend a hand to the unemployed, Southern Pacific established a worker- and corporate-sponsored relief fund. Under the company-sponsored plan, employees contributed 1 percent of their earnings, which the company matched, to a no-interest loan fund. Unemployed workers vested under the plan could apply for loans with no interest and with payments not due until "circumstances permitted." The generous credit plan loaned around $349,000 to three thousand out-of-work families before the program terminated in 1932 because of declining employee contributions.[18] Company support of unemployed workers was one thing. However, nonwhites and noncitizens found it difficult to qualify for state relief. Against this discriminatory policy of entitlement, the Mexican immigrant community was unable to cope with the severity of the economic depression. Because of the lack of jobs, some immigrants opted to return to México.

Acting on the advice of President Herbert Hoover's Emergency Committee on Employment, federal officials believed that wholesale deportation of nonauthorized immigrants would free up additional jobs for (white) citizens. Accordingly, they began to apprehend people suspected of being in the United States without authorization. When Secretary of Labor William N. Doak sanctioned the Bureau of Immigration to deport undocumented foreigners as a way of whittling away at public relief rolls, and in an effort to provide job opportunities for citizens, he in fact legitimized an indiscriminate practice of expelling citizens and noncitizens alike for dubious reasons. Not surprisingly, the federal drive to offset hard times by deporting Mexican people encouraged ordinary citizens, fraternal and religious organizations, and state and municipal politicians to act against immigrant Mexicans.

Unemployed Mexican laborers became subject to systematic and extensive deportation efforts. In California the Interstate Commerce Commission approved a plan whereby Los Angeles County paid the Southern Pacific Railroad a reduced "low charity rate" of $14.70 for each nonlegal Mexican resident transported to México's border.[19] In 1932 the municipal governments of East Chicago and Gary, Indiana, agreed to cover the expense of returning thirty-three hundred people by train to México.[20] The deportation

of Mexican immigrants became systemic. In the Pacific Northwest the director of the Oregon State Bureau of Labor raised the issue of Mexicans being
employed by Southern Pacific while white residents suffered for lack of jobs.
The Southern Pacific's Oregon Division, state officials contended, should
replace all Mexicans with white labor. Although the company refused to
concede, it did adopt a Depression-era reverse affirmative action policy
whereby whites had preference over Mexicans in subsequent hiring.[21]

Deportation, a Band-Aid solution to serious national economic hemor-
rhaging, fell hard on other nationalities as well, especially nonwhite immigrants. In the case of Filipino nationals, the federal government provided
one-way fares back to the Philippines. Mexicans were markedly represented
among the apprehended.[22] The most documented instances of the wanton
apprehension and deportation of Mexicans took place in southern California and the upper Midwest regions of the nation. Mexicans faced economic anxiety and psychological stress related to repatriation efforts that
were place everywhere. By the end of the Depression, the United States had
deported approximately 650,000 Mexicans, including many with U.S. citizenship.[23] Of course, the idea of creating employment for American citizens
did not warrant the abrogation of civil rights of citizens and constitutional
protections guaranteed to immigrants.

When farm prices dropped and factories went bankrupt, freight revenues plummeted precipitously, casting railroad workers into already burgeoning unemployment lines. The overnight loss of jobs generally started
in low-skill entry-level track and "back shop" operations (two areas usually
dominated by Mexican laborers). Adding to the woes of the workers, some
railroad companies transferred maintenance jobs away from predominantly
Mexican communities.[24] Employers consented to mounting public pressure
by systematically dismissing Mexicans employees, leaving them to fend for
themselves. The railroad companies, including other employers, had relied
on this practice before but never during a period of such great public anxiety over unwanted Mexicans. Under the circumstances, the term "Mexican"
took on an added meaning of contempt, loathing, and hatred unequaled
since the years after the Mexican American War. In Idaho, and elsewhere in
the Pacific Northwest, many whites started to regard Mexicans as beyond
"undesirable" and served them with what became popularly known as "ski-
doo" notices.

* * *

As the Depression worsened, railroad companies sought to modernize in order to survive the tight economy and regain the decline in passenger service and freight shipments. In the 1930s the Southern Pacific began to put in newer and faster trains to boost passenger and freight revenues. Increasing speed to cut travel times required improvements to grades as well as curve reductions on existing track beds. Beginning in 1936, carriers started to lay new higher-capacity track on their most profitable lines. Enhanced efficiency required using heavier ninety to ninety-four pound per yard rail to sustain faster and heavier loaded trains.[25] Companies also introduced centralized traffic control systems, allowing for more efficient routing on existing lines.

Despite these advancements in rolling equipment and track, railroad traffic continued to face constant and stiffening competition from motor vehicle transportation. Trucks and buses slowly became more efficient and profitable, cutting steadily into rail freight and passenger service. Unlike the railroads the truck and bus transportation industries had a competitive advantage by circulating on roads and highways constructed and maintained at public expense. Railroads, however, had to build their own right of ways and keep them serviceable without public compensation. Passenger buses and freight trucks had another competitive advantages. Railroads, engineered to transfer high volumes, were not able to contract with shippers to move small freight consignments (called "less-than-carload" freight) efficiently or economically. Motor vehicles traveling on public avenues operated more flexibly with varying schedules and routes, allowing them to pick and choose from the best value freight and passenger lines. In this manner, trucks sliced into rail freight by hauling smaller loads faster and more economically than trains over short-haul distances.

Faster and higher-capacity buses also challenged railroad passenger service by entering into emerging lucrative interurban transportation markets. Between 1930 and 1935 in the western states, the number of intercity passengers using flexible and convenient bus lines more than tripled. The number of customers using longer-route interstate buses to travel inside and across state lines also doubled. In addition to buses and trucks, privately owned automobiles also contested the railroad industry. Resulting from a combination of improvements in car design and better engineered roads, private automobiles challenged for intercity passenger traffic. So many people embraced cars as an effective, reliable, and independent means of transportation that by 1926 automobiles accounted for nearly 75 percent of all intercity travel. All the while, urban rail coach travel continued to decline steadily.

The railroad companies were well aware of the increasing competition emerging from these newer forms of transportation, but they moved slowly to respond competitively. Throughout the 1920s the industry believed that train service could offset the challenge of motor carriers. Modernization resulted in increased efficiency and profits, but in the long run this "why do today what you can put off until tomorrow" mentality proved costly, especially as the Depression wore on. In an all-out effort to respond to changing business and public preferences concerning transportation, railroads launched new campaigns to make trains more appealing to passengers and shippers alike. For example, the Southern Pacific and Union Pacific promoted their modern luxury "super speed" trains. Advertisements called attention to the latest railroad technology, modern streamlined designs with such evocative names as Hiawatha, the Treasure Island Special, and the Zephyr. The Milwaukee, Chicago, and Pacific Road, operating on a more practical level, opened a state-of-the-art, half-million-dollar receiving-and-transfer station to expedite freight arriving and departing Chicago. At the same time, the company reached out to shippers by rolling out new equipment that drastically reduced delivery time of freight between Chicago and Seattle in some cases by as much as twenty-four hours.

From California to Washington, railroad companies faced the reality of increasing vehicular competition and a changing transportation market by abandoning hundreds of miles of rail lines that were no longer cost-effective. Against the backdrop of the severity of the Depression, industry profits ranged from poor to dreadful, forcing companies to begin curtailments in service or outright abandonment of unprofitable lines. By 1931 the Southern Pacific had abandoned all-electric intercity commuter train service from Portland south into Willamette Valley communities.[26] Gasoline-powered buses began to replace streetcars in Salem, Eugene, and Portland. Across the industry, layoffs hit track laborers hardest even though companies still had to retain a workforce equal to the maintenance requirements brought by the increasing weight and speed of trains. Reductions in labor resulted from changes in construction methods and track design, including labor-saving machinery, the use of longer lasting ties, deeper ballast, and heavier and stronger rail. Reduction in track curvature and elevation translated into shorter travel times, lower maintenance requirements, and fewer track repairs. All told, track laborers, albeit in smaller numbers, remained essential to the railroad industry.

For those still employed or searching for work, personal connections and union affiliation were key during the difficult circumstances of the Depression. It was especially helpful to have an employed family member, particularly a father or other relative, to even have a chance for part-time work. This meant that non-BMWE members like Mexicans and other nonwhites stood little chance in the extremely slow job market that was now solidly underpinned by an explicit white-preference policy. As carriers economized expenditures at all levels, those track laborers fortunate to have work dealt with ongoing reductions and fluctuations in wages. In 1932 railroad employees had agreed to a one-year temporary industrywide 10 percent reduction in wages. During the next two years, workers conceded to another cut in wages, lasting until midyear of 1934. At this time, the railroads restored 2.5 percent of the wage reduction. Six months later, workers got another 2.5 percent increase, and employers eventually reinstated the outstanding 5 percent wage reduction in April 1935.[27] Business for the railroad industry finally began to improve in 1936, when a combination of new business strategies and a surge in the economy put the carriers on the road to partial recovery. The following year, track workers and other nonoperating employees received an additional five-cent per hour increase in wages.[28]

\* \* \*

Track workers clearly fared badly during the early days of the Depression. But they also benefited from general public sentiment in favor of federal legislation benefiting labor. The Railroad Act of 1934 provided new protection to many but not all workers and unions through the National Mediation Board. Workers welcomed into the industry were now free to join any labor organization of their choice without fear of retribution from management. The bill created the National Railroad Adjustment Board to arbitrate grievances, disputes, or interpretations of standing agreements covering pay, rules, and working conditions. That same year, the Railroad Retirement Act created a retirement program for workers. The legislation provided full annuities to people fifty-six years or older after thirty years rail employment. Although challenged and declared unconstitutional in some courts, the retirement program won permanent approval in 1935.

Under the Washington Job Protection Agreement of 1936, other workers became eligible to receive displacement compensation as a result of the negative effects of consolidations or mergers in the industry. Organized labor considered compensation for workforce reductions to be a major issue because jobs disappeared as carriers unified, consolidated, or pooled facilities or operations to cope with the ongoing sluggish economic downturn. In 1935 unions estimated that the Association of American Railroads had considered as many as six hundred consolidations of various kinds to economize expenditures. Accordingly, 250,000 workers stood to lose their jobs when many were already unemployed. In addition to the Washington Job Protection Agreement, the Social Security Act of 1933 extended unemployment insurance to railroad employees. Thus railway workers gained from New Deal legislation that produced unprecedented job protections and entitlements to the American working class. Finally, the enactment of the 1938 Fair Labor Standards Act resulted in another major income boost. Administered by the Wage and Hour Division of the Department of Labor, the act established a floor for hourly wages and a limit of the number of work hours per week for railroad employees. To be in compliance, the railroad industry had to offer twenty-five cents per hour for the incoming year, thirty cents for the next six years, and forty cents thereafter.[29]

Even as conditions seemed to improve for the railroads, in 1938 things suddenly worsened, prompting notification to employees of an impending 15 percent reduction in wages. The industry had entered a downward slide as a result of changes in transportation technology. Facing challenges from the automotive industry, air transport, highway construction, and inexorable use of private cars, the railroad industry and its workforce appeared hemmed in by insurmountable limitations. This time, however, labor quickly contested the cut in wages by calling for mediation through the Railway Labor Act and the Presidential Emergency Board. In the end the decision favored labor; mediators determined that despite the industry's claims, "no horizontal reduction upon a national scale of the wages of railway labor should be pressed by the carriers at this time."[30]

The economy began to improve a year later as the war in Europe began. As the United States became involved in the war through the lend-lease program of assistance to the allies, railroad companies began to rebuild their workforce to transport increasing amounts of freight across the nation and for destinations in Europe. Once more, shippers called on the railroad industry to move high volumes of food and manufactured goods in volumes previously unheard of. In the fall of 1939 business boomed so much that the Association of American Railroads in cooperation with military preparedness officials designed a traffic system to address railcar congestion at East Coast ports. An ever increasing demand for food and fiber from western farms suddenly imposed a severe burden on carriers to ship materials to eastern ports for delivery to Europe. Without a doubt, escalating freight orders marked the first stage toward a wartime resurgence for the industry. Southern Pacific attributed 81.2 percent of all earnings to freight revenues alone.[31] The resurgence in freight shipments meant railroad companies began to hire back workers. Now, twice as many Brotherhood of Maintenance of Way Employees members had jobs than during the worse years of the Depression. Railroad companies looked forward to increased profits, and track workers became increasingly optimistic of better times.

Indicative of improving stability in the industry in 1940, Southern Pacific added more than eighteen thousand workers to its West Coast lines and an additional twenty-one hundred on the Texas and New Orleans Railroad to handle freight and for track work.[32] Even as Southern Pacific increased the number of employees, finding workers in a rapidly tightening labor market became problematic. By February 1941 railroad executives announced some companies were "undermanned" and unable to respond to the nation's transportation requirements without additional employees.[33] According to Southern Pacific, unreasonable federal regulations, such as "full-crew laws" that required several brakemen on freight shipments, tended to exacerbate the problem.[34] The industry contended that between February 1940 and early 1941, overtime work shifts had actually masked a critical serious shortage of seventy-five thousand workers. Indicative of the mushrooming labor issue, the Railroad Retirement Board confirmed the company's claims of an estimated shortage at fifty-five thousand workers, 80 percent of which were necessary for maintenance-of-way work.[35]

By the end of 1940, railroad companies (particularly those operating in the West) defined the labor shortage as a serious impediment to the European war effort. By linking the lack of workers to the nation's responsibility to assist its allies abroad, an industry labor problem turned into an issue of national importance. Railroads were now in a position to seek assistance from the federal government. Echoing the agricultural industry's earlier petition for help through the use of contracted farm labor from México, the Southern Pacific Railroad made the first request to recruit track laborers from México.

\* \* \*

Between the two world wars, the railroad industry, along with labor, had gone from abundance to near collapse during the Great Depression then rebounded after 1939. Despite the hard economic times and challenges from the automobile, bus, and truck industries, the railroad companies emerged intact. On the horizon the U.S. entry into World War II would test the capacity of the railroad industry as never before. The railroads would reconfigure their operations as much to regain their position as the nation's most vital mode of transportation as to support the national and global war effort. In both normal and depressed economic times, labor played a critical role in sustaining the railroad industry. A more extensive industrywide labor scarcity brought on by World War II would demonstrate just how essential labor would become.

# Chapter 3

# We Will Need the Mexicans Back

In 1941 the U.S. declaration of war against Japan, Germany, and Italy pulled the U.S. railroad industry out of the economic gloom of the 1930s. During the World War II, rail carriers regained the premier position among the nation's transportation industries as it moved unprecedented levels of freight and passengers. Hardly one year into the war, industry executives reached back to their experience during World War I and began making plans to once again import Mexican railroad contract laborers. The railroad labor proposal closely resembled the agricultural industry's justification and contractual language that had been used to bring temporary workers from México.

Shortly after the United States declared war, México had severed diplomatic relations with Japan but without totally committing to the Allied cause. In May 1942, however, a German submarine operating in the Gulf of México torpedoed the Mexican oil tankers *Potrero del Llano* and *Faja de Oro*. The surprise attack and loss of Mexican lives immediately pushed México directly into the world conflict.[1] On June 1, following a near unanimous vote in the National Congress, President Manuel Ávila Camacho officially announced México's declaration of war against the Axis powers. "The United Mexican States," he declared, "are found in a State of War with Germany, Italy, and Japan."[2] After this announcement, México and the United States moved rapidly to build a spirit of Pan-American assistance to address their immediate and shared interests in national security, defense of the West Coast, and ultimate victory abroad. The existing U.S. Railway Mission to improve México's railroads served to launch and solidify an unequivocal binational commitment to the war. At a September 16, 1942, Fiestas Patrias celebration in Los Angeles, Vice President Henry Wallace stressed the importance of unity and mutual aid between the Mexican and United States armed forces.

Six weeks later, the *New York Times* reported that President Camcho
had committed Mexican troops for overseas combat. This announcement
took México by surprise, since Camacho's declaration of war had included
a pledge that its military would not serve outside of the republic. Indeed,
Mexican land forces had never traveled overseas during the war, but 150 officers and enlisted men trained in various U.S. military installations, including Fort Benning (Georgia), Fort Monroe (Virginia), Fort Monmouth (New
Jersey), March Air Field (California), Pocatello (Idaho), and Randolph and
Kelly Air Field (Texas).[3] One month later, a group of Mexican air force pilots
arrived to train at March Air Field. Eventually, the complete contingent of
officers and mechanics attached to Mexican Fighter Squadron 201 arrived
at the Pocatello Air Base in Idaho to qualify flying P47 Thunderbolts. Un-
beknownst to the Mexican pilots, training missions occurred over areas of
southern Idaho and eastern Oregon and Washington, where an extensive
land army of their compatriots labored under the auspices of the World
War II bracero farm and railroad programs.

Under a Lend Lease Agreement the United States transferred considerable quantities of outdated railroad and military equipment to México. Because México's transportation industry did not have the ability or capacity
to move heavy war material, the U.S. agreed to construct liberty ships for
México's use. On April 14, 1943, the wife of General Felipe Rico, comman-
dant of the Second Military Zone, Ensenada, Baja California, christened
the *Miguel Hidalgo* at the California Shipbuilding Corporation yards in
Wilmington, California. The act of commemorating Mexican patriots with
U.S.-built vessels worked to strengthen the alliance between México and the
United States and simultaneously build up binational trade. In a separate
accord to amplify the two armed forces, the two nations agreed to authorize the conscription of resident aliens, excepting students, border crossers,
and braceros. Reciprocity notwithstanding, no United States citizen living
in México entered the Mexican armed forces. By June 1945 more than 15,632
Mexican nationals had served with distinction in the U.S. military in the
Pacific and European theaters.[4]

The spirit of binational cooperation during the war compelled México
to temporarily overlook the humiliating memory of having thousands of
its citizens forced back across the border during the Great Depression. The
United States had to embrace the sincerity of demonstrating goodwill toward México. These were not easy steps for the two nations to take. Strained

relations between the two countries stretched back to the Mexican American War of 1848 through the Revolution of 1910, when the United States invaded México. While xenophobia festered on both sides of the border, a few years before World War II, anti-Americanism escalated in México when the United States contested México's right to expropriate foreign property. The hostility intensified when the United States demanded compensation for oil, railroads, and other properties nationalized by México. A lingering disagreement between California and México over water rights from the Colorado River further soured international relations. Across the United States during the Depression, a discernible pattern of ethnic and racial prejudice resulted in systemic deportations of Mexican nationals and commonplace segregation and mistreatment of Mexican American citizens. On June 4, 1943, several days of violent racial riots broke out in Los Angeles when U.S. servicemen began an indiscriminate attack on Mexican American youth. Widely publicized in newspapers, the anti-Mexican riots eventually spread to other American cities. This type of racial and ethnic animosity directed at Mexican-origin residents seemed paradoxical with the federal efforts to improve wartime relations between México and the United States.

Despite these societal and political distractions on both sides of the border, the importance of winning the global war and addressing strategic hemispheric defense and trade issues established an overall sentiment of goodwill between the United States and other Latin America countries. Like México, other Latin America countries had vital war resources, adding urgency to the establishment of strong Pan-American unity. Fascism emanating from Spain and Italy enjoyed nascent interest in Argentina as well as other Spanish-speaking countries, including México. Therefore, in establishing a good neighbor policy toward México, the United States's strategy was to leverage an ideological platform to engender greater Pan-American collaboration against fascism and the Axis.

The highlights of the U.S.-México good neighbor policy emerged in the form of the U.S. Railway Mission to México and the bracero agricultural and railroad labor agreements. Early in the war, the United States turned to México for strategic minerals and materials, such as petroleum, copper, zinc, mercury, mahogany and other hardwoods essential for medicine, and aircraft and naval construction. México also became an important conduit for Central American shipment of durable goods, including bananas, coffee, pineapples, cattle, and other foodstuffs vital to the United States. Although

México had historically exported enormous quantities of raw products to
the U.S., trade slowed considerably after México's 1917 Constitution nationalized and shielded key sectors of the Mexican economy from export.

In light of the attack on México, the wartime emergency allowed the government to circumvent existing trade barriers. México's badly dilapidated
and substandard national railway had to be reconstructed in order for the
United States to procure essential war materials. From the U.S. point of
view, a reliable and efficient railroad system in México became imperative
for reasons other than trade. The threat of German and Italian submarines
and the diversion of merchant ships to wartime activities interrupted the
long-established maritime supply line between the United States, México,
and Central America. Hemispheric defense, especially at the Panama Canal,
required great quantities of machinery, equipment, and supplies to travel
through Mexican railroads. México, and for that matter the United States,
could not keep pace with its own intensifying export and domestic wartime
economy without a reliable Mexican railway network.

Escalating war production coupled with an interruption of maritime
shipments of essential goods compelled the United States to recognize
México as a key supplier of strategic raw materials and agricultural products. In 1940, México ranked first in the world in silver production, second
in antimony, third in lead, fourth in mercury, fifth in zinc, sixth in gold, and
seventh in petroleum and graphite. Mexican agricultural production of bis-
muth, guayule rubber, sisal, henequen, mahogany, alcohol, coffee, sugar,
and chicle were just as critical to the U.S. war effort. The war in Europe and
Asia significantly disrupted imports from other nations. As a result, in the
summer of 1941 the U.S. contracted to purchase México's entire production
of many essential raw products.[5]

The growing U.S. dependency on Mexican economic output immediately revealed the inadequacies of México's railroad transportation system.
As the United States ambassador in México pointed out, "Mexican railways
are of vital importance to the United States in both peace and war, but particularly now, in a time of war, when Mexican raw materials, minerals, and
agricultural products must be transported to our Nation by rail."[6] Given the
urgent need for vital materials, the U.S. approached México with a proposal
to upgrade its railway system in order to allow material to flow more readily across the two countries. The negotiations quickly produced a binational
agreement in December 1942 to establish a U.S. Railway Mission. Nelson A.
Rockefeller, together with a delegation of fifty experienced railroad techni-

cians, arrived in México City in 1943 to aid in rebuilding México's railway system.

The political context leading to the Railway Mission reveals critical insights into U.S. policy regarding México. Twelve months before entering the war, President Franklin Roosevelt established the Office for the Coordination of Commercial and Cultural Relations between the American Republics, with Rockefeller as coordinator. Under the guise of addressing commercial and social affairs, Rockefeller's office also served as the headquarters for the Latin American branch of the U.S. Army's intelligence, G-2 Division. Until the summer of 1941, the office functioned mostly to contest German, Italian, and Japanese commercial and political propaganda in Latin America. In July 1941, U.S. intelligence-gathering functions moved to the state department office in México City. Rockefeller, now with the Office of Inter-American Affairs (an outgrowth of the Office for the Coordination of Commercial and Cultural Relations between the American Republics) continued to gather important economic intelligence. To avoid suspicion, the Office of Inter-American Affairs announced plans to construct public facilities, including water supply systems, hospitals, sanitation, housing, and communication facilities. Ironically, but consistent with its military intent, the public projects were not designated in places where they were most needed but rather at key strategic military points identified by G-2 intelligence.[7]

* * *

The interplay between Rockefeller's role before and after the arrival of the Railroad Mission to México in 1943 tells much about U.S. political posture toward México. Where México anticipated that the Railway Mission would improve its transportation system, the U.S. viewed the program as a strategic economic and military objective. Quite swiftly, the American technical personnel reported the Mexican rail system, along with other key transportation industries, as wholly inadequate and close to complete collapse. The reasons for the degraded Mexican rail system were not hard to find: the Mexican revolution, ongoing civil disturbances through the late 1920s; and the economic depression of the 1930s took a severe toll on the nation's railroad infrastructure and rolling equipment. Efficiency continued to erode in 1938 after President Lázaro Cárdenas expropriated the national railroads of México and turned complete operational control of the railroads over to the powerful and politically influential Mexican Railroad Workers Union.[8] Subsequently, most revenues went to salaries, leaving little for investments to improve the railway system. Since the union exercised total control of railway operations, patronage flourished and in cases of incompetence, the workers organization protected employees against dismissal. In December 1940, President Camacho began to wrest operations back from the Mexican Railroad Workers Union by establishing a railroad administrative council composed of three members selected by the union and four members appointed by the president.[9]

The poor state of the Mexican railway system can just as well be attributed to the U.S. railroad companies. For years, U.S. companies expediently disposed of older, depreciated, or obsolete equipment by dumping them in México at substantial profit. Later, the Mexican railway system began to default on its payments for the used equipment, incapable of making repairs or regular maintenance. For these reasons Mexican locomotive equipment did not cross into the U.S. for repair work; American creditors were waiting to seize the equipment to satisfy payment of debts. The Baldwin Locomotive Works company, for example, maintained regular surveillance in El Paso hoping to seize Mexican railway equipment in payment for six steam locomotives purchased by the national railways of México in 1937.[10]

The lack of cooperation between the Mexican National Railways and the U.S. railroad industry stemmed from a deeply rooted atmosphere of mistrust on both sides of the border. U.S. businesses alleged México had defaulted on numerous debts extending back to the early 1900s and on remuneration for privately owned property expropriated in the 1930s. In 1941, as evidence of goodwill and binational economic cooperation, the two countries agreed that México would pay $40 million to U.S. railroads and businesses as settlement of all outstanding claims. Because it did not produce its own equipment until 1944, Mexican railways continued to operate with older depreciated steam locomotives manufactured in the United States. Domestic production of rolling stock came much later and nearly a decade after the war's end.[11] Consequently, México's inability to repair its equipment or have repairs done in U.S. facilities translated into an unsafe, inefficient, and oftentimes unproductive train system.

Aware of these issues, and in order to solidify México's contribution to the war, President Roosevelt traveled to Monterrey, Nuevo Leon, to meet with President Camacho on April 20, 1943, ending a thirty-four-year span where no U.S. president had visited México.[12] The governments mutually announced an agreement to create a joint Commission for Economic Cooperation with the goal of finding the means to increase deliveries of U.S.

equipment, supplies, and tools to the Mexican industrial sector. In bolstering México's industries, the economic commission expected to complement the efforts of the U.S. Railway Mission and stimulate increased productivity of much needed minerals and industrial raw products.[13]

On June 30, 1946, the Railway Mission had successfully completed its work to improve México's rail infrastructure.[14] During the Railway Mission, the U.S. expended $6.8 million to upgrade the system while México expended $10 million.[15] The attainment of the Railway Mission can be measured at two important points. First, critical supplies from México and as far away as Central America were able to reach the United States. Second, in México the binational railway agreement resulted in a successful upgrades of track, some repair facilities, and improved practices within the industry. Mexican passenger service grew tremendously during 1943–45, a surge not seen again until 1965, but the increase was largely a result of the train loads of braceros headed to the United States to work and returning back to México when the work was completed.[16] In fact, officials urged that all braceros be transported on México's national railway to call attention to the successful work of the Railway Mission.[17] While the improvements to the Mexican railroad network were effective to achieve the desired results, any lasting improvements were more symbolic than representative of expansion in México's industrial capacity as a result of the success of the Railroad Mission itself.

By all accounts, the work of the U.S. Railway Mission to México revived the national railways of México so that it could ship strategic supplies to the United States. In its farewell note to México, the Railway Mission wrote: "We of the Mission will never forget the magnificent resolution and cooperative spirit displayed by men of the National Railways System when our two Nations made common cause of keeping your rail lifeline open for the steady flow of strategic materials from México and Central America into the United States stockpile."[18]

\* \* \*

The noteworthy foreign policy strategy of the U.S. Railway Mission to México marked the first massive American technical assistance program to a foreign nation—well before the post–World War II Marshall Plan of 1948. The mission served as a valuable means to facilitate the transportation of hundreds of thousands of bracero laborers north to the United States. When México granted the United States the authority to recruit Mexican labor for the agriculture and railroad industries, it demonstrated the same unity of action that underscored mutual defense matters, the construction of liberty ships, the U.S. Railway Mission, and bilateral trade in technology and raw products.

In the United States, labor shortages, especially in the developing West, became disconcerting to employers and government officials alike. The need for Mexican workers, preferably men, began when the U.S. Congress started to limit the entry of Asian immigrants to the United States.[19] In 1905 matters worsened for employers when President Theodore Roosevelt closed a loophole that had permitted Asian immigrants to enter the country through México. Closing the Mexican border to Asian immigrants hit employers so hard that labor agents began to smuggle Chinese workers "from México" for jobs as far away as Portland, Oregon.[20] At the same time, Mexicans entered the United States freely, barring a few unenforced restrictions. As the swell of Mexican workers spread across the geographical expanse of the country, it led to early binational labor conferences on the issue. The first of these conferences occurred in 1909 between President William H. Taft and México's Porfirio Díaz. The conference resulted in a gentleman's agreement to authorize employers to contract Mexican workers. Also in that year, temporary contracted workers (the forerunners of the braceros of World War II) arrived to western and midwestern sugar beet farms and railroad companies. Some job contracts carried Mexican laborers still farther north for employment in Alaska's fish-processing and canning industries.

Later, during World War I and as employers faced increasing labor shortages, Congress initiated legislative hearings aimed at curbing Mexican immigration. This became a serious national issue because until the establishment of the Border Patrol in 1924, public anxiety heightened over unlawful border crossings from México. Caught in a dilemma between calls for immigration restrictions and a shortage of workers, employers sidestepped the issue by calling for legally admitted temporary Mexican contracted workers held to specific labor terms, including type of job and wages. All things considered, any solution to the labor problem had to balance with the civic and political concern over legal and undocumented immigration. The Immigration Act of 1917, however, prohibited the entry of foreign contracted labor into the country. Only after extensive lobbying by the agriculture and railroad industries did the secretary of labor suspend existing literacy and tax requirements leveled against persons intending to immigrate legally to the United States. The waiver granted employers permission to recruit Mexican contract workers starting on May 22, 1918.

Building on the earlier Díaz-Taft labor agreement, the United States and México sanctioned the first comprehensive bracero program, officially called the Temporary Admissions Program of World War I. This binational agreement required employers to file an official request specifying the number of workers, the type of job, wage, and place of employment to obtain laborers. Employers wanting to hire contract labor from México also had to comply with all state housing regulations and cover all transportation costs from México to the work site. The language of the worker's labor contract fixed the person to a particular job and for a specified length of time while in the U.S. To further secure the worker to an employer, the agreement deducted a percentage from each worker's wages not refundable until the end of the work period. In the event that a worker broke the contract, the employer could notify the Immigration Bureau to revoke the worker's legal temporary status to remain in the United States. These clauses, which served as insurance against workers skipping their contracts and not returning to México, addressed the public's fear that Mexican temporary workers would become permanent residents.

When the World War I bracero program ended in 1921, the U.S. and Mexican governments and the workers themselves considered the Temporary Admissions Program a near failure. A lack of enforcement nullified the intent and provisions of the agreement, rendering the worker's contract useless. In the end, only farmers and the railroads benefited from the government-sanctioned labor initiative. Lacking enforcement or effective sanctions, the Temporary Admissions Program did little to curb Mexican immigration and encouraged it instead. Twenty years later, at the onset of World War II, the agricultural and railroad industry resurrected the Temporary Admission Program to petition the federal government for assistance in procuring vitally needed Mexican workers. Unlike the earlier war, the scale of World War II generated an unprecedented demand for labor. Farms required record amounts of labor to produce enough to feed and clothe the nation, the military, as well as to provide for our allies. Coming out of the Great Depression, the railroads faced a similar dilemma. Large numbers of workers were imperative to quickly upgrade the existing track system so vital to move troops, civilians, and the nation's entire agricultural and industrial production. These two industries faced a narrow labor market and had to contend with increasingly competitive wage structures.

The first call for laborers from México came from western farm operators on the eve of World War II, in 1939. Reminiscent of the pre-Depression years, growers began to assert that Mexican labor was indispensable to a healthy agricultural economy. Indeed, well ahead of the war, President Roosevelt's New Deal initiatives returned some agricultural crops back to 1929 production levels. Sugar beet cultivation, for example, expanded from tariffs on imported Cuban and Hawaiian cane sugar. In many parts of the West, hop acreage multiplied dramatically following the repeal of prohibition. Agricultural production expanded due to new technologies such as improved field-to-market transportation, irrigation methods, and soil conservation projects. The war-driven demand for increased food production for national consumption and export to Europe functioned as a powerful incentive to stimulate agricultural producers. By the beginning of 1940, California farms increased the pressure on the government to help secure essential Mexican laborers.

Publicity over the mounting labor shortages set off an uncontrolled flow of immigrants across the U.S.-México border. In McAllen, Texas, the Mexican consul reported that an expanding population of undocumented Mexicans had developed in the state in response to the widespread call for laborers. Even through 1940, aggressive farm lobbying failed to persuade the immigration service to allow contract workers into the United States. The U.S. declaration of war called for still higher levels of farm production even as the economy moved to full employment. In response to farmers, U.S. Secretary of Agriculture Claude Wickard instructed the Department of Agriculture to draft several contingencies justifying the importation of workers. The prospect for the use of contracted labor increased significantly in the summer of 1941, when Secretary Wickard spoke in favor of a binational bracero program at the Inter-American Conference on Agriculture in México City. Governor Culbert Olson of California added his voice to the powerful state agriculture producers in a telegram to the secretaries of agriculture, labor, and the state department. "Without a substantial number of Mexicans," he wired, "the situation is certain to be disastrous to the entire victory [war] program."[21] In April 1942 the Departments of Justice, Labor, State, Agriculture, and the War Manpower Commission began to study the feasibility of importing contract workers from México.

When federal and business representatives met to address the escalating scarcity of labor, they had to cope with similar issues faced by the original bracero program twenty years earlier. Outside of the Great Depression, the railroad and agricultural economies had historically relied on Mexican farm and track labor. Now, the unprecedented demand for economic production brought about by the war had the potential of resulting in an uncontrollable exodus of Mexican immigrants. To address this possibility, officials agreed that a modified World War I type of contract labor program seemed the most expedient method of delivering temporary Mexican help to employers. The new contract labor program had to satisfy three principal concerns. First and foremost, Mexican contract workers were only allowed into the country in order alleviate the wartime labor shortages. Second, language of the workers' contracts had to lock them to specific jobs and geographic locations. Finally, the contract labor program had to satisfy the public disquiet over the perception that temporary workers, once in the U.S., would remain permanently.

To meet these conditions, the federal government modified the World War I bracero program to meet the current needs of the agricultural and railroad industries. To help win México's cooperation the new bracero program conceded minimal safeguards and guarantees to the imported workers regarding wages, housing, return transportation, and against racial and social discrimination. The U.S. government agreed to allow Mexican government labor inspectors to inspect work sites and monitor contract compliance. During June 1942, U.S. officials along with farm representatives from California and Texas, traveled to México City to address several key issues pertinent to the binational labor program. The concerns came mainly from México, centered around the number of workers needed in the United States and how the men would be treated on and off the job.

México's negotiators questioned the logic of officially sanctioning the use of contracted workers when Mexican and Mexican Americans already experienced disparate social discrimination in the United States. México recalled that at the end of World War I, Arizona cotton growers had failed to provide return transportation to the braceros, leaving them destitute in the United States. Mexican officials were just as concerned with the possibility that once the contract workers became accustomed to higher wages in the U.S., they would demand similar pay at home and disrupt the Mexican farm wage scale. Finally, to ensure that braceros did not return completely penniless, México proposed that employers withhold a percentage of all wages earned by the men in the United States, refundable upon their return. Recognizing that the U.S. military drafted large numbers of young men, México also wanted assurances that the temporary workers would not be conscripted during their stay in the United States.

In light of México's concerns and despite the existing spirit of goodwill between the two nations, negotiations lasted ninety days before officials signed the binational agreement on August 4, 1942. By September, trains brought the first group of fifteen hundred contracted Mexican workers to California. Two months later, similar groups of braceros were employed in Washington State's sugar beet harvest. In principle, the language of the binational agreement and the corresponding individual worker's contract provided for fair and equal treatment of every bracero during his stay in the United States.

* * *

Negotiations moved to consider allowing Mexican contract laborers to enter the U.S. for railroad track maintenance. In calling for contracted Mexican track workers, the railroad companies brought up the dwindling supplies of labor and the precedent already set by the agricultural industry. However, the labor requirements across the two industries differed. The need for labor varied widely among carriers and depended on location, organizational divisions, time of the year, and unanticipated circumstances related to track construction and maintenance. Unlike agriculture, which had successfully prevented workers from organizing into unions, railroad workers were well represented, organized down to the level of track section hands. The success of agriculture notwithstanding, the complexity and nature of these problems meant that the railroad industry had to articulate its entitlement to foreign contract labor in a forceful and persuasive argument.

Chapter 4

# Railroad Track Workers Needed;
# Where Are the Domestic Laborers?

In order to obtain the authorization to receive braceros, the railroad industry had to convince federal authorities that labor shortages were genuine. Therefore the industry painted the shortages as putting the war effort in jeopardy. Any plea for help from México also had to address sensitive immigration issues, the concerns of the Brotherhood of Maintenance of Way Employees (BMWE), an ingrained racially sensitive railroad worker culture, along with political opposition from other potential sources of labor. In México a second call to add railroad laborers to the thousands of farm workers already engaged in the bracero program raised questions and concerns surrounding domestic farm production. Similar to agriculture, the railroad industry had benefited from various New Deal initiatives; railroad shipments of farm production rebounded toward the end of the 1930s. Railroad agricultural shipments, which continued to slump nationally, enjoyed a dramatic increase in western states. By 1939 the principal agricultural-producing areas in the West relied once again on local rail carriers to move produce to concentration points along the main lines. From these shipping sites, agricultural products moved across the country by rail to processors and consumers in the central and eastern parts of the United States.

After 1939 a general increase in nonfarm freight traffic brought additional business to the railroads. War preparedness necessitated hauling immense quantities of raw materials to production centers and eventual shipment overseas. Due to improvements made in track and equipment sectors during the Great Depression, carriers had the capacity to ship more without experiencing a substantial increase in maintenance-of-way labor. Between 1939 and the attack on Pearl Harbor in December 1941, the Southern Pacific Railroad (SP) alone ordered sixty-four million dollars in modern cars and locomotive power.[1] Such railroads as the Union Pacific (UP); Chicago, Milwaukee, St. Paul and Pacific (CMStP&P); Northern Pacific (NP); Great Northern (GN); and the Atchison, Topeka and Santa Fe (AT&SF) introduced new high-speed diesel-electric locomotives that reduced freight times dramatically.[2] Freight cars were designed with greater capacity to match the increased power of the new generation of locomotives. During World War I freight cars carried on average of forty-two tons per load. However, by World War II freight traveling on new cars over longer distances and carrying heavier loads averaged fifty-two tons.[3] In 1940 the Association of American Railroads boosted that efficiency as measured by amount of freight carried per train, average locomotive speed, better utilization of freight cars, and overall industry performance set "new high records."[4] Still, over the long run, and particularly under a war economy, railroad companies coped with the persistent problem of insufficient labor.

In some part of the United States, railroads had little difficulty hiring additional workers. Near industrial centers, for example, turnover rates in railroad jobs were so high that any net effect of additional hires was negligible. In many West Coast areas the continual replacement of railroad workers hired by shipyards and construction contractors kept track crews in a constant state of below-par job performance. Despite adding eighteen thousand new employees between 1940 and 1941, the Southern Pacific maintained that its operational workforce remained "undermanned."[5] In September 1941 the company presented its first request to the federal government for permission to import Mexican labor.[6]

In addition to civilian-related shipments, before the attack at Pearl Harbor, war trains transferred military supplies and troops across the nation. After the attack, President Franklin Roosevelt invoked executive emergency power to create the Office of Defense Transportation to ensure, in every possible way, an increased efficiency of the nation's railroads. Various federal and state regulatory bodies and departments, War Production Boards, the War Manpower Commission, civilian transportation associations, and all branches of the military cooperated with the Office of Defense Transportation and the railroads on these matters. The railroads collaborated and operated in alignment with military and manufacturing industries to avoid a federal takeover the industry had experienced under the U.S. Railroad Administration Act during World War I.

The magnitude of responsibility felt by the railroad industry during World War II was unprecedented. No previous circumstances had required the economy to furnish such record quantities of troops and war-related materials for national and military consumption abroad. War mobilization created a sudden increase in the volume of people moving across the country as well. The surge in manufacturing, with large quantities of raw materials and partially finished parts shipping to various parts of the nation, imposed unparalleled demands on the railroads. Among the five principal transportation industries—pipelines, ships, aircraft, highway, and trains—the railroads would shoulder the bulk of the shipment burden.

As the war intensified and millions of workers traded their jobs for military service or employment in the mushrooming defense industries, the railroad labor shortage worsened. To enable trains would run at peak efficiency, the Office of Defense Transportation and the War Manpower Commission began to prevent some railroad employees from transferring to other jobs.[7] As worker shortages continued to reach alarming levels, the industry developed several methods of addressing the problem. First, in 1942, the government classified the Railroad Retirement Board (RRB) as a war agency. Almost immediately, the RRB devoted greater attention to the recruitment and placement of railroad employees in an effort to stem the tide of the labor crisis.[8] Using graphic and colorful posters, the board marketed the need and importance of railroad employment in sustaining the war effort. Carriers followed the RRB's lead by establishing hiring offices in selected cities and advertising employment opportunities to particular ethnic groups such as Mexican Americans.

Because of competitive wages, the greatest worker shortages developed in track crews in urban areas near war industries. The high turnover of workers drawn away from roadbed employment by better salaries and working conditions in aircraft plants and shipyards kept rail companies scrambling for labor. In agricultural districts the railroads were more effective securing help because the prevailing wages were comparable or higher than farm labor wages. However, by the time the war was well under way, job opportunities in other industries resulted in a significant rural-to-urban migration of workers. Among the remaining men and women not already employed, very few were willing to transfer away from their homes for railroad work.

These wage differentials only partially explain the labor shortage railroad companies experienced. Compulsory military service further exacer-

bated retention problems, especially among the low-skilled workers. One
year into the war, 185,000 workers entered military service.[9] Experienced
railroad employees served with distinction in several transportation battalions. The military decided on the Southern Pacific as the first railway for
training in the Railway Operating Battalions of the Transportation Corps,
Army Special Forces. Two-thirds of the men and officers of the 727th Battalion (and the first to complete training) were pulled from the Southern
Pacific. Similarly, Santa Fe railroad men comprised almost the whole of the
713th Battalion.[10] Although these experienced men were vital for repairing
roadbeds and running a military train in the African and European theaters
of operation, they represented a substantive loss of labor for the industry
at home at a most critical time. Railroad companies did attempt to obtain
deferments for employees from the draft, but they faced the same problem
as did the agriculture industry. Selective service boards remained unconvinced that unskilled track laborers, like farm workers, were essential to the
war effort at home. Later, the War Department authorized the Railroad Retirement Board to employ thousands of off-duty military personnel to assist
with shipments during peak periods.[11]

* * *

The railroad industry experienced difficulty solving the puzzle of recruiting and retaining new workers, especially track laborers. Various companies, with the cooperation of the Office of Defense Transportation, issued
patriotic appeals to local businesses to grant temporary leaves of absence
to employees willing to take railroad jobs. Generic pleas in newspapers and
billboards along busy highways appealed directly to the public sentiment.
To offset the potential loss of workers to other industries and the military,
railroad companies sought to hire young men right out of high school with
the hope of engaging them to a lifetime railroad career.[12] To accommodate
these young workers, railroads lowered their qualifications, including standards of skill, age, and physical requirements. Targeted circulars toward
college professors, women, and Native Americans were issued, which did
produce results but not enough to make up for the chronic labor shortage
in the rail industry.

The SP used well-crafted promotions intended to catch the attention
of middle-class Americans. One job advertisement ("Why Professor Tate
spends his week-ends as a Section Hand") urged college professors to take
track employment. Of course, the work culture of railroad men was wholly

incongruous with middle-class college academicians. Most professors lacked the physical stamina demanded by the job and veteran track foremen, but the Southern Pacific assumed that college faculty had idle time. On many campuses, however, especially research institutions, professors worked evenings and through the weekends on class materials and scholarly investigation. The total number of college faculty in various states was comparatively small. Few faculty, even for weekends, were willing to exchange their elitist status and intellectualism for backbreaking shovel-and-pick duty.

In a similar example, the Southern Pacific produced an advertisement titled "Indians on our Warpath." One paragraph read: "Garbed in purple and scarlet shirts, wearing bright headbands, the Indians form America's most colorful and unique section gangs. Under the brilliant Arizona sky, they swing picks and tamp ballast with the easy grace and endurance for which the Indian is famous." The promotion appealed directly to Native American cultural and civic pride. It spoke of "patriotic Redmen" who "came from the reservations and from scattered hogans in answer to our wartime call for extra manpower."[13] The railroads had a terrible employment record with Native Americans, many of whom found it difficult to accept such employment considering that their forefathers had strongly opposed the railroad for its destructive effects on their communities and personal lives.

During the 1928 hearings in the U.S. House of Representatives on Mexican immigration, southwestern railroad companies were so determined to secure Mexican labor that they overlooked Native American communities as an alternative source of labor.[14] Like many others, Native Americans were turned off by the poor wages and arduous nature of track employment. Despite this, however, the railroads had some success working through the various Indian agencies and reservations, especially among the Navajo. The hiring of Native Americans became easier when permanent jobs were located adjacent to tribal communities with high levels of unemployment.[15] Once employed, however, companies like Southern Pacific and Union Pacific persuaded Navajos from Arizona to accept reassignments to extra gang crews operating in faraway areas like Pocatello, Idaho.[16]

Railroad companies also used recruitment posters to recruit women into track maintenance work to keep the trains rolling. "ANGELS guard our right of way" read one poster featuring "Track Forelady Blanche Tuttle" at work while her husband served in the army. The poster pictured a crew of track workers comprised entirely of white women. In reality, one half of Blanche Tuttle's team consisted of Latinas from Watsonville, California, including Bertha Montalvo, Rosie Montalvo, and Sara Soto; each woman had family members serving in the military. Women were no strangers to railroad employment. In the early years, railroad companies had placed them in low-paying office and other clerical positions. During World War I, because of the absence of men, women began to fill some male-dominated jobs. In 1918, Mexican and European immigrant women took light cleaning as well as machine jobs in SP repair shops in Sacramento, California. For the most part, the railroad companies considered women too "delicate" for the physically strenuous car and engine shops or track crews. Even in some higher-level office positions, male supervisors considered it inappropriate to entrust women with important responsibilities like scheduling or communications. But the attitude of the male-dominated railroad industry changed with World War II. A new respect for the ability of women workers to perform at any level developed once national mobilization got under way. Changes came about when the military began to organize female corps to perform highly specialized duties beyond the traditional tasks of nurses or stenographers.

The agriculture industry had customarily employed large numbers of women farm workers. As food production became increasingly vital to the war effort under the War Food Administration, farming essentially became a wartime industry. Unable to compete with higher-waged industrial jobs, farms lost scores of men and women workers, jeopardizing production. By 1943 farm extension authorities in the western states organized a "women's land army" to come to the aid of farmers.[17] The railroads reacted differently. Supervisors resisted employing women for as long as possible, preferring to call retirees and other men ineligible for military service. Managers and unions felt it was inappropriate to hire women to fill jobs that were considered traditionally male. In mid-October 1942, however, the first all-woman Southern Pacific road maintenance crew began work on tracks in Eugene and Springfield, Oregon.[18] The practice spread quickly, and by 1943 women section crews were found tamping ballast and lifting and lining rail on roads and yards across the nation, except in the Southeast, where male dominance held fast. In general, a substantial number of women hired into the railroad industry but only a fraction took track jobs. Among 1,452 women employed by the Northern Pacific west of Livingston, Montana, in January 1945, only 33 were track laborers.[19]

* * *

Recruiting alone could not solve the difficult problem of insufficient track labor. Despite advertisements that exaggerated the healthful benefits of working outdoors and touted the patriotic contribution of track labor, workers tended to shy away from these jobs. Railroad labor recruiters experienced this firsthand. On one occasion, the Southern Pacific solicited every government employment agency for help in finding unemployed workers. Altogether, 2,896 men responded to the call, but 113 men refused to board the trains that would carry them to the job site. En route from the East Coast to the West Coast, another 722 had second thoughts and disappeared altogether from the train. Eventually, 2,061 men arrived, but 267 refused to go to work and another 406 recruits failed their physical examinations. In the end, the Southern Pacific gained fewer than 50 percent of the original number of employee referrals.[20]

Attracting African American workers from the eastern areas of the country to the proved particularly complicated for western rail companies. In 1943 the federal government issued a series of directives urging employers not to discriminate on the basis of "race, creed, color, nationality or lack of citizenship." Existing and strident Jim Crow ordinances interfered with the ability of employers to place African Americans, however. On the one hand, the government advised employers to remove barriers against training or hiring African Americans as a way of addressing the labor scarcity; on the other hand, federal officials and the railroad companies had to comply with local and state-imposed racial measures that mitigated recruitment efforts.

In May 1944 a War Manpower Commission (WMC) official held a meeting to discuss employing African Americans with two hundred representatives of the Central Railroad of New Jersey. To loud applause, each spokesperson responded "that under no circumstances would the men they represent agree to work with Negroes." Hoping to persuade the crowd to step away from deep-seated racism, an African American official of the commission attempted to address the gathering. The white workers bluntly refused to listen.[21] Racial animosity notwithstanding, in June 1942 the Railroad Retirement Board initiated a plan to recruit maintenance-of-way workers from the Mississippi Valley and Texas for Southern Pacific's western lines. Despite expending $135,000, the plan failed to impact the labor shortage. According to the SP, the results were very "unsatisfactory as most were colored" and "a very poor class of labor."[22]

The Brotherhood of Maintenance of Way Employees insisted that surplus labor in Cleveland, in Pittsburgh, and in various southern cities could be transferred to the West to offset any want for track labor. In a four-week period between June 17 and July 17, 1942, the RRB offered jobs and transportation west to 2,896 men. Along the way, or shortly after arriving, 1,395 of the prospects simply deserted. Only 1,501 new recruits actually went to work, with many quitting altogether after only a few days. In the opinion of the railroad company, the recruits had taken advantage of the free passage and subsistence to earn higher wages in other West Coast industries. Between 1942 and early 1943, Southern Pacific tried again to get workers from other parts of the country to the West with dismal results. All told, between 1942 and 1943 the company recruited 16,182 track laborers; 16,136 abandoned railroad work for other jobs, leaving the company with a net gain of 46 laborers.[23]

Carey McWilliams had a different view of Southern Pacific's attempts to lure workers west. In 1942 he penned a report outlining the problems inherent in recruiting African Americans for employment with the SP in southern California. Among the 330 to 400 workers arriving daily in Los Angeles in late summer 1942, 98 percent were African American. Company officials recruited these workers to California with little coordination or foresight about the tight housing market in Los Angeles and "white only" rental practices. Upon arrival, African Americans had no option but congregate at the train depot, prompting the Los Angeles police department to arrest and charge the arriving workers with violating city vagrancy laws.[24] According to McWilliams, the company lost 15 percent of the workers en route to Los Angeles. Upon arrival, only 50 percent went to work and 15 percent refused the company's offer of employment. After a short time, one in five workers walked off the job for employment elsewhere in Los Angeles's booming job market. McWilliams estimated that of the total number of men recruited by Southern Pacific, just one in two went to work for the company and with little assurance of remaining on the job permanently.

Mexican Americans fared no better. When Congress debated immigration restrictions after World War I, Mexican Americans became the target of xenophobes who characterized Mexicans as inferior in all ways to European immigrants. The human despair of the Great Depression had magnified racial animosities to new heights as thousands of white migrants fleeing the Midwest settled in many Idaho, California, Oregon, and Washington communities. Victims of economic hardship themselves, these new arrivals added their own brand of southern racism and applied it toward Mexican Americans and other nonwhites. In time, whites transferred the same racial epithets directed against African Americans to Mexican Americans, Native Americans, and other nonwhites. Well into the 1950s and 1960s, Mexican Americans were shunned in some barbershops in such rural towns as Grandview, Washington, and Nampa, Idaho, where some business owners prominently displayed "No Mexicans Allowed" placards in their establishments.

The Fair Employment Practices Committee, set up in 1941 to abolish racial discrimination in federal employment, eventually began to hear testimony from Mexican Americans. In San Diego the committee heard testimony from the Industrial Council regarding tension between the "Mexican element in the population and the majority group." Whites, according to the testimony, blamed the Mexicans for lowering wages. The situation became explosive, prompting the council to summon Ernesto Galarza to help diffuse "imminent violence" between the two working communities. The council charged the San Diego police force with being "guilty of gross brutality and stupidity" as it used force against Mexican laborers.[25]

* * *

Despite their many years of experience, the railroad companies were unprepared and ineffective in signing up labor in a worker-scarce situation. In past years companies had relied on the commissary companies for their labor and foremen and track supervisors to hire men "at the work site." In assessing the railroad industry's attempt to acquire the much needed workers, one RRB official described it as "unbelievably bad and inadequate." "It is reported that that they have no employment office," he said, "not even signs and no personnel office except perhaps a vice president at national headquarters." Making matters worse, the working conditions were inferior to those offered by plant employers in the same area. The Office of Defense Transportation accused the railroads and their employment effort as "so disorganized as almost to preclude the possibility of success." McWilliams went further in criticizing the railroad industry: Some companies, like Southern Pacific, were furtively operating to contract laborers from México, so it did not cooperate fully with the government to successfully recruit African Americans and others.[26]

Hiring "green" or inexperienced men and women usually translated into a drop in the efficiency of the track crews. More students than college faculty answered the railroad industry's plea for help. These youthful workers were more casual in job habits, often highly independent and insubordinate with crew foremen. Lowered physical and age requirements lead to below-average job performance. Calling retirees back to work had a similar negative effect since these older men could no longer accomplish tasks as in their younger years. Before the war, track foremen usually rejected men thirty-five years of age or older. Now, track foreman increasingly exacerbated the problem of poor performance by pushing inexpert crews over longer hours to offset their own ineptness.

Although the output of crews did not diminish in all cases, industry investigators calculated that overall job efficiency had declined as much as 75 percent from prewar days. To compensate for decreased worker productivity, companies had to hire above actual requirements in an already tight labor market. At the same time that job performance fell and new workers were hard to find, train traffic expanded across the railroad industry. The heavier transportation pressures sharply increased the average employment needs of individual carriers. The burden on railroad companies to transport changed from seasonal peaks and valleys to a sustained year-round flow of wartime materials and passengers. By 1942 few if any workers experienced the usual fall and winter layoffs due to the sustained need to keep roads open and in safe operating conditions.

# Chapter 5

# Bracero Railroaders, "Soldiers of Democracy"

Sporadic labor shortages began to appear along the West Coast track lines in early 1940. Rapid economic growth fueled by the growth of war industries and military construction projects impeded the employers' ability to locate workers. In typical times, railroad companies struggled to maintain full track crews; now the robust economy presented new labor troubles for western railway companies. Against this background, and in early 1941, the Southern Pacific Railroad (SP) submitted an application with the Department of Immigration for permission to bring workers from México. The company's initial proposal to offset its labor problems with foreign workers was met with considerable opposition from railroad unions, forcing Southern Pacific to withdraw the request. However, between May and September 1942, conditions became more favorable for Southern Pacific to renew its request for help from México. These petitions eventually went to the War Manpower Commission (WMC) and the approval to begin contracting track workers from México began in December of that year.

The decision to authorize the railroad industry to import Mexican workers must have seemed hypocritical to many Mexican Americans with vivid memories of the systemic Depression-era deportations. Despite the lingering anti-Mexican sentiment that underscored those repatriation drives, Washington, D.C., acting on behalf of the railroads, now asked Mexican laborers to *return* to the United States. México and U.S. relations were similarly strained when the war began. The deportations of the 1930s and violent attacks during 1942 against Mexican American youth by military personnel and police in Los Angeles strained goodwill between the two nations. Simmering issues involving the United States reflected negatively in México.

Complicating matters included General John J. Pershing's retaliatory military expedition across the border in pursuit of the popular revolutionary General Francisco Villa, the intrusive landing of naval forces at Veracruz, and the compensation paid by México to U.S. owners of expropriated properties. Under these circumstances, U.S. administrators prepared to negotiate for importing Mexican track workers on behalf of the nation's railroads. This became the second binational labor agreement the two countries reached in fewer than forty years.

Pan-American relations notwithstanding, Southern Pacific also faced internal opposition to the idea of bringing in outside labor, particularly Mexicans. When the railroad company made its requests for Mexican laborers alleging the shortage of labor jeopardized critical war-related transportation, there was strong opposition from unions, the WMC, and the Railroad Retirement Board (RRB). Before getting permission to contract workers from México, the railroad industry had to assure the federal government it had exhausted all available sources of domestic labor. Because of standing racial, ethnic, and gender discrimination in the United States during these years, Mexican Americans, African Americans, and women were not always considered for railroad employment. The industry first had to demonstrate it had made an honest effort to enlist laborers from these communities.

Regarding Mexican Americans, the railroad companies developed special appeals to the large Mexican-origin communities in the United States. One help-wanted advertisement produced in Spanish urged Mexican Americans to do their part to win the war: "Men! If you really want to help the war effort, here is your opportunity. This is healthy work in the open air . . . particularly for inexperienced men. The SP needs you to work on the track so we can keep the war trains rolling."[1] Other companies asked Mexican American employees to write their relatives and friends, including those in México, to consider working for the railroad. Through these efforts the railroads succeeded in adding some Spanish-speaking employees. Later, companies promoted some of these new hires into supervisory positions over the incoming braceros. Yet the overall response to this ethnic-focused plea had mixed results. Patriotism only went so far. Time had done little to assuage many individual's recollections of being earmarked for deportation, often losing their jobs because of their ethnicity. This is not to say Mexican Americans were unresponsive and therefore lacking in patriotism, however. Indeed, many Mexican Americans demonstrated their nationalism and loyalty repeatedly and in varied ways during the war, particularly in the military. Unemployed Mexican Americans were simply no different from other workers who shunned railroad employment for higher-paying positions and often safer jobs in other wartime industries.

In an effort to fully utilize all persons able to work, the U.S. Employment Service ordered that all able men and women be purged from public community projects with the Works Progress Administration. Even though companies preferred to employ men over women, federal officials insisted that the railroads make the most of all resident labor regardless of gender. Going into the war, a greater percentage of African American and Mexican American women already held jobs outside of their homes than their white counterparts. When the number of war-related job opportunities opened for women, the number of black and Mexican American females gainfully employed increased substantially, especially in manufacturing and transportation. The African American population shift from rural farm areas to manufacturing centers during these years went beyond an important demographic change; the migration represented upward social movement as women went from farm to factory employment.

In the railroad industry the majority of women held janitorial or food service jobs, while a few joined section or extra gang crews and shop crews during the war. Restricting women to low-level and poorly paid jobs amounted to de facto gender segregation. African American women faced more explicit segregation, as some company policies instructed supervisors that "colored labor . . . would be required to be segregated" to comply with explicit racial state and local ordinances.[2] Even after President Franklin Roosevelt issued the fair employment practices decree, racial and gender discrimination and segregation often remained the order of the day. Despite the WMC's attempt to convince employers that full employment of nonwhites and women furthered the war effort, deep-seated discrimination continued to hinder complete and equal employment. These prevalent social practices exacerbated the industry's labor problems and indirectly cemented the eventual contracting of Mexican labor.

The Brotherhood of Maintenance of Way Employees (BMWE), in particular, opposed the idea of contracting Mexican track workers for several reasons. Unlike the agriculture industry, the railroad companies were soliciting Mexican laborers for jobs where the BMWE was the accredited representative of all track workers. The union was concerned that the braceros would lower the prevailing wage and work standards. Just as important, the BMWE and other union representatives sought concession that employment of contracted labor would be temporary, both in terms of the individual bracero and the program itself. In its opposition the union accused the railroads of already favoring Mexican immigrants and making it practically impossible for a "white person" and "American citizens" to obtain employment. It accused Southern Pacific of systematically giving Mexicans "an exclusive right to positions of laborer" on divisions from Santa Barbara and Fresno, California, then east to Tucumcari, New Mexico. According to union spokespersons, some "Americans" and "Italians" were working in the Salt Lake, Sacramento, and Portland divisions only because of the efforts of local chambers of commerce and community organizations pressuring for the employment of residents.[3] The union charged that the railroad had made no effort to explore obtaining local labor as several million people remained unemployed. In the BMWE's opinion the supposed dearth of track labor and the need for Mexican laborers could be resolved if the railroads sought local residents and offered decent wages instead of "starvation rates of pay."[4]

The WMC's decision to develop a bracero railroad program did not originate entirely from Southern Pacific's application to import Mexican laborers. The commission, already aware of serious labor shortages on American farms, clearly forecasted potential labor problems in other sectors of the economy. For this reason, the U.S.-México agreement to contract workers for the American farmers signed in August 1942 had already anticipated employing additional braceros in "nonagricultural sectors." George S. Messersmith, U.S. ambassador to México, reminded México's president Manuel Ávila Camacho that "the possibility of the recruiting of other than farm labor was likewise foreseen at the time when the agricultural labor agreement was signed."[5] Southern Pacific's petitions, however, prompted the War Manpower Commission to survey its state directors concerning the availability of track workers in Arizona, California, Nevada, Oregon, and Utah. Not unexpectedly, the state directors had discouraging news. Under the existing Southern Pacific wage scales, the company's labor needs could not be realistically met in these western states. To determine if other carriers would require Mexican track workers as well, the WMC surveyed various railroads. Realizing that other companies faced similar labor problems, the WMC moved forward to develop the Mexican railroad bracero program.

The bracero railroad program began to take shape at a conference in Chicago during October 24–26, attended by railroad executives, union representatives, and federal agencies, including the RRB and the WMC. Labor and management disagreed on two basic issues. The railroad companies wanted to bring Mexican workers to fill jobs without any conditions set forth by the brotherhood of railroad workers. BMWE union representatives wanted to ensure that carriers would not lower working conditions or violate existing industrywide contracts by hiring cheaper Mexican labor. At the end of the conference, both sides agreed to consider imported Mexican labor strictly for maintenance-of-way employment. Several meetings followed to spell out the principles and details of the proposal leading to the WMC's decision to contact labor in México to offset the shortage of track workers.

By December 1942 the commission had sufficient information from labor organizations, the railroad industry, and federal agencies to outline the railroad bracero program. The bracero railroad contract would preserve all the guarantees and provisions extended to agricultural workers. However, railroad workers and carriers would be subjected to provisions of the collective bargaining agreement. One new development included paying bracero track labor time and a half after eight hours work. Until that time section workers received time and a half after eight hours but not extra gang laborers, where most braceros worked. If wage negotiations covering track workers resulted in an increase, braceros already in the United States would also receive a retroactive adjustment.

With the basics in place, the State Department began preliminary negotiations with Mexican authorities from January until April 1943, when it reached a preliminary agreement for the "temporary migration of nonagricultural workers." An exchange of notes between the U.S. Embassy in México City and the Ministry of Foreign Affairs put the agreement into effect on April 29. The short time frame was the result of several key factors. Already one year earlier, following steady requests from the United States for farm laborers, President Camacho had established a federal commission comprised of the ministers of the Departments of Government, Foreign Relations, and Labor and Social Welfare to study the feasibility of answering the U.S. need for labor. Thus the resulting agricultural bracero agreement signed on August 4, 1942, had been in operation for nearly eight months before the railroad labor program. The railroad companies agreed to lend their equipment to transport the agricultural workers from the international border to the work sites. With each trainload of braceros delivered to farmers, the railroads understood that, like agricultural workers, contracted Mexican track workers were the solution to their labor troubles as well.

One week after the approval of the railroad program, Immigration and Naturalization authorized, and the U.S. attorney general approved under the 9th Proviso to Section 3 of the Immigration Act of February 5, 1917, the temporary admission of unskilled Mexican nonagricultural workers for railroad track and maintenance-of-way employment. The authorization stipulated that railroad braceros could only enter the United States for the duration of the war. On this basis the first group of six thousand braceros received contracts for railroad employment in the U.S. between May 10 and June 15, 1943. The Southern Pacific Railroad received thirty-five hundred workers; twenty-two hundred signed with the Atchison, Topeka and Santa Fe; and three hundred went to Western Pacific. Within six weeks nine more railroad companies submitted requests for 9,360 additional laborers.[6] The Mexican National Railroad Workers Program of World War II had begun.

\* \* \*

Under the terms of the program, the War Manpower Commission, acting on behalf of the United States, entered into an agreement with participating railroad companies to select, employ, and transport each bracero to his place of employment. Separately, the federal government signed another bilingual contract called the "individual work agreement" approved by the Mexican government with every worker participating in the program. This contract outlined the general procedures, principles, and protections applicable to the worker and to the railroad companies. Under the general principles, workers entering the United States would not be subject to military service or discriminatory acts of any kind. In accordance with México's Federal Labor Law, the workers were entitled to transportation, subsistence, and repatriation to and from the U.S. at no cost to the worker or his family. With regard to working conditions, the braceros were to receive no less than forty-six cents per hour or they were to paid at the prevailing wage, whichever was higher or lower. Wages were to be paid in full and not subject to any deduction except those required by law. In no instance could employers use contract labor to displace or lower the wages or standards of U.S. workers. As a further safeguard, once contracted, braceros, with the consent of the Mexican government, had to approve any transfer to another type of employment.

The Mexican government also negotiated several conditions regarding the braceros' social welfare. The most significant of these stipulations reflected the Mexican government's desire that as the workers benefited from their employment in the United States, México gained as well. This would come about as braceros returned home with new skills, technology, and a portion of their earnings. Article III of the Mexican labor code already permitted wage deductions for the purpose of creating a worker savings plan.[7] The idea to set aside a portion of a worker's earnings in the United States got a boost from Manuel Gamio's study of the social characteristics of Mexican immigrants in the United States during the late 1920s.[8] Commissioned by the U.S. Social Studies Research Council, Gamio keyed in to the benefits derived from the tendency among returning migrants to bring back practical tools and other appliances from the United States. Based on his field studies in the U.S., Gamio began to theorize how structured temporary Mexican migration to the United States could in fact help modernize México. Not surprisingly, he emerged as one of the drafting architects of the World War II bracero program.

México hoped to create a Bracero Farm Workers Fund (Fondo de Ahorro Campesino) in the Agricultural Credit Bank (Banco de Crédito Agrícola). The fund had two purposes. First, the deductions amounted to an individual compulsory savings account. Second, the fund would methodically finance the purchase of much needed farming equipment from the United States to be used by the returning men in México. To that end, the worker's contract instructed employers to withhold 10 percent from each worker's earnings for deposit into an individual savings fund. Officials attached the idea for a savings plan to the railroad braceros as well. Upon their return to México, the railroad braceros could invest directly in México's economy after withdrawing their funds from the Banco del Ahorro Nacional.

México guarded the social welfare of the workers in other ways. The contract prohibited minors under sixteen from joining the bracero program. Under the terms of the agreement, the braceros were entitled to lodging and kitchen and sanitary facilities comparable to other workers in the employment area. Although the railroad companies relied on commissary companies to provide food and other personal supplies to their workforce, the braceros had the option to purchase these items where it was most convenient. Finally, the contract guaranteed medical care for occupational diseases and accidents at levels enjoyed by domestic workers pursuant to state and federal legislation. To enforce these contract provisions, the braceros were at liberty to elect their own spokesperson to represent them before an employer, unions, or other interested parties concerning any violations or interpretation of the worker agreement. As an important measure of compliance, the United States agreed to allow Mexican consuls and field labor inspectors of the Mexican government free and open access to the braceros to investigate any complaints. Ninety days after giving notice, either government could renounce its participation in the agreements.

The individual worker contract and the WMC's agreement with railroad companies were a continuation of the language of the earlier agricultural bracero accord. Some operational problems had already surfaced among farm braceros, but neither government made any substantive adjustments in the railroad contracts. Eluding the attention of both governments, for example, were issues related to the inevitable loss of life or long-term health problems among braceros on or off the job. The negotiators also failed to adequately consider how cultural dislocation, linguistic differences, and food preferences in particular would impact the bracero workers. The contract guaranteed full employment 75 percent of the time but failed to consider leisure time activities for the young and all-male workforce. In many respects both governments placed too much faith in the contract itself and neglected to take into account compulsory compliance. In the end the contract became little more than a failed promise to safeguard the interest of the braceros and their families.

One thing is certain: México had the upper hand and failed in negotiating the terms of employment and providing for the social welfare on behalf of its citizens. At the time the United States desperately needed México's young workers because they were vital to the bustling war economy. Beyond that, the United States considered it imperative that México lend its full cooperation for the war effort. Earlier, in 1940, México had warned the Axis governments that any aggression toward any American nation corresponded to hostility against México. The following January, the U.S.-Mexican Joint Defense Commission provided for complete military collaboration between the two nations in the mutual defense of México's land and sea coast. This allowed U.S. aircraft to fly over Mexican territory and touch down inside México. The Mexican government also allowed U.S. warships to enter its waters and naval bases. Under this pact, U.S. troops could enter Mexican territory if necessary.

Because of the distance to the Panama Canal and other strategic defense points in Latin America, the United States required México's full cooperation. Aside from direct military-related issues, México's agricultural and mineral resources were also of considerable importance to the United States. The same held true for much needed agricultural commodities from Central America. Germany proved it could threaten maritime shipping from Central America to the United States when it sank two Mexican oil tankers in the

Gulf of México. As a precaution against similar attacks, freight traveling to the U.S. had to pass through Mexican air space or move overland on Mexican rail. In 1942 alone, an estimated 1.3 million tons of essential northbound rail traffic traveled across México to reach the United States.[9] With this strategic advantage, México was able to leverage more effective protection for its workers while still upholding the spirit of Pan-American cooperation in winning the war.

Looking back, however, it is apparent that Mexican negotiators failed in their responsibility to forcefully assert the braceros' best interests. This became evident as scores of immediate and serious problems surfaced almost as soon as the men arrived in the United States. The complexity of the issues and lack of clear lines of accountability in both countries meant that resolution of the men's concerns would linger unsettled for decades as the youthful workers reached old age. Delivery of the braceros from México to U.S. employers operated on a very straightforward manner and was shaped by the increasing U.S. demand for the track labor. The railroad companies, after making an honest effort to hire domestic workers, placed their order with the Railroad Retirement Board for as many braceros necessary to keep the track in good working order. At the same time, the carriers executed contracts with the War Manpower Commission to employ and transport the workers at the company's expense. Each employer also had to post a departure bond with a surety company for every worker to assure the Immigration and Naturalization Service that the bracero had returned to México at the end of the work contract. The employing railroad assigned the authority to the WMC to select men on their behalf fitting specific physical qualifications from a pool of Mexican recruits.

In México hundreds of workers left their communities, from all parts of the country, sometimes for the first time in their lives, and traveled to México City, the focal point of the program. The story of Paracho, a small community in Michoacán, illustrates how the call for Mexican workers brought an inactive culture of male outmigration back to life. Well before World War II, Paracho had developed into a principal labor-exporting area for employment in the United States. Beginning in the early 1900s, Parachoans customarily left for the U.S., some permanently and others leaving and returning in a cyclical pattern of annual migration. According to residents, the first Parachoans left in 1904 during the austere period of the Porfirio Díaz regime. When the worker returned with encouraging anecdotes of his experiences in the north, it marked the start of a euphoric culture of migration; subsequent groups of young men left and returned home, encouraging others to follow.

From the early 1900s, the pipeline of seasonal and permanent migrants from Paracho to the southwestern United States swelled until the Great Depression. When the economic crash of the 1930s led to the forced repatriation of Mexican immigrants, migration ended as no more than three Parachoans left during the entire period.[10] During the 1930s, when Parachoan men stopped migrating to the U.S., the population of Paracho actually expanded until World War II began. Then, abruptly, the call for contract laborers (for both agricultural and railroad work) for U.S. employment restarted the exodus of laborers out of Paracho. All but a few men left as braceros. This pattern repeated itself across Michoacán and other areas in México. During the first year of the war, Michoacán accounted for more than one quarter of the total number of braceros contracted to U.S. employers. For the entire duration of the war, no other Mexican state supplied as many workers to the U.S. economy.[11]

* * *

As news of the renewal of job opportunities through the bracero program reverberated across México, experienced workers and neophytes alike were determined to qualify for U.S. employment. Some, hoping President Camacho could intervene on their behalf, wrote to the president pleading their circumstances and asking for special consideration. Others sent letters reminding him of special connections, either having family members who were former employees or somehow connected to friends of the president to heighten their chances of being selected. In order to bribe local officials for sanction to leave for the recruiting centers and to cover travel expenses, men borrowed money, placing themselves and their families deeply in debt.

At the start of the bracero program, the Mexican government's only reception center was located in the National Stadium in México City. Masses of men arrived, some carrying *permisos* issued by town mayors or other officials. All desperately hoped for a spot in the program. From this point on, anyone could be disqualified through a careful selection process called the *sorteo* coordinated by the WMC, the RRB, and the minister of labor and social welfare. The first step involved becoming an *aspirante* by joining the cue of men in the selection line process. This required an enrollment card issued by the Ministry of Labor and Social Welfare that was not always easy to acquire as the number of potential recruits exceeded the demand from the

U.S. employers. This being the case, officials controlled enrollment based on patronage. Men either purchased the authorization card, received it by bribing officials, or got it by knowing someone with the right political connections. The process quickly became corrupt, making it hopeless for those unable to pay a bribe or lacking the right connections.

Those *aspirantes* fortunate to receive an enrollment card proceeded to one of four public health service baths in the city for "cleansing." U.S. and Mexican health workers examined and treated the men for infestations of body lice, common in poor rural populations outside of México City. As the men assembled in the National Stadium, the parasite moved easily among the men, passing through shared clothing, blankets, and close personal contact. To treat the problem, officials ordered the men to strip down and enter an empty room carrying their clothes. After shaving their underarms and pubic hair, the men stood naked with their clothes at their feet and devoid of respiratory protection, inhaling a white fog of DDT or lindane pumped into the sealed room.[12] Public health nurses pulled out a sample of the first hundred *aspirantes* for serological testing for evidence of venereal disease.

A preliminary interview regarding previous work experience and a physical examination followed. At this point officials dismissed men for being too tall, too old, disabled, or lacking dexterity. To exclude any physically unqualified men, U.S. railroad officials also used a "hand examination" method, checking for spurious calluses to turn back men deemed physically weak or unaccustomed to hard labor. Questions probed the men's personal backgrounds, including whether the individual had already worked in the United States. Throughout the life of the bracero program, more men were rejected than selected. Those disqualified were left destitute, even after going so deeply in debt as *aspirantes*. With their lives and that of their families in despair, the men were forced to choose between returning back to their homes empty-handed or heading for the United States on their own.

Those accepted into the bracero program received a processing card containing personal data, name, age, marital status, address, and hometown. Three physicians from the U.S. Public Health Service and seven from the Mexican Public Health Service, working in teams in spaces below the National Stadium, conducted a physical, psychological, and general medical examination of each individual. The evaluation began at the head, checking eyes, ears, mouth, throat, teeth, and lymphatic system. Doctors then examined upper and lower extremities, heart, lungs, genitalia, and rectum. The medical test concluded when physicians checked for hernia and any indication of color blindness. Later, health authorities added a test for syphilis. Barring health or physical problems, the men received a chest X-ray suggestive of a clean bill of health. The men moved to the final stages of the process, where a cameraman photographed each worker. This photographic image, together with a record of fingerprints, became part of each man's Alien Laborer Identification Card. In the next to the last step before receiving an actual work contract, Mexican nurses vaccinated each worker against smallpox. By design, and from the beginning to the end, the exacting physical and medical selection process ensured that only the most physically able and healthiest men became braceros.

The men assembled in groups of twenty-five or more to meet with officials from the Mexican Ministry of Labor and the War Manpower Commission to get last-minute instructions and sign their name to the individual work contract. Whether they knew it or not, this meeting provided the men with the last opportunity to raise questions or concerns about a number of different and binding papers spanning the individual work contract, their government ration book, and stamps to obtain work shoes. The forms contained complicated language authored by various U.S. agencies: the WMC, the U.S. Public Health Service, and the Office of Price Administration. Everyone also had to sign a savings fund deposit slip permitting the Banco del Ahorro Nacional to credit employer-deducted earnings in the United States.

The long, grueling, and costly experience of being a bracero had just begun. As a consequence of their own marked levels of illiteracy, the men were reluctant to ask too many questions for fear of jeopardizing their good fortune in advancing this far. They were now in the final stage before departure to the United States. By putting their signature on the work contract, they ceased being *aspirantes* and officially became braceros authorized by both governments to work in the U.S. After a long period of waiting through stressful uncertainty, the newly inducted proceeded to the Buena Vista Train Station for departure. The War Manpower Commission scheduled all train departures out of México City by pooling outstanding requests for track workers with the supply of men cleared to leave for the United States. At maximum capacity, the passenger trains could transport between 750 and 850 men. In México these trains became known as *los trenes especiales* (special trains) because once loaded, railroad officials cleared locomotive engineers to speed north with special priority over other rail traffic.

The men approached the actual moment of departure from México City with anxiety if not fear. As the train suddenly jolted forward, many workers reached out from the cars for a last touch from the hands of the few family members standing or walking alongside the train as it lurched forward. More often than not, family members were not present. It is quite conceivable that as the train began roll the inescapable reality of leaving their families and homeland for a distant and unknown location had a melancholy effect on the men. Aware of the angst, officials designated the braceros as more than ordinary workers but *soldados* and used white chalk to write "Trabajamos para la victoria de las democracias," "Viva America," and similar catchphrases on the outside of the railroad cars. They affixed large banners to the sides of the some of the cars.

The government designed these propaganda slogans with dual intent. First, the sayings cast the braceros as more than laborers, but rather as México's most important contribution to the global war for democracy. As the first bracero trains left the capital on May 13, 1943, Secretary of Labor Francisco Trujillo Gurría characterized the laborers as "soldiers of democracy of México who are on your way to battle with that patriotic spirit vibrating in every Mexican."[13] He continued to support the departing braceros and later wrote: "You constitute the first brigade of track laborers who are going to cooperate in the maintenance and development of the network of communication of our allies. You represent as one of the most effective elements with which México is carrying out its obligation to help democracy defeat the forces of cruelty. Uphold your dignity with the assurance that you are fulfilling the most sacred duty as behooves a man at this historic moment."[14] Officials carefully crafted the slogans to appeal to the whole of the decidedly nationalistic Mexican populace in an effort to win support for the state-sponsored transfer of labor to the U.S. war effort. Months after the braceros began leaving, the newspaper *El popular* reinforced the patriotic messages. The temporary loss of México's workforce was not an issue but a ray hope, the paper wrote, a "magnificent reborn force from which all México should benefit."[15]

\* \* \*

Once on board the trains, the men began experiencing the real life of a contracted laborer. If the men had contracts along the western states, the route out of México City took them west to Guadalajara, Jalisco, then north of the border at Nogales Sonora. Workers holding contracts for employment in the Midwest or the eastern part of the United States traveled north from México City to San Luis Potosí and then directly to the international crossing at Lar-

edo, Texas. Regardless of the route, representatives of both governments together with Mexican railway security agents guarded the men to the border.
While the braceros rode north in second- and first-class coach cars owned
by Ferrocarriles Nacionales de México, the trip was far from comfortable.
The passenger cars were already old, having been expropriated from private Mexican companies by President Lázaro Cárdenas in 1938. Before that,
much of the motive power and cars had arrived to México as surplus depreciated equipment from the U.S. railway companies.

The trip to the U.S. border took three days, and all the while the men sat
three abreast in fixed seats separated by an aisle running the length of the
cars. They stored their personal items, limited to seventy pounds, in over-
head racks or beneath their seats. En route, the trains rarely stopped and
then only to switch or service equipment or change operating personnel.
When the trains did stop at stations, the men were not permitted to disem-
bark. Still, they were besieged through the car windows by food vendors
and crowds of Mexican men wanting to learn how they could also join as
braceros.[16] Already organized by officials into smaller groups of ten or so
workers, the journey gave the men the chance to get to know each other and
informally select group spokespersons. These personal bonds became important later on in negotiations with employers and WMC officials in the
United States.

At the port of entry, the WMC took custody of the men. Every bracero
was cleared through an Immigration and Naturalization security check,
where inspectors reviewed work contracts and U.S. social security numbers
and a brief final medical exam. Barring any discrepancy or cause for rejection, the WMC assigned each bracero to a specific employer. Braceros assigned to nearby railroads reported to the job site within a day of arriving in
the U.S. Other crews contracted to northwestern or northeastern railroads
transferred to U.S. carriers for an additional one to three days of travel to
their final destination. The border crossing provided another opportunity
to reinforce the patriotic Pan-American message previously administered
in México City. For effect, a Mexican American railroad employee boarded
each train and, moving car to car, handed out flags of both nations along
with keepsake cards while reading the following welcome in Spanish:

> We are very grateful to your country for having made it possible for you
> to come to help us in this hour of need. I am very proud that our neighbor

México is our ally in this war for freedom. I am very fond of México and
the Mexican people, and I hope you are as happy to come here as we are
to welcome you. Many of your fellow countrymen have long been in the
employ of the Southern Pacific and have proved themselves industrious
and worthy workers. I am sure these and other employees with whom you
work will do everything they can to make you feel at home, and to show you
how much we appreciate your coming to this country to help us win the war
by keeping our railroad tracks strong and safe for our fighting forces.[17]

The affective tone of the scripted message lifted the men's spirits and for the
moment, many shouted, "Thank you, we are very happy to help out." Soon it
would become apparent that the binding and detailed language of the work
contract, the patriotic speeches, and their personal motivation for enlisting in the bracero program took on a different meaning outside of México.
The meaning and implications of the braceros and their life experiences in
México were not the same in the United States and nearly every experience,
action, and social situation was suddenly unfamiliar. Braceros found themselves in unfamiliar political spaces where the U.S. government and railroad
companies had the benefit of inclusive jurisdiction for the life of the contract. Linguistic and social differences, widespread racial hierarchies, and
the public ardor to win the war at all costs further exacerbated an already
one-sided relationship between the braceros and their employers.

México failed to act to enforce all the carefully crafted provisions of the
contract. In time, the official nationalistic fervor that underscored the agreement to ship workers to the United States rang hollow among the braceros.
From far away, México could not realistically expect to enforce contractual
conditions regarding living and other social conditions and the terms of
employment. Besides, in México these guarantees were beyond the reach of
Mexican workers. As a consequence, and despite the inadequate conditions
in the United States, no sooner did the workers arrive back in México, but
many began planning their return as undocumented or legal immigrants
with or without governmental permission. The idea that returning braceros
could stimulate modernization of the Mexican economy through a manda-
tory savings plan also proved illusory. Many men returned just as poor as
when they signed up as braceros. Just as many workers never invested in the
national economy, as they were unable to access to their savings accounts
when they returned home.

# Chapter 6

# Contractual Promises to Keep

For several reasons, the flow of braceros finally became operational. The growing U.S. demand for labor and war materials during the war, the upgraded Mexican railroad system, an operational War Manpower Commission (WMC) recruitment administration in México City, and a general easing of tension between the two nations all contributed to the braceros railroad program finally getting under way. The contractual obligation of the U.S. government to see that its own duties—and those of the employer—followed the letter of the work contract suffered partially because of ambiguities and weaknesses in the terms of the agreement. The U.S. government guaranteed only the most basic conditions (housing, medical services, exemption from military service, and safeguards from social discrimination), but it had no real intention to deliver on these minimal promises. The weak agreement resulted in negative unintended consequences. How could officials guarantee social equality to Mexican braceros when it could not protect its own Mexican American citizens against ethnic and racial discrimination in public places and employment?

Railroad braceros differed from agricultural braceros, who could be placed in former Farm Security Administration housing. The contracted track laborers, however, would reside in private railroad-company-owned accommodations, very often under substandard conditions. Federal and state governments had little or no oversight of the living conditions of the track laborers. For an employer to adhere to the labor contract and provide adequate accommodations would mean altering decades of entrenched industry and social norms. The vague terms and unrealistic guarantees of the imperfect worker contract created a situation where every entity, including the braceros (whose signature made them a party to the contract), breached some aspect of the agreement. Many of the Mexican railroad workers would

endure unexpected hardship at the hands of indifferent officials and employers. The unintended consequences could have been avoided as the U.S.
and the Mexican governments had enough time to strengthen the language
of the railroad worker contract. When the railroad workers began to arrive
from México in late 1943, the WMC had already experienced months of difficulty enforcing the provisions outlined in the agricultural bracero program.[1]
Despite this prior knowledge, both governments did nothing to address the
ambiguous language of the previous contract. Instead, the WMC pulled the
language for the railroad workers' contract directly from the agricultural
work agreement. A similar pattern of contravention was to be expected with
the railroad agreement.

The issues for the railroad workers were far more complex and challenging to resolve, however, because of conflicting interests among the Brotherhood of Maintenance of Way Employees (BMWE), the Railway Executives'
Association, the WMC, the Railroad Retirement Board (RRB), immigration
authorities, and the State Department. Bureaucratic regulations and concerns complicated even the simplest dispute. The agricultural program, in
contrast—not without problems of its own—essentially involved three entities: the bracero, the farmer, and the WMC. Upon crossing the U.S. border,
and before the braceros boarded American trains, buses, and trucks for the
last leg of their journey, Spanish-speaking officials arranged the men into
clusters of ten, led by a designated group spokesman chosen by the men.
Depending on the location of the work, the second leg of the men's travel
could last a few hours or several days of additional travel. Facilitators went
with the braceros to arrange for meals and other necessities along the way.
Upon arrival at the place of employment, a company road master or crew
foreman assumed responsibility for the braceros. From this point on, except
for Sundays, officials tried everything possible to systematize and standard-
ize the braceros' workday to maximize productivity.

Employers quickly arranged work schedules at the work site. In the first
hours after arriving, the men would be directed to their living quarters and
told to sleep or rest so they could commence working the following day. Issues with the living quarters surfaced immediately. The WMC had promised the braceros sanitary housing facilities similar to those offered to local workers. While it is true that companies historically housed white track
laborers in very poor quarters to begin with, by the time the braceros arrived, only the worst of accommodations were available. The braceros actually provided employers with a convenient and welcomed escape from

the nagging problem of managing segregated crews and living quarters. In some regions of the country combined track crews of Greeks, Italians, Polish, African Americans, and Mexicans sometimes worked together, which necessitated living together or in close proximity to each other. Under these circumstances, however, established racial norms intensified interethnic and racial animosity. Consequently, labor segregation grew, in part, from the employers' realization that separate crews and nonintegrated living areas were much easier to manage. Thus a justification for segregated work crews and housing developed across the railroad industry.

The imported workforce was distinctive and identifiable not only along racial or ethnic lines but also by the reasons for their presence in the United States. As employers saw it, segregated bracero work crews and housing did not constitute a violation of the antidiscrimination clause in the binational agreement. The braceros reacted negatively to their substandard living conditions. After all, many returning migrants had spun exaggerated stories about social and work conditions in the United States. To assuage the fears of *aspirantes*, Mexican and WMC officials had assured the braceros that the state of housing would be similar to that offered to nonbracero workers. In many circumstances the living quarters were unlivable. The braceros complained immediately when their living arrangements did not match expectations.

As track workers, approximately 48 percent of the braceros roomed in two types of company-owned box cars situated next to the work site. Extra gang workers assigned to floating repair crews occupied temporary mobile box cars, while section and maintenance workers settled into more permanent stationary box cars adjacent to repair shops or yards. Another 18 percent of the workforce were provided small bunkhouses designed to accommodate multiple workers. Large barracks and rooming houses sheltered the remaining workers.[2] In some circumstances the railroad companies improvised by creating makeshift lodging in work or storage areas in plants and maintenance shops.[3] In November 1945, Southern Pacific reported 147 separate worker camps in Oregon alone, an indication of the large number of Mexican track labor camps.[4]

Box cars represented the most degraded type of housing. Originally constructed to haul freight or passengers, but now well beyond their useful life, these wooden cars were converted by the railroads into makeshift living quarters. During the summer, when temperatures reached 90 degrees or more in many areas of the West, the old steel freight cars became unbearably hot. In the winter, when temperatures plummeted, the cars were excruciatingly cold. Being mobile, however, the box cars were practical. Companies could easily move the laborers from work site to work site or situate the cars somewhere as semipermanent quarters. Inside, a single wooden partition often divided the interior to lodge separate groups of workers or two or more nonbracero families per unit.

To enter the box cars, the men had to climb onto iron steps attached to the outside, located about two feet off the ground. When the railroad companies converted the cars to stationary housing, mechanics removed the wheel assemblies so the units rested directly on the ground. The box cars were arranged in groups from two to twelve or more. They offered meager accommodations: a single woodstove per partition, a wooden table, chairs, and bunk beds. Bunkhouses and barracks were a slight improvement over the box cars, so employers designated them for domestic seasonal or permanent track workers. The bunkhouses and barracks generally had electricity, water, and simple plumbing. The upgraded accommodations stopped there, however; these quarters offered rudimentary bunks to sleep and simple stoves to prepare meals. Older units were already severely dilapidated from use by generations of nonbracero workers. Because building materials of all kinds were in short supply, even newly constructed quarters provided braceros little more than shelter with a minimal space to sleep and eat.

Given the poor state of the bracero housing, living accommodations became an immediate operational concern and remained problematic for the duration of the railroad labor program. Despite the work agreement guaranteeing adequate lodging, officials had little interest in the condition of the braceros' housing and were not compelled to become involved until the braceros brought attention to the issue by refusing to work or by complaining to the Mexican consuls. Prevailing local health regulations regarding housing were almost never enforced at most railroad camps, regardless of the residents' concerns. The Railroad Retirement Board, charged with ensuring the braceros had suitable housing, had no prior housing standards or system to routinely check if living quarters were indeed adequate. In fact, the officials had not even examined the adequacy of living conditions before the arrival of the braceros. When the RRB finally moved to inspect the living accommodations, it was a reactive response to workers' complaints when housing conditions were most likely at their worst.

At the camps RRB inspectors encountered a wide range of living conditions. Where the contracted workers joined domestic section crews and close to other railroad worker communities, the inspectors found generally well-maintained and constructed housing. Here employers provided, among other things, stoves, chairs, cots, food storage areas, electric lights, running water, bathing and lavatory facilities. Some companies also supplied tubs, so the men could wash their work clothes. Screened windows and doors kept flies and other insects out of the living spaces and allowed for ventilation. Outside toilets and open ground pits where workers could dispose of the garbage gave these camps a tidy appearance. The well-being of these quarters stemmed from the fact that these were originally constructed for families but were left empty when former railroad workers migrated to better opportunities in other burgeoning war industries. Now vacant, the railroads set aside this constructed housing for the braceros.

Upon arriving to examine the living quarters for braceros in more remote areas, however, the RRB inspectors came up against a very different set of conditions. Out of sight from public view, this housing represented some of the most unpleasant and deplorable conditions faced by the Mexican railroaders. In 1943, Armando Suárez Rodríguez, a spokesperson for several extra gang crews assigned to the Texas & Pacific Railway Company, filed a complaint of racial discrimination over housing with the War Manpower Commission. According to the braceros, the railroad deducted one dollar per week for lodging and beds but did not report the deductions. While the company furnished cotton mattresses to non-Mexican workers, the braceros slept on straw bedding.[5] In September, just months after the Mexicans arrived, an RRB inspector responded to worker complaints at a Southern Pacific Railroad bracero camp located in the Shasta Division. His report described the degraded state of the site in vivid terms:

> Without doubt these quarters are the worse [sic] I have seen anywhere. They are a collection of small shacks, dirty, unsanitary, unsightly, verminous and utterly unfit for human habitation. The employer recently attempted to fumigate them, which was a waste of human effort because there are so many cracks in the walls that fumigation is ineffective. These hovels should be burned and decent quarters provided. It is strongly urged that the employer be required to provide immediate correction for this condition. It is understood the employer plans to abandon these quarters and erect others at another location. This should be done without delay.[6]

In addition, bedbug infestations were commonplace throughout the railroad camps even before the braceros' arrival. The parasite thrived in the crowded environment described by the RRB inspector. The general lack of sanitation and a high worker turnover rate resulted in serious outbreaks of bedbugs. Once the clothing or the bedding of the men was infested, the bugs traveled easily from one camp to another.

Until DDT came into use, simple fixes such as switching to metal beds from wooden cots with cracks and crevices were common. Sprays made by combining arsenic, mercury, and water were also used. Other toxic insecticidal concoctions deemed lethal to bedbugs(such as turpentine, gasoline, kerosene, benzene, and alcohol) did little to suppress infestations but caused human health problems and safety concerns due to the chemicals' flammability. By the time the braceros arrived, fumigation for bedbugs consisted of burning sulfur or spraying.[7] The presence of bedbugs led to the stigma associated with a perceived lack of cleanliness of the Mexican workers. Connecting a lack of hygiene with being a potential carrier of disease served to further denigrate and racially stigmatize the braceros. The discomfort of sleeping in quarters plagued with bedbugs affected braceros' morale and productivity.

RRB officials reported one of the worst cases at a Chicago, Burlington and Quincy Railroad bracero camp in Selbina, Missouri. In response to worker complaints, an inspector approached the first bunk and reported finding "bedbugs of all sizes" and in "great quantities together with eggs for generations yet to come." The railroad supervisor at the site, however, described the infestation as prevailing in many camps and "common to all extra gangs."[8] These experiences were not isolated. In Oregon, inspectors touring Southern Pacific camps from Corvallis north to Beaverton and east to The Dalles discovered a wide range of similarly improvised, grimy quarters. At one location the braceros were living in hurriedly erected tent camps and at another Southern Pacific work site, the men lived in old dismounted railroad car bodies.[9]

RRB inspectors visiting the Western Pacific Railroad Company Extra Gang No. 8 camp at Lyoth, California, observed that the men's living quarters comprised of eleven box cars in the hot and dusty San Joaquin Valley. The workers in three of the cars slept on a one-inch mattress on metal bunk beds without pillows or sheets. The other cars lacked bedding of any kind. During daytime, light entered the cars through four unscreened side windows. Oil lamps provided night visibility, and each car had one coal-burning stove. The cars had no other conveniences, as the RRB field supervisor did not see a single chair, table, or even a wall of foot lockers to store personal

effects.[10] Farther north, Southern Pacific stationed braceros at their roundhouse complex at Crescent Lake, Oregon. At an altitude of 4,455 feet, Crescent Lake winter temperatures often plummeted below zero, with snowfall
accumulations as high as 169 inches from September through May. When
RRB inspectors arrived on October 31, 1944, they found a crew of four braceros crammed into an eight- by twelve-foot bunkhouse. Each man worked
separate twelve-hour shifts in the roundhouse, making it necessary for some
to try to sleep while others cooked, washed clothes, or rested. The braceros
did not complain about the congested quarters, as they had more pressing
concerns: two months into the winter, the men were not prepared for the
medical and physical toll that resulted from the unbearably cold temperatures inside the bunkhouse.

Earlier in the year, Southern Pacific carpenters had constructed the
bunk space using green lumber, which eventually dried and left large cracks
throughout the whole structure. Under these circumstances and with one
small stove for heat, the braceros found it essentially impossible to warm
the bunkhouse. The Railroad Retirement Board immediately determined
that the men were in danger and ordered Southern Pacific to take swift re-
medial action. "The winters at Crescent Lake are very severe," the RRB reported, "and it is necessary that the Mexican Nationals have adequate protection from the winter elements." Already, officials added, the braceros
had requested permission to return back to México unless Southern Pacific
repaired the living quarters. Twenty-one days later, and despite the RRB's
urgent request for corrective steps, Southern Pacific's master mechanic in
Portland had taken no action.[11] Finally, in November, the railroad company
sealed the bunkhouse exterior.

* * *

As the RRB began to make routine surveys and file reports, a more compos-
ite picture of bracero housing developed. In some Santa Fe camps near San
Diego and Del Mar, California, for example, the accommodations had no
lights and the housing sites provided no toilet or bathing facilities. Lacking
bunks and mattresses, the men were forced to sleep on the floor. In one Spokane, Portland and Seattle Railway camp in Washington, as many as nine
men could be found living, cooking, and sleeping in a single bunk car. Inside, inspectors found one small stove, a kerosene lamp without kerosene,
steel cots without straw ticks or mattresses, and not a single chair or table.
The men bathed nearby in the Columbia River for lack of facilities, a prac-

tice that alarmed inspectors as the area where they bathed was known for being "swift" and "dangerous to swim in."[12] Workers in Saline, Utah, assigned to Southern Pacific lived in similar conditions. Despite the company's general housing repair program (supposedly in operation), inspectors reported that no "facilities whatsoever are available for bathing; there is adequate water but there is not even a tub or barrel at the camp in which the men might take some sort of a bath."[13] The braceros' only source of water came from a cistern filled twice a week by passing trains.

Large water storage boxes constructed in the ground and topped off by passing trains, cisterns were commonplace among rural railroad camps. In earlier times the water came directly from the tender used to supply water to steam locomotives. With the introduction of electric locomotives, trains added tank cars to service the cisterns to provide water to work crews. In either case, the workers were dependent on trains regularly resupplying the water. The cisterns at the camps had inherent problems. Unless the company or the workers constantly maintained them, water rapidly became dirty and contaminated. They were generally loosely covered, so mud and other debris entered the reservoir and eventually lined the cistern bottom. Standing water tended to attract snakes as well as provide habitat for mosquitoes and frogs. Still, cisterns were the only water many braceros had. In other instances, the delivery tank cars supplying the cisterns were unclean. As a result, the workers' water supply could arrive already polluted. The combination of filthy cisterns and dirty tank cars exacerbated deplorable living conditions at the braceros' camps.

RRB officials recorded an account after responding to bracero complaints about oil-contaminated water at an Atchison, Topeka and Santa Fe Railway Company camp in southern California. The company had used a tank car previously operated to haul petroleum products to deliver water to the work site. When the inspectors confronted the railroad with the allegation, the company defended itself by pointing to a stencil mark indicating the tank car had been cleaned two weeks earlier. But in the course of interviewing the braceros, one of the braceros went to the tank car to wash. As he opened the water valve, the RRB officials stood in shock as a gush of "very rusty water which ran dirty and rusty for several minutes" spewed from the tank car. Workers also objected forcefully to the lack of any shower facilities at the camp. According to the men, to cleanse themselves after work, they had been squatting beneath the valve on the same tank car so they could sponge-bathe with the oily water.[14]

The haphazard structure and construction of the camps themselves led to them becoming a magnet and breeding ground for flies, rats, and other annoying and unhealthy vermin. Flies and rats multiplied until they swarmed around the outdoor privies and garbage strewn about the camp-grounds. Toilets and housing areas very often lacked screens, enabling flies and rats to move undeterred from place to place. In camps without running water, where eight or more men shared one stove to prepare their meals, living conditions were generally filthy with dirty dishes and spoiled food. These untidy circumstances became an open call for camp parasites to enter the men's quarters completely unmolested. Lacking adequate sources of water and bathing facilities or a way to launder their clothes, it is understandable that the men often had a slovenly unshaved appearance and wore the same soiled work clothes for days at a time. Even in camps with improved living conditions, track repair and maintenance, and railroad work in general, quickly coated the men's bodies and clothes with layers of creosote, oil, and dirt, making it impossible for the men to stay clean. In the northern states, extreme cold temperatures added different challenges when the men attempted to wash their work clothes. During the winter, clothes hung outside quickly froze stiff, leaving the men little choice but to dry them inside their tight quarters.

During the spring months in eastern Washington and elsewhere, fierce dust storms added to the men's woes by coating them with dirt and dust. In the summer, braceros employed in the West's open and hot arid areas became drenched in sweat and caked in grunge after only a few minutes at work. Gonzalo Salazar, working in southern California after the war, recalled that as soon as the sun rose he and his companions were already sweating; by 10:00 a.m. they looked like they had been in a "swimming pool."[15] The evening hours brought some respite from the hot sun as perspiration on the worker's clothes dried, but not without first leaving a telltale stiff starched-like appearance on the clothing. Unless they had a day off to launder, braceros everywhere were back on the job the next day wearing the same soiled and rank-smelling undergarments, pants, and shirts.

* * *

Worse than the braceros' living arrangements, the contracted workers found the food unsuitable if not downright repugnant. They expressed markedly stronger objections to the quality and kinds of meals. The controversy over the food services developed from the start of the railroad program, catching the War Manpower Commission entirely unprepared. Each subsequent group of braceros arriving at the railroad camps protested the food provided by the railroad companies or the commissaries as well as the lack of Mexican ingredients for the workers to prepare their own food. Complaints about the meals were much more prevalent in the first year of the program and in areas further away from the Southwest.

The government arranged food services for the braceros in one of three ways. Commissary companies contracted by the various railroads provided meals directly to the braceros in the larger complexes. At other camps, employers hired local cooks to prepare food for the men. Among smaller work crews and in remote locations, employers contracted with local restaurants or the workers cooked their own food as long as a kitchen or other cooking facilities were available to them. Regardless of the method of food preparation and service, similar grievances surfaced over the quality and quantity of meals. The railroad companies had a long history of contracting commercial commissary companies to feed and provide other necessities to the labor force. The arrangement between the railroads and the commissaries amounted to a monopoly for the braceros working for that particular railroad.

The commissaries used every hook imaginable to maximize profits, especially by selling cheap and low-quality goods at top prices. Conditions changed only slightly under the bracero railroad program because the commissaries now operated in a more structured and regulated market economy, where prices and supplies were managed by the federal government because of the war. The commissaries sometimes found it impossible to obtain adequate supplies of food and other necessities. Regardless of sufficient stock of supplies, the work contract fixed the braceros to their jobs and by extension to the commissary. The commissaries often used a shortage of supplies to their advantage as an excuse to not provide adequate food services and other commodities to the Mexican labor force.

Despite wartime rationing, the federal government had to ensure every Mexican railroader could obtain enough quantities of food and other personal items. To address the concern, the War Manpower Commission and the Office of Price Administration (OPA) decided to issue separate ration books to each bracero so he could obtain critical food items and work clothing. The ration books were valuable and considered better than currency as many items could only be purchased with ration stamps. To guard against lost or stolen ration books, officials held all the ration books for safekeeping until the braceros entered the United States. The WMC tried to convey the value of the ration books and provided practical steps for safekeeping. Instructing the men on how to use the ration stamps presented a further challenge. Countless Americans, let alone the non-English-speaking braceros, found the system of purchasing rationed commodities complicated.

To address the language barrier, the OPA developed a guide titled "Hoja de Instrucciones para los Mexicanos Bajo Contrato con la War Manpower Administration." Even with instructions in Spanish, however, the braceros had difficulty following the complex system of expiration dates, points, colors, and letters used to purchase much needed items; many of them were functionally illiterate. Stores where the braceros shopped posted helpful information in English but not in Spanish. Along with the explanation of how to redeem the stamps, the OPA underscored the value of the ration stamps by cautioning the workers not to lose, sell, or loan the book. All of these warnings had little effect because unless the men prepared their own food, the OPA directed them to turn over their ration book to the person responsible for providing their meals.[16]

An opportunity for the potentially dishonest use of braceros' ration books was thereby developed. By relinquishing the ration book to the food provider, the bracero entrusted this valuable asset to the goodwill of the employer, cook, or worse yet the commissary company. Braceros were susceptible to fraud at several levels. In the wrong hands little prevented commissary officials, store clerks, or anyone else from unlawfully using a bracero ration book to provide for their own needs, pass them on to others, or sell. Venders knew that braceros could not call the police or report a crime. Store clerks could easily tear more stamps than the value of the purchase without the bracero knowing. The high probability of corruption and theft with the ration books existed because of racism and as the growing social conditions of shortage of food, clothing, and other basic supplies grew across the nation. A corresponding black market in stolen and counterfeit ration stamps grew. Given the situation, the braceros themselves were not above stealing from each other.

Ration books could be lost at work, in public places, while traveling, or somewhere in the largely unsecured living areas. Once lost, only the slimmest chance existed of recovering ration books. Like many other contract workers, Southern Pacific bracero Juan Ponce Herrera took steps to safeguard his two most important documents by inserting the work contract into the back of the ration book. Despite being careful, however, Herrera lost both documents, which were later found after he had already returned to México City.[17] Even when ration books could be securely protected, the braceros did not always make the best use of their allocation of stamps. In one dispatch the chief engineer for the Texas and Pacific Railway notified the War Manpower Commission to request "supplementary coupons" so 405 braceros could purchase work shoes. The men, he wrote, "are badly in need of work shoes. Many [are] now working in sandals [huaraches]." Unaccustomed to the work conditions the men had used their ration stamps to purchase inferior grade shoes that soon wore out.[18] At other times the men purchased fresh meat, milk, or vegetables in more quantities than they could consume, only to have the food spoil for lack of ice boxes or appropriate food storage areas.

Beyond the many difficulties in using the ration books, food in general garnered the most angry and resentful complaints from the braceros. In a matter of days after entering the United States, the majority of the braceros found themselves surrounded by unfamiliar food and a difficult experience adjusting to schedules for main meals. In the opinion of the inspectors, the worst food conditions existed where small groups of men lived together and prepared their own food. Crowded unclean rooming quarters, a lack of running water, and inadequate cooking stoves were the root causes of many of the complaints. Cleanliness and sanitation aside, it was unreasonable for eight or more men living in the same congested space to take turns preparing both breakfast and lunch on a single stove and without a kitchen table. At one location, flat-top cooking stoves were not even available to the men unless they were willing to rent them at fifty cents per month.[19] Also, that braceros coming from a male-dominant culture where women did all of the cooking could suddenly learn how to prepare their meals surely was difficult for many of the workers. In some cases, inspectors found ten men trying to prepare both breakfast and lunch on a single small stove before going to work. After a ten-hour workday, the men returned to grapple with one another to try to fix their evening meal. Outside of the Southwest and some parts of the Midwestern states, familiar and traditional foodstuffs were not available to the braceros. Many times when such products were sold locally, the braceros were stationed miles away from the nearest store without any means of transportation.[20]

To address the complex food issue, the Railroad Retirement Board recommended that railroad officials provide transportation for braceros to shop at stores stocking food "suitable to the Mexican menu." Where transportation could not be arranged, officials proposed that the railroads could deliver "these foods" directly to the track section where the men were employed. In cases where the commissary companies, hired as independent contractors, provided food to the camps, the RRB suggested that they instruct braceros how to order and prepare balanced meals, which they stressed for its "important psychological benefit" among the men. Since the rudimentary living quarters did not ordinarily have ice boxes or a regular supply of ice, the RRB also recommended that the OPA allow the workers to receive extra ration food stamps for them to purchase more canned and dried foods than the normal ration book allowed. Aware of the gravity of the food issue, the RRB sent a directive to all railroad companies employing braceros to install one stove suitable for making tortillas for every four workers in each railroad camp.[21]

The improvements ordered by the Railroad Retirement Board were only effective in addressing complaints over food if implemented. As a rule, the RRB's instructions went directly to company officials, who passed them on to a mechanical engineer or the crew foreman. Immediate corrective action followed in some cases, but the camp supervisors or crew foreman did not always follow the RRB's orders. Much depended on the availability of materials and the goodwill of local company officials, particularly the crew foreman who was ultimately responsible for the well-being of the braceros. For years, supervisors were accustomed to having complete control over all aspects of track work culture until the RRB contested their authority at the start of the bracero program.

\* \* \*

The specter of racism often entered into decisions affecting the braceros. Supervisors of the Mexican men struggled with the idea of accommodating the imported workers when other ethnic groups and white track laborers were not regularly provided ice boxes, sinks with running water, and other amenities. As far as the supervisors were concerned, their main responsibility was to ensure freight and passenger trains ran on efficiently and safely; food services were of secondary concern to proper track maintenance despite the obvious link between poor health and food conditions and decreased productivity. In the beginning, some railroads did not consider themselves responsible for providing provisions to the contracted men. When federal officials began to hold them accountable, the railroad companies had to consider the unbending attitude of their own supervisors as well as the scale of the food issue. Hence they turned to past practices and gave the responsibility over to experienced commissary companies.[22]

A close look at the commissaries identifies the significant levels of swindling. As a rule, workers with Southern Pacific track crews could expect to pay twice the retail price for most clothing and apparel. At a bracero camp near Montezuma, Arizona, for example, the Threlkeld Commissary Company priced cotton work caps at $1.50, while the identical item sold for $.60 at a nearby supply store in Phoenix.[23] At Del Mar, California, workers accused the Holmes Supply Company of inflating the value of merchandise sold at the camp store. The same braceros alleged that Holmes Supply store clerks were taking an excessive number of sugar ration stamps then limiting each worker to 1.5 pounds of sugar per month. According to the workers, for the same amount of sugar stamps they could purchase 5 pounds per month at an off-camp grocery store.[24]

Not only were prices high, but the commissaries encouraged its captive market of buyers into making all purchases at the company's store. In this way, according to the commissary, the braceros could accumulate additional points from the rationing boards entitling them to more supplies above the usual allocation. Although the qualifying points technically went to the men, the commissaries made effective use of the supplementary stamps to stock more supplies and all the more to sell to the braceros. For example, the Threlkeld Commissary recognized that some of the men arrived from México wearing light duty shoes or in some instances *huaraches* and thus the men were ill-equipped for track work. The commissary seized on the opening to sell the appropriate work boot to the braceros. First, the commissary took sufficient shoe ration stamps from the braceros so it could qualify for an allotment of "safety shoes." Next, the camp store turned around and retailed the safety shoes to the laborers at $4.50, nearly a day's earnings.[25]

Food purchases and charges for board returned considerably higher profits to the commissaries. While the charge for meals varied among the commissaries. Southern Pacific set the charge at $1.20 per day or $33.50 monthly. Workers with Northern Pacific paid $1.30 daily plus a $1.00 monthly blanket-use fee. Maintenance crews contracted to the Atchison, Topeka and Santa Fe earned $0.49 an hour while paying $1.03 per day for their meals. It did not matter if the braceros boarding with the Holmes commissary kitchen took their meals or not. Regardless, the railroad made deductions against the workers' pay on behalf of the commissary.[26]

Where workers cooked for themselves, inadequate kitchen facilities and
a lack of variety of provisions were the principal complaints. Upon arrival at
Southern Pacific section houses, workers purchased food supplies from the
Threlkeld Commissary ranging from seven to nine dollars. Regardless of the
price, workers received mostly raw groceries consisting of rice, canned vegetables, dried beans, and chile peppers, considered to be an "inadequate diet"
by RRB inspectors.[27] Bearing in mind that refrigerators and ice boxes were
not available to the braceros, any perishable food would spoil in a matter
of hours. At Manteca, California, in August 1943, fifteen members of Southern Pacific extra gang 3, along with the camp cook, came down with food
poisoning after an evening meal of spoiled turkey. The cook explained the
difficulty of obtaining supplies to serve the men. One day, for example, the
kitchen had three cans of canned salmon and some oysters to feed dinner to
the entire camp. According to the cook, the commissary supplied the meat
to the camp, and "it usually contained a very large portion of bone and fat,
thereby cutting down the amount available for consumption." The braceros
had complained about the food all summer, but meals remained unappetiz-
ing, lacking in nutrition, and unhealthy. When one of the workers returned
to México, he filed a complaint with the Mexican government hoping to improve food services at the Manteca camp.[28]

Braceros who ate at the commissary kitchen protested the most, as the
gastrointestinal discomfort associated with going from a Mexican diet to
"American food" began immediately. One bracero en route to a work site
at Wenatchee, Washington, relayed a gruesome tale. According to him, all
the braceros got diarrhea after the evening supper before their arrival in
Wenatchee. Although difficult to ascertain the actual source of the illness,
the braceros alleged that officials purposefully wanted the men to arrive
with "clean" and empty stomachs.[29] Braceros working in California for the
Santa Fe attributed stomach pain to sour, nauseating beans and the poor
quality of meals. Since their arrival, the kitchen had served vegetable soup
on a daily basis.[30] To avoid cooking for every meal, camp cooks preferred
to keep leftover soup and serve it repeatedly until the original amount was
consumed. Soups and beans were easy to prepare and reheat, so cooks constantly served them to the braceros. But unless refrigerated, beans were
prone to spoil especially in hot summer temperatures. This practice among
camp cooks led to an outbreak of dysentery at an Atchison, Topeka and
Santa Fe track laying crew in Canejo, California, in 1943.[31]

Similarly, RRB inspectors responded to complaints from workers during a camp inspection of the Chicago, Milwaukee, Saint Paul, and Pacific Railroad in Mowery, Idaho. Their report confirmed the men's charges. Not only were the cooks employed by the Olympic Commissary Company "very poor" but also had been serving "spoiled meat" to the braceros.[32] The conflation of poor food preparation, rationed provisions, and unfamiliar and repetitive menus precipitated bracero work stoppages in various railroad camps. The RRB considered this type of labor disruption an unacceptable obstruction because it originated from the poor feeding program.

After continuous protests from the braceros, the Railroad Retirement Board seriously addressed the issue of food. As a first step, the RRB urged the feeding companies to make every effort to obtain ample and improved food supplies from the local rationing board. Officials pushed the commissaries to hire better-trained cooks. Where possible, cooks familiar with Mexican cuisine were a better fit in kitchens feeding the bracero workforce, according to the RRB. This commonsense idea received a quick response. The John J. Grier Company, for example, bid to recruit Mexican cooks exclusively for extra gang crews with Chicago, Burlington and Quincy Railroad, Colorado and Southern Railway, and Fort Worth and Denver City Railway. One year into the railroad program, the State Department began to explore the feasibility of contracting Mexican cooks for bracero kitchens with U.S. Ambassador George S. Messersmith in México City.[33]

It did not help the recruiting effort of contracted workers in México when a State Department official in charge of the Mexican labor program addressed the food issue in stereotypic language of the time, describing worker complaints as silly and ridiculous:

Mexico's Juan Trabajador [worker] traditionally asks only the most modest comforts in life; he possesses a genius for devising his own recreations; he is rarely a heavy eater, but he likes his corn-meal tortillas, his beans, and his chili, and no amount of ham "sanweech" will quite satisfy him as a substitute. In common with most strangers in a strange country, he entertains doubts and fears about new foods that taste queer. A Mexican consul recently had to investigate complaints from one group of workers that the cook was giving them for breakfast a "bitter water" which they thought suspicious. It turned out to be grapefruit juice.[34]

However, a dramatically different view came from Adolfo Morales Matamoros, an ex-Southern Pacific track worker testifying before the director of
social provisions in México City.

> The commissary obligates us to consume food that is completely vile and
> sickening that even dogs will not eat it. They fed us tripe, smelly liver, oat
> meal that looked like starch, and very little sugar.
>
> Health officials told us we had no reason to protest the food because
> according to them it was perfect. We, Mexicans, were accustomed to eating
> tortillas and frijoles [pinto beans] and would benefit from a different meal.
> We responded that the work contract obligated them to serve us food as if
> we were "American" citizens. They didn't pay attention to us and continued
> serving the same food.[35]

Manuel Gamio, despite being a very staunch advocate of the bracero
programs, corroborated the worker's testimony. After returning in November 1944 from a tour of railroad camps in the United States, Gamio wrote
a confidential summary to Mexican president Manuel Ávila Camacho describing the "conditions much more deficient than in the agricultural bracero camps."[36] Each new wave of workers continued to complain about the
food, repulsed by constant servings of potatoes, roast beef, and the lack of
fresh vegetables. In the end the War Manpower Commission, working with
the Threlkeld Commissary, came up with a different solution to the ongoing
food dilemma. The request to authorize the contracting of cooks for the bracero railroad camps went nowhere politically. Already, thousands of agricultural and railroad bracero workers were in the United States. Adding yet
another category of contract workers, in this case cooks, made little political
sense as protests against the bracero programs continued to mount.

Acting on the advice of the Threlkeld Commissary and bearing in mind
the latent but virulent anti-Chinese racism that existed in both México
and the United States, the two governments agreed to yet another separate
grouping of bracero workers: ethnic Chinese Mexicans, "accustomed to the
Mexican ways," would be in charge of the bracero camp kitchens.[37] In 1944
the Threlkeld Commissary received permission to begin recruiting Chinese
Mexican cooks in Tampico and México City, both sites of significant concentrations of Chinese ethnic communities. To aid in selecting the cooks, Fon
Wing Fun, a Chinese national employed by the Threlkeld Company in San
Francisco, traveled to México City to work with WMC officials. The initial au-

thorization allowed the commissary to bring 175 contracted bilingual cooks familiar with Mexican food.

The WMC decided to conduct all health examinations of the Chinese cooks in Tampico for fear of taking them to México City, where they would mix with Mexican bracero recruits. This helped avoid the possibility that allowing the Chinese to mingle with other Mexicans "might raise a good many thorny questions which would be difficult to explain."[38] When chosen as cooks, the Chinese Mexicans received hourly wages of $0.46 and could remain in the United States for up to two years by renewing their contracts.[39] Taking into consideration the exclusion of Chinese immigrants to the United States and aware of the smuggling of Chinese immigrants from México north to Portland, Oregon, and beyond, the Threlkeld Commissary posted a thousand-dollar surety bond per individual. This guaranteed that each cook would be repatriated to México. The total amount of the bond for the Chinese cooks came to $175,000 and was deposited at the Crocker National Bank in San Francisco, California.[40]

Although intolerance against the Chinese in México had lessened slightly by the 1940s, the Mexican railroaders brought their bigotry with them. In many cases the Mexican workers made life difficult for the Chinese Mexican cooks, compelling them to desert and gravitate to the nearest Chinese community. Others requested a return back to México, alleging mistreatment from the braceros and failure of the Threlkeld Company to abide by the contract. This treatment of cooks forced the commissary to be constantly replacing the returnees and deserters. As a result, the initial allocation for 175 Chinese Mexican cooks increased to 250 and on to 525.[41] The WMC also took into consideration that racism toward Chinese immigrant communities was as deep-seated in the United States as in México. In addressing the issue of anti-Chinese sentiment, the Threlkeld Commissary assured the U.S. Department of State in México that it was aware that the Chinese cooks "may come in contact with people who, through ignorance, may not at all times treat them with the consideration that we always want our Chinese to have." The commissary, however, had a record of employing Chinese for forty-five years and would make use of that experience with the bracero camp cooks.[42]

Not all ethnic Chinese camp cooks came from México under the auspices of the bracero cook agreement. Some of them were longtime residents in the United States and hired on with the various railroads or commissaries. Still other Mexican-born Chinese cooks entered the U.S. on their own using aliases. In fact, a smuggling operation involving cooks, sometimes with their own kitchen assistants, developed in Tampico once the contracting of the Chinese Mexicans got under way.[43] Not every commissary kitchen served terrible food. In Pocatello, Idaho, for example, the Union Pacific railroad hired Felicitas Pérez García to assist a Chinese cook by preparing tortillas, "frijoles," and other food items much to the satisfaction of the braceros.[44]

\* \* \*

Still the ubiquitous complaints of the braceros concerning the food spoke to the magnitude and seriousness of the problem. Regardless of whether the men prepared their own food or took their meals at the commissary, they were correct in feeling wronged by the lack of adequate provisions. Considering the food issue alongside abject living quarters, the braceros had legitimate reasons to feel victimized. At the very least, they expected better conditions in the United States. When the men could interpret their work agreement in light of the regrettable state of affairs, they believed the guarantees of the work contract had been violated. Yet as bad as the braceros felt about the food and their living conditions, they would experience worse treatment on the job.

**Figure 1.** Labor recruiting agency in Wyoming. The Spanish sign on the right reads: "Railroad workers needed for the Southern Pacific Stockton Division." Mexican railroaders moved from Stockton to Oregon's Portland Division. *Source*: Lawrence Cardoso Papers, American Heritage Collection, University of Wyoming.

**Figure 2.** Wedding at a Southern Pacific Sacramento, California, upholstery shop between a bracero and a Mexican American bride. Note the all-women workforce. *Source*: California State Railway Museum.

**Figure 3.** Women track workers Bertha and Rosie Montalvo, Blanche Tuttle, Myrtle Tracy, Sara Soto, and Gina Everett (from left), all with family members in the military. *Source*: *Southern Pacific Bulletin*.

AMERICANOS TODOS
★
LUCHAMOS POR LA
VICTORIA

★ **AMERICANS ALL** ★
LET'S FIGHT FOR VICTORY

**Figure 4.** Notwithstanding Depression-era deportations of Mexicans and Mexican American citizens, the war encouraged a new effort to promote racial and ethnic unity. *Source*: War Information Office, RG 208, NARA.

**Figure 5.** Referred to as "railroad soldiers," Southern Pacific braceros stand in military-like formation. *Source*: *Southern Pacific Bulletin*.

**Figure 6.** Bracero railroad workers crossing the border into the United States. *Source: Southern Pacific Bulletin.*

**Figure 7.** Pan-American unity extolled on the cover of the October 1943 issue of the *Southern Pacific Bulletin. Source: Southern Pacific Bulletin.*

**Figure 8.** Southern Pacific braceros from the Portland, Oregon, Division. *Source*: *Southern Pacific Bulletin*.

**Figure 9.** Bracero extra gang crew at work with the New York Central. *Source*: *Railway Age*.

**Figure 10.** The Southern Pacific Tucson Band organized as a leisure activity for its Mexican American employees. Braceros bitterly complained about the lack of similar opportunities. *Source*: Mexican Heritage Project, Arizona Historical Society.

**Figure 11.** Union Pacific car shop crew at Pocatello, Idaho, in the 1970s. Miguel Rivera (standing fifth from left) is the only nonwhite worker. The position of the lone woman is also telling of the postwar work culture. *Source*: Author's collection.

**Figure 12.** Northern Pacific poster used to locate deserters at the end of the bracero railroad program. *Source*: Minnesota Historical Society.

**Figure 13.** Northern Pacific Baldwin steam locomotive at Pasco, Washington. Pasco was an important railroad juncture and site of employment for braceros during World War II and for Mexican Americans after the war. *Source*: Author's collection.

Chapter 7

# The Perils of Being a Bracero

While negotiating the bracero railroad workers agreement, the United States assured México that, unlike the agricultural workers agreement (whereby state and federal administrators regulated the contract workers), the Railroad Retirement Board (RRB) would be solely responsible for enforcement. This was after all a government-to-government agreement, meaning the U.S. government, not the railroads, employed the track workers. In the same way that the RRB oversaw the feeding and sheltering of the railroad braceros, it also had the responsibility to monitor all employee relations with the railroad companies. According to an official War Manpower Commission (WMC) investigation during the summer of 1943, however, no one had bothered to inspect the facilities for the railroad braceros before their arrival and no inspection was scheduled. Administrative procedures for managing the men were also nonexistent, and the railroad companies had not adopted any personnel program for the managing them once they arrived in the United States.[1]

Even though the U.S. government employed the braceros, the railroads had a proprietary interest in each individual worker before his arrival in the country. By the time the contracted workers departed México City, representatives of the U.S. Railway Mission and the U.S. railroad industry had earmarked workers to specific employers. From the start, they thus began to view and treat the laborers as commodities. The Association of American Railroads and the Western Association of Railroad Executives (WARE), as well as management from the U.S. Railway Mission and representatives from the employing companies themselves, had actively collaborated in the recruitment and picking of braceros in México. This became more evident when WARE assumed responsibility for program operations in México in 1944. When the WMC or WARE assigned a bracero to a particular company and the workers signed the individual work contract, they became inextricably tied to their employer. From that point on, each railroad company traced its braceros from the recruiting centers in México, through the border crossing into the United States, and ultimately to the work site.

The railroad companies' ownership interest in the braceros developed at several levels. When the WMC recruited braceros in México, it did so with the goal of filling an explicit request for workers from railroad companies in different regions of the United States. Through active participation in the screening and selection of the braceros, company officials in México had a direct hand in selecting workers to meet the interests and needs of their particular railroad. The WMC required that each railroad pay twenty dollars for a five-hundred-dollar bond per bracero with an authorized bonding company. In effect, this deposit guaranteed each worker's exit to immigration authorities. The deposit meant that although the workers and the War Manpower Commission signed the work contract on behalf of the United States, in actuality (and legally) the company posting the departure bond assumed possession of and responsibility for the worker. In principle, the failure to repatriate a bracero to México at the end of the employment period meant forfeiture of the bond. Unlike other violations of the contract where officials often looked the other way or underplayed the infraction, the U.S. government did not cancel the surety. It held the employing railroad responsible until the company provided proof that the bonded worker had crossed back into México. The cumulative worth of the bonds (deposited for every bracero) became substantial and expanded with the growing demand for Mexican track workers.

The reason for requiring companies to deposit a bond is obvious. From the beginning of preliminary discussions to authorize contracting Mexican track laborers to the United States, the Brotherhood of Maintenance of Way Employees (BMWE) adamantly argued for assurances that the workers would not undermine the union by remaining in the country after the war. The braceros therefore were temporary workers, and companies stood to forfeit the surety if a bracero became a permanent free wage earner in the U.S. Just as important, the bond acted to mitigate the larger public's fear that the railroad bracero program would open the floodgate to permanent immigration so soon after the Depression-era deportation of Mexicans. Public anxiety over Mexican immigration had previously shaped the World War I bracero program and the congressional debates of the 1920s, and it clearly influenced the decision to make use of a security bond to compel companies to return every contracted man to México.

Employers were thus accountable for the repatriation of the workforce, but there was no language in the individual work agreement calling for repercussions for employers who defaulted on their workers' rights. The contractual obligations to their workers were straightforward but often lacked specificity. For their part, railroad companies agreed to furnish travel to and from the work site and employment for a six-month period. The contract also stipulated that railroad braceros were entitled to wages and pay adjustments equivalent to union and nonunion workers employed in a similar capacity in the same work area. In contradiction to the ambiguity in some sections of the contract, the language laid out the workers' responsibilities very clearly. The men agreed to properly and diligently perform the work assigned to them for a minimum six-month period under the supervision and direction of the employer.

Generally, the men commenced work the day after their arrival at the work site and kept busy for 180 days, except Sundays and legal U.S. holidays. When disputes arose between the contracted men and the employer, the WMC through the U.S. Employment Service (USES) had the ultimate authority to resolve the issue.[2] When workers filed complaints, the USES could hold hearings open to the RRB, Mexican consuls, Mexican labor inspectors, and railroad representatives. At the start of the bracero railroad program, the Mexican government denied or made light of the maltreatment of its workers in the United States.[3] Later in negotiations between the WMC and the Mexican government, México gradually asserted its right to intervene on behalf of its citizens. However, this did not change the WMC's position as exclusive arbitrator, thus limiting the effectiveness of Mexican government involvement.

U.S. railroad companies had a long history of contracting labor by working with private recruiting agents. In this respect, Mexican immigration before World War II constituted a de facto bracero program. A number of these men with previous knowledge of railroad work and labor contracts were also in the mix of the wave of arriving World War II Mexican railroaders. Experienced as they were with the hazardous and demanding task of lifting rails, putting down ties, and the importance of a properly prepared road bed, in general conversation the older (and former) immigrants were helpful to the neophyte braceros by explaining the precarious nature of being a contracted worker in the U.S. This meant that by the time the braceros arrived to the work site, they were in some cases conscious of their rights and on the alert for infractions. This partially explains why some groups of braceros wasted little time in defying the stereotypes held by employers.

As the WMC and the railroad companies soon found out, Mexicans were far from passive and very often ready to stand up to mistreatment. One official surmised that the braceros were "sharper" in contrast to domestic Mexican American workers employed as track laborers. The braceros, he said, were more "conscious of their contractual rights, and it was our observation, less easily satisfied than our own native workers."[4] On the job, each arriving wave of braceros was immediately confronted by the powerful nexus of racism, social injustice, and the authoritarian power of supervisor over worker. The coming together of these powerful social forces often made already grueling work unbearable. Contracts do not enforce themselves; the workers, government, and employers could act to implement or disregard the provisions of the bilateral agreement. In the majority of cases, employers and the government overshadowed the capacity of the braceros to force compliance with the foremost conditions of the contract.

Entering World War II, the railroad companies and the War Manpower Commission saw México's labor-rich labor market as the answer to many of the labor issues brought about by the war. In designing the bracero railroad program to tap México, however, the focal point became managing the transfer of labor along qualitative lines with built-in assurances that any international movement of labor would be temporary. Of course, for the duration of the war the transnational shift of labor was short-term, but the railroad and agricultural bracero programs had the opposite effect. The World War II bracero programs placed in motion unprecedented immigration of Mexican labor lasting until the end of the century. At the start of the program, the WMC located the administration of the bracero railroad program in México City. Although many *aspirantes* came from the urban metropolis, many more came from rural communities as the BMWE strongly and successfully opposed the entry of skilled men; this meant that a good number of the recruits were common rural laborers.

For example, rural Michoacán communities had a long history of dispatching labor to the United States (except during the Great Depression). A renewed exodus set off by World War II occurred in Paracho, Michoacán. According to community lore, the first Parachoan left in 1904 during the austere period of President Díaz's regime and later returned with encouraging anecdotes of his work experiences in the north. This placed in motion a euphoric and sustained culture of migration until the Depression, when no more than three men left the community.[5] The U.S. war economy almost instantaneously recharged the flow of laborers out of Paracho, and all but a few men left under contract with the bracero programs. In the first year of the World War II, Michoacán accounted for 26.73 percent of the total number of braceros contracted to U.S. employers; for the duration of the war no other Mexican state supplied more workers to the United States.[6] The indigenous racial makeup of many of the bracero laborers from Michoacán, and other parts of rural México, determined whether the officials selected them as braceros. In 1940 the Mexican national census identified 51.2 percent of the total population was living at the level of "indigenous" communities. The weight of this socially defined population varied across México. "Indigenous" communities, for example, accounted for nearly 50 percent of all residents of Michoacán.[7] Residents in some rural communities pinpointed much higher concentrations of mixed race or indigenous people. In Jaripo, just south of Paracho, for example, the people recalled that in the prewar years very few whites lived in their community and the majority of the residents spoke Spanish but were mostly "dark like Indian."[8]

Writing in 1935, Manuel Gamio, a key architect of the bracero program and a visionary of a modernized México, identified the majority of the pre–World War II Mexican emigrants to the United States as being "mestizos" or "full-blooded Indians."[9] The racial composition of the exported labor force did not change by World War II, given the significant indigenous racial composition of the Mexican population and its concentration in key bracero-recruiting areas. When the recruitment of railroad braceros moved from México City to San Luis Potosí and Tampico, the percentage of "indigenous" persons in the surrounding population surpassed that in Michoacán. San Luis Potosí's population consisted of 52.9 percent "indigenous" and nearby Veracruz, 63.3 percent.[10]

At the request of U.S. employers, in the beginning of the program, WMC officials in México City used race to select the bracero labor force. To make their subjective determination, officials decided selection on the physiognomy and cultural characteristics of the men. Indigenous racial identity, coupled with related social attributes such as illiteracy, lessened the chance of joining the railroad labor program. The subjective use of race is another reason why small numbers of braceros came from states with heavy concentrations of indigenous people such as Oaxaca.[11] However, a higher manifestation of "whiteness" and literacy enhanced the probability of joining the U.S.-bound labor force. Racial discrimination against indigenous and other "nonwhite" men in the selection process caught the attention of the WMC: in the fall of 1943 it urged employers to no longer request particular workers and exclude others on the basis of "color" and "race."[12] The racial composition of the bracero laborers did matter in the United States, but not much is known about the workers' day-to-day routine unless the Railroad Retirement Board investigated a complaint from the Mexican railroaders. For the most part, the braceros worked and lived in segregated crews, so little is understood about interplay among themselves and with other laborers. Their interaction with the crew supervisor, however, does provide some insight.

The majority of the railroaders coming from México during World War II served in the western region of the country and the bulk were assigned to unskilled arduous work with extra gang crews. Despite México's hope that railroad braceros would acquire modern industrial skills in the U.S., most of the men performed ordinary hard labor unloading rail and ties, preparing the road bed, laying ties, and securing the rail. On D-Day in 1944, nearly eight of every ten Southern Pacific track jobs were held by braceros.[13] The railroad unions imposed their views on race and membership on the Mexican laborers. At the start of World War II, eleven railroad unions (including the AFL and independents) excluded nonwhites, particularly African Americans, from complete membership.[14] They did this in several ways. Some unions had clauses excluding nonwhites from membership. When nonwhites were not denied membership by provision, new members could only join if recommended by an active card holder. In practice, nonwhites were rarely invited to enter the union. In other cases, nonwhites could belong to auxiliary unions, which had no representation in general meetings of the organization. Basically, the railroad unions were the exclusive domain of white workers and functioned to eliminate nonwhites from partaking in any of the benefits of collective bargaining.

* * *

Instructive here is the public's unwarranted anxiety and fear of the Japanese Americans during the war. This captures the social atmosphere that Mexican railroaders were stepping into in the United States. At the outset of the war, white railroad workers directed their racial animosity toward Japanese immigrants and Japanese Americans in ways reminiscent of the hostility Mexicans and Mexican Americans had felt during the Great Depression. Now, across rural communities in Washington State (such as Klickitat, Wenatchee, and Goldendale) white railroad workers met to vehemently oppose employment of Japanese and Japanese American track workers.[15] In Wenatchee, for example, the community empowered the sheriff to remove all Japanese Americans working or living on Great Northern railroad premises.[16] In the minds of these white railroaders, the treacherous Japanese could easily cripple rail travel since they had switch keys and access to powerhouses.

Described as "yellow Aryans," Japanese Americans in urban area railroad shops and roundhouses were intensely persecuted. On January 24, 1942, the complete workforce at Seattle's Great Northern roundhouse threatened to "sit down" if and when "Jap" members of Local 764 were reinstated to their jobs. Of course such opposition called into question the validity of a shortage of railroad workers. Even after the war ended, the loathing against the Japanese Americans persisted. Representatives of all Great Northern craft unions at the Seattle roundhouse met to vote whether to permit Sam Saki and Jimmie Saki to be re-employed. In unanimity, the vote was a resounding no. They did "not want the above mentioned or any other Japanese employed at the Seattle roundhouse."[17] Depriving Japanese Americans endured in rural areas as well. Hoping to reclaim a job he had held as a section hand since 1928, Kuhei Tsuchida wrote to the Great Northern Railway Company in September 1945 while being held at the Topaz, Utah, internment camp for Japanese and Japanese Americans. The war had ended and Tsuchida wanted to return with his five children to Auburn, Washington. A month later, the military released Tsuchida and his family to Ogden, Utah.[18]

Despite preference of the Brotherhood of Maintenance of Way Employees for the employment of braceros over prisoners of war and other "suspected aliens," Mexicans were also considered nonwhite and treated as such many years before World War II.[19] The BMWE and other unions had been reluctant to accept the importation of railroad workers from México. Writing after the war, the newspaper *El tiempo* reported that the overwhelming majority of the braceros were artisans, workers, or farmers, twenty-one-year-old men or younger.[20] Most of the men found themselves tied to hard labor or pick-and-shovel gang work repairing and maintaining track lines throughout the country. As the war labor shortages deepened and the braceros proved themselves adroit workers, railroad companies sought permission from the War Manpower Commission and the BMWE to upgrade certain braceros to other similarly unskilled low-wage jobs, such as mechanical and stores departments, truck drivers, structural helpers, assistants, and timber treatment plants.

The Pacific Fruit Express (PFE), primarily a shipper of fresh perishable food commodities, relied mostly on braceros as icemen and ice pullers at its western icing stations. The bracero ice pullers worked in the freezing rooms manipulating large ice blocks and moving them to storerooms. The icemen loaded the refrigerated cars by moving the ice along elevated wooden platforms and dropping them into roof openings of the refrigerated bunkers. The work was undesirable, hard, and hazardous. At the PFE Los Angeles icing stations, 75 percent of the workers were braceros. The percentage of icing braceros at Modesto, California, was 65 percent; it was 80 percent at the Roseville station. At Wallula, Washington, braceros accounted for 77 percent of the total number of ice plant workers. Pocatello, Idaho, braceros were 31 percent of the total. Braceros at Sparks, Nevada, totaled 50 percent; 55 percent at Ogden, Utah; and 38 percent at Laramie, Wyoming. Without the bracero ice men, the PFE figured a substantial amount of perishable food would not be available for civilian and military consumption.[21]

Unfamiliar weather conditions, coupled with a different diet and meal schedule, presented other challenges to the railroad bracero workers. The majority of the braceros originated from the Mexican central states of Michoacán, Guanajuato, and Jalisco, and they were often sent to repair track in extreme weather in the northern latitudes of the United States. From northern California, north and east, deep winter snow, biting wind, and ice brought difficulties to those working at high altitudes to keep the lines open. These conditions required hearty men appropriately dressed to withstand the extreme temperatures. During the first winter of the railroad program, the Mexican Civic Committee of the West Side of Chicago called on President Manuel Ávila Camacho to request winter clothes and shoes for the bracero railroaders. With temperatures commonly dropping from 20 to 10 degrees below zero during winter, the group pointed out that the braceros were susceptible to respiratory illness and tuberculosis. "We have seen braceros arrive at these latitudes with straw hats, thin underclothes, canvas shoes with rubber soles, without jackets of any kind, and have seen them covering themselves with newspapers or blankets," they wrote to the president. "These scenes are painful and denigrate the nation (México) and can be easily remedied, since the railroad companies can easily provide the necessary clothes to the work force." The Mexican Civic Committee requested

the railroad companies provide each bracero destined for winter jobs outside the Southwest with two changes of underwear, rubber shoes, leather
shoes, three pairs of socks (at least 30 percent wool), warm jackets, sweater,
work gloves, and a cap with ear coverings.[22]

WMC officials were well aware of the potential for hypothermia in below-
zero weather, particularly in the northern states and that a failure to protect
the braceros would be "inconsistent" with the binational accord.[23] Early in
the program, an RRB official sounded the alarm over braceros working in
severe winter weather: "I believe that we are going to face some difficulty in
the handling of Mexican Nationals in the territory where it gets very cold
and where they have a great deal of snow during the winter months." Yet
the only steps taken by the War Manpower Commission were to issue blankets at the border and urge the braceros to purchase adequate protection for
their own "health and welfare."[24]

Where the braceros struggled to cope with the extreme temperatures in
the northern latitudes, they also worked in extreme summer heat throughout much of the West. Despite the persistent ignorance among railroad officials that Mexican men were by nature accustomed to working in "hot
weather," many of the braceros originated from the more temperate central
highlands of México.[25] Braceros pained under the 100 or more degree temperatures, not just in the Southwest but in eastern Oregon and Washington
and much of Idaho. The strenuous and demanding nature of track labor
meant that the men were exposed to the open sun. Supervisors cautioned
against the workers seeking the shade of railroad cars for fear of the braceros being accidently crushed. Instead, they dispensed salt tablets and
tried to provide water to combat heat prostration, a condition not uncommon during summer months. The combination of being malnourished and
dehydrated accounted for some deaths from "heat prostration" and "sunstroke."[26] In recognition of the seriousness of working in extremely high
temperatures, the Southern Pacific distributed a bilingual Spanish and English pamphlet outlining symptoms, prevention, and treatment of "heat sickness."

Track work required workers to become familiar with the demands of
the job but also to be conscious of safety procedures. The war brought added
pressure to the job as passenger service increased and the railroads had to
move enormous quantities of heavy materials over great distances. Wartime
conditions placed unusual demands on the industry, which filtered down to
the braceros repairing the damaged and worn track. Working on the track

under extreme conditions, often surrounded by moving equipment, put the arriving braceros at greater risk of suffering accidents and resulting fatalities. Braceros assigned to extra gang crews could be sent to different locations and work environments a dozen times or more during the length of their contract. Often, just when the men became accustomed to a particular work site, the company could assign them elsewhere to fill labor shortages or to go where more experienced braceros were needed. Even though most of the men worked for a period of six months and not over an extended period, they were still prone to experiencing physical trauma from repetitive motion. Constant heavy lifting and physical exertion had the potential of causing moderate to severe back and neck injuries.

Exercising caution and wisdom on the job came with experience. Once seasoned, the braceros could more easily evaluate a track's condition with a quick visual inspection and by listening to the sound of traveling trains. With time they learned to avoid the perils of riding on moving equipment, working around double tracks, repairing and switching yards, and performing their jobs on challenging terrain. But they could not be expected to gain this knowledge overnight, even with previous experience in México. The demands of the job, difficult working conditions, and concomitant attitudes were simply too great. In addition, language differences between the braceros and their supervisors tended to exacerbate an already strenuous and hazardous work environment.

Spanish-speaking supervisors and foremen were common in many parts of the Southwest but not always available elsewhere to provide critical instructions to the braceros. In the late summer of 1943, when braceros arrived at the Southern Pacific motive power department in Eugene, Oregon, for example, not one supervisor could speak Spanish. In due course, the company located and designated an English-speaking shop employee who had been to México to interpret and fit the braceros with protective goggles, shoes, and other safety gear.[27] Recognizing the limitations and risks associated with haphazard translations, Northern Pacific, as well as other companies, wisely produced Spanish-language safety pamphlets called "Instrucciones de seguridad para trabajadores Mexicanos" and made them available to the workers. The pamphlets welcomed the men and pointed out that the company had a long history of employing Mexican track workers. It also stressed that track work was not dangerous unless the men themselves made it so. The company urged the men to always follow the instructions of their foremen to avoid being hurt on the job. The printed instructions, however, were impractical unless the Spanish-speaking braceros could communicate with what were generally English-speaking supervisors.[28]

Elsewhere, companies addressed this critical issue by setting up evening English classes where the braceros could study basic railroading words to better understand their work.[29] As a last resort, and not always effective, supervisors invented their own jargon of Spanish words, used hand gestures, or resorted to physically direct the men. It is baffling that the WMC and the railroad companies failed to anticipate the significance of being able to instruct the arriving braceros in basic job and safety procedures in their own language. Men working around moving railroad equipment, heavy and complicated machinery, slippery and uneven surfaces, facing fatigue and strain, were in constant danger. In the case of the non-English-speaking braceros, the risk of accidents multiplied. Not only were they unaccustomed to working around passing trains, flying metal, and inhaling and exposure to toxic fumes and chemicals, but they could not fathom the danger without adequate instruction.

Numerous deaths occurred from a combination of interrelated factors. Southern Pacific reported 105 braceros deaths during the life of the railroad program. The company classified fifty-one of these fatalities as being job related and another twenty-five due to natural causes. Another four men committed suicide, and the remainder died in physical altercations, due to alcoholism, auto accidents, and drowning.[30] In March 1944, Southern Pacific bracero Carmen Ortega stood up from repairing track and was run over by a moving freight car.[31] Months later, a careless driver of a private oil truck struck a crew of thirteen Southern Pacific braceros working at an intersection in Portland, Oregon. Four of the section hands suffered serious fractures as well as head and face lacerations resulting from the accident. One of the four, Ignacio Espinoza, died six days later at Good Samaritan Hospital from leg, ankle, and head injuries. Authorities charged the thirty-five-year-old driver with reckless driving and set bail at $350.[32]

Even as the war's end neared, careless accidents continued and one took the life of Enrique Zapata when he was hit by a passing Southern Pacific train in Woodburn, Oregon.[33] Although the railroad company assumed some responsibility for these fatalities, little investigation followed other than canceling the worker's contract to secure a replacement bracero. In some cases the families of the braceros themselves pressed for a complete explanation of the circumstances surrounding these deaths. The official report tended to attribute the fatalities to worker negligence. Work-related deaths of braceros occurred across the industry and for the life of the program. In Pocatello, Idaho, a passing train hit and killed José Espinoza Gonzales while he was repairing rail. In 1944 another train struck thirty-four-year-old Carlos Mendoza Morales while he was walking along the tracks at Winlock, Washington, depot. According to investigators, the engineer repeatedly tried to warn Morales. Still, the accident occurred just nine hundred feet from the Winlock depot, when the train should have been travelling at a reduced speed.

That same winter, three braceros died in the same vicinity. On September 30 a crew of braceros discovered Medosa Vargas, age twenty-two, lying dead across the tracks just six hundred feet from the same depot. Three braceros were initially arrested for questioning, but they were later released when authorities concluded that a train had struck the worker. Nearby, at Vader, Washington, another group of braceros found Salomón Yllescas Cano lying dead across a track. Because no one came forward as a witness to the accident, officials concluded that a train on the double track had stuck him. For the most part, these types of accidents can be attributed to the failure to fully instruct the braceros of the dangers of working in close proximity to moving and passing high-speed trains. These casualties could have been easily avoided with proper supervision and instruction in safe working practices. While repairing an elevated bridge without the use of safety lines, Lorenzo Guerro Carrillo fell and died from sustained massive injuries. In another case, a foreman motioned Ventura Mireles Serrano away from two trains passing on double tracks in opposite directions. For a moment he moved to a safe distance from one of the trains but then accidently walked into the path of the other train.

Lack of safety awareness and plain carelessness posed other risks to the Mexican workers who were being taken to and from work sites in overloaded and speeding motor cars. Such was the case on November 1, 1943, in Seattle when a motor car carrying braceros and traveling on the Lake Washington Beltline derailed. The injuries from this mishap were serious enough to send Jesús C. Gutiérrez, José Flores, and José López to the hospital. In some cases, injured braceros had to verify the pain or wound in order to be compensated and excused from working. Such was the case of Gildardo Sánchez Vences with extra gang 13 at Tacoma, Washington. Upon returning to México, Vences filed a claim of liability against Northern Pacific for an injury suffered while working. According to the claim, he lost a finger, for which Northern Pacific paid seventy-five dollars. The company disputed any claim of liability for the lost finger and counterclaimed that the finger had merely been injured. They asserted that when Vences lost the finger, it was not the result of his employment with the railroad.[34]

Even when working away from passing trains and assigned to various car shops and yards, braceros were endangered by the utter failure of instruction regarding safe work practices. At the Southern Pacific locomotive shop in Eugene, Oregon, for example, Teodoro Fregoso's supervisor assigned him to guide heavy engine components moving on a track along an elevated catwalk and then release the parts into a deep tank full of powerful toxic cleaning solvent. While performing the task, Fregoso accidently slipped and fell into the chemical tank. Although workers saved him from drowning, Fregoso ingested enough of the cleaning chemical that he succumbed to death six hours later.[35]

* * *

The Mexican workforce clearly suffered from injury and loss of life. But the story does not end here. Railroad work also involved serious health and social issues connected to employment within the railroad industry. Exposure to heavy metals, asbestos, and harmful chemicals routinely occurred. Without knowing it, some of the braceros were exposed to toxic chemicals, which caused neurological damage and other long-term medical conditions. In 1942 the industry treated wooden cross ties and the wooden infrastructure with various combinations of creosote, zinc chloride, chromate zinc chloride, and zinc-met-arsenide.[36]

Especially troubling was the industry's use of tar creosote, for example—a carbon by-product of coal that prevented decay in wooden crossties and warded off wood-boring insects. A thick dark sticky oily substance, tar creosote repels water. For the same reason that it is toxic to insects, tar creosote posed health risks to track workers in constant contact with the material. Repeated exposure to the substance, common in working with or near treated ties or contaminated soil, can cause skin irritations, watery eyes, and respiratory problems. More serious health risks can follow when tar creosote enters the body. Because federal authorities did not regulate the use of tar creosote at the time, the braceros were at risk in several ways. Without adequate washing facilities at the work site, the men unknowingly carried the toxicant on their hands and clothes back to their living quarters. The box cars often lacked a proper place to clean up or to wash work clothes, so the braceros lived amid the chemical. The men were likely to ingest traces of tar creosote when drinking or eating with soiled hands in and around contaminated environments.

Numerous injuries and illnesses presented several problems for the employing railroad companies. Employers understood that if they had five braceros on a crew one day, next week they may only see four workers. Given lax safety procedures, companies ironically took steps to anchor the labor force and keep them on the job. Since they were obligated to provide health care and hospitalization to the braceros, operators such as Southern Pacific (where 78 percent of all track workers were Mexican on D-Day) considered employing Mexican physicians dedicated to care for the Spanish-speaking workers.[37] Physicians were critical to the employers, as they made the clinical determination of when and if an injured man could return to work. If a doctor determined injuries were permanent and disabling, the railroad company had to officially cancel the individual's work contract and make arrangements to return him to México. Only then could the employer request a replacement bracero.

The death of a bracero brought additional concerns, obviously, to the survivors of the deceased worker. During the negotiations of the work contract, both governments and industry officials in México and the United States had to be aware of the dangerous nature of railroad employment. The Office of Defense Transportation reported a 41 percent increase in 1941 in the number of injured railroad workers and 40.5 percent more fatalities than in 1940. According to the report, the increases were attributed to work conditions and the mental strain resulting from long hours spent on the job. The trend continued into 1942 and beyond, when the untrained braceros began to arrive.[38] One of the most serious accidents occurred in Amsterdam, New York, where eight braceros contracted with the New York Central Railroad were struck by a train and killed in June 1945.[39]

It is incomprehensible that officials drafting the work agreement did not address the probability that some braceros would be fatally injured or die for other reasons while in the United States. When the early bracero casualties began to occur, the railroads returned the bodies to México in accordance with the language of the agreement, which guaranteed transportation from the point of recruitment to the United States and back to México. As the number of fatalities mounted, however, returning the dead to their hometowns became too expensive and troublesome. The War Manpower Commission obtained a ruling from the Mexican government that permitted employers to bury the deceased workers in local cemeteries. When a bracero died, the WMC notified the worker's family by way of a very brief explanation of the cause of death. The WMC offered a $150 survivor's benefit on the condition that the deceased would be buried locally at the employer's expense, not to exceed $130 in funeral expenses.

If the worker's family wanted the body to be returned to México, the employer rescinded the survivor's benefit and transported the body to the point where the worker had entered the bracero program. The expense of transporting the deceased from the recruitment center to his hometown fell to the family. This unofficial but industrywide arrangement offered to the workforce by the railroad companies became known as a "goodwill" measure or a "gentlemen's agreement." The War Manpower Commission had totally overlooked death and funeral benefits in the official work contract, thus the "gentlemen's agreement" was at best an informal expression of goodwill coming from the employing companies. This sort of "benevolence" saved the railroad companies the expense of transporting the dead back to México.

When a death occurred, the WMC inventoried and packed the worker's personal effects and shipped him to the Mexican consul in El Paso, Texas, for return to México. Examining the personal effects of the braceros after death reveal much about their lives in the United States as part of the bracero railroad program. For example, Aristeo Ortiz Hernández, who succumbed to a malignant tumor, possessed the following:

| | |
|---|---|
| 1 pair of shoes | 1 pair of overalls |
| 1 pair of under drawers | 1 sock |
| 1 lock and key | 1 wallet with papers |
| 1 pair of overshoes | 2 shirts |
| 1 clothes bag | 1 social security card |
| 1 pencil | opened letters |
| 1 pair of sandals | 1 key on chain |
| 1 shawl | 1 opened letter |
| 1 package of paper and | 1 sealed letter |
| Envelopes | |

Hernández also had $78.72 in cash and a Pacific Fruit Express payroll check in the amount of $18.30.[40] His possessions were hardly enough to build a future on had he returned to México and certainly ran counter to the belief of bracero program architect Manuel Gamio that the braceros would benefit materially from their time in the United States.

Death, understandably, exacted a toll on surviving family members as well as fellow workers, as they had little to say about the disposition of the bracero's body. When braceros had deserted from their place of employment, funeral arrangements became more complicated. In the case of Alfonso Sánchez Carrasco, who was killed by a car in Los Angeles, Southern Pacific disavowed any obligation for the funeral expenses because he had already walked off the job. To the railroad company and the War Manpower Commission, the "gentlemen's agreement" did not apply in specific ways in Carrasco's case. When the accident occurred, Carrasco was no longer considered an employee of Southern Pacific. The "gentlemen's agreement"—simply an expression of goodwill toward the braceros—therefore did not apply since Carrasco was technically no longer a bracero. The bracero work contract did not reference any death and funeral agreement, so the city wanted to cremate the body at public expense. This prompted the Los Angeles Mexican General Consul to intercede and argue for a Catholic burial in accordance with man's faith and church teachings. In instances such as these the Mexican consuls authorized using any wages or money due to the deceased or took up a collection among friends to cover burial and funeral costs.[41]

Examining death records of the braceros brings other situations to light. There were cases where siblings worked at the same work site. Juan Sánchez Muñoz died of heat prostration while working for the Atchison, Topeka and Santa Fe (AT&SF) railroad in 1943; his brother was faced with the hard decision about Muñoz's final resting place. Far from México, and only temporarily employed as a bracero, he consented burial for his brother in Emporia, Kansas.[42] In a separate incident involving another pair of brothers, Carmen Ortega and Jesús Ortega, who had contracted by Southern Pacific to repair track, Carmen died while moving into the path of a passing freight car. Southern Pacific buried Carmen in Saint Joseph's Cemetery in San Pablo, California, at company expense and then tried to notify his mother about the $150 death benefit using an address in Aguascalientes, México. In order to receive the death benefit, the surviving brother, Jesús, disclosed to the company that the family was actually from Jalisco but they had deceived WMC authorities with a false address because the quota for men from Jalisco had filled.[43]

At other times, the War Manpower Commission failed to notify surviving family members in cases of death. For example, Elpidia Macías de Casas learned about the death of her husband, Otilio Casas Gómez, in a railroad accident from a family member of another bracero who worked with him in the Midwest. Despite the accident, Mrs. Casas had not been notified by the Mexican government, the railroad company, or the WMC. Writing to the Mexican consul in Kansas City, she demanded to know the circumstances of her husband's death and how to file liability claims against the AT&SF railroad.[44] In fairness to the WMC, many times the proper address of family members was incorrect or missing from the official files. Despite U.S. health officials in México thoroughly examining each bracero's head, eyes, ears, mouth, teeth, throat, neck and lymphatic system, skin over the entire body, upper and lower extremities, heart, lungs, genitalia, and rectum before their acceptance into the bracero program, deaths also occurred upon their arrival in the United States as a result of "natural causes." The most common reasons included ruptured appendix, "intestinal obstruction," streptococcus pneumonia, leukemia, tuberculosis, and other severe illnesses. These deaths generally happened while the men were hospitalized.

Braceros also experienced high levels of stress and serious mental illness. Reasons for this included psychological strain of working in unfamiliar social spaces, pressure by supervisors to labor tirelessly, and an inability to communicate with their families. Such was the case of Juan Martínez, contracted to the Northern Pacific, who became ill, unable to cope, and incapable of working. After physicians diagnosed him as being "mentally ill" but not violent or aggressive toward anyone, the company returned him to México accompanied by another person.[45] When physicians diagnosed braceros as "insane," "lunatics," or "irrational" and subject to violent spells, officials ordered them to make the trip back to México in straitjackets, confined in the baggage car.[46] The number of men diagnosed as suffering from some level of mental illness is difficult to ascertain, but the records point to persistent psychological stress that resulted in mental strain. Cases of mental illness among the bracero workforce were well known in México. On April 19, 1944, the Matamoros, Tamaulipas, newspaper *El regional* printed this headline: "Numerous Braceros Have Become Insane in the United States."

Psychiatrists described another disabled and emotionally unstable bracero, Daniel Sánchez Luna, as "deranged" and ordered his return to Juarez across the border from El Paso.[47] In yet another case, Northern Pacific physicians diagnosed Marcial Figueroa Bustamante as "deranged, "irrational," and "subject to violent spells," and recommended that he be taken into custody and sent to El Paso.[48] In Washington State, in 1944, Juan Patiño-

Velásquez suffered a serious mental breakdown while employed with Northern Pacific. In December the company contacted federal officials that arrangements were in place for Patiño-Velásquez to be repatriated to México at El Paso on January 11, 1945. In the meantime, the bracero's condition worsened to the point that doctors refused to release him and instead ordered his confinement to the psychopathic ward at the Western Washington State Hospital for the "insane" near Tacoma. Weeks later, the Railroad Retirement Board wired WMC officials in México City that Patiño-Velásquez, described as a "violent case" requiring "straight jacket," would cross into México on February 8. Like many other braceros, Patiño-Velásquez had likely viewed program as an opportunity to get ahead, but for him the experience resulted in a return to México, mentally ill and physically immobilized. Although officials notified the Mexican government of his arrival, it is unlikely that he ever received any professional medical psychiatric care in México.[49]

Psychiatrists evaluated bracero Jorge Romero Candia and determined his mental illness to be so severe that he could not be repatriated to México. Doctors treating the ill braceros determined the men's fates, as illustrated in the case of Antonio Cervantes Gómez, who died at Dunsmuir, California, in August of 1945, after being diagnosed with "acute mania." The accounts of mental illness, some seriously misdiagnosed, are numerous in federal and railroad company archives. Doctors diagnosed worker G. Ávila Vera as suffering from severe alcoholism and dementia. Committed for treatment, Ávila Vera possessed enough sanity to plot a successful escape from confinement and later disappeared by walking away from the hospital.[50] Figueroa Bustamante, a Northern Pacific bracero working in Montana, suffered a mental breakdown and was judged to have become insane. Authorities described him as having gone "wild," refusing to keep his clothes on and threatening to jump out of windows. Unable to cope with his condition, Northern Pacific left Bustamante in the custody of the Yellowstone County sheriff, who booked him into the Billings, Montana, county jail.[51]

When hospitals asked police authorities to intervene in psychiatric cases, the results were tragic. On August 1, 1943, bracero Antonio Gómez, who had been assigned to Southern Pacific in Castella, California, suddenly became ill, unable to work, and was admitted to the hospital in Dunsmuir. When a doctor examined Gómez, his pulse and respiration appeared normal with no signs of any serious medical condition. After taking a mild laxative and sedative, Gómez improved but soon began exhibiting marked signs of nervousness and agitation. Within a short period of time, his mental state deteriorated. Fearing he was dying, Gómez instructed that his wages and personal belongings be sent to his mother in México. Thereafter, the hospital reported that sedatives no longer had any effect on Gómez's nervous state and increasingly violent disposition. Five days after being admitted to the hospital, Gómez was ordered by doctors, in an attempt to cope with his erratic behavior, to be placed in a straitjacket.

Then, in an inexplicable move, the hospital called the Shasta County sheriff to take custody of Gómez. The sheriff arrived, took charge of Gómez, and placed the very mentally ill bracero in the back seat of his police car. According to a doctor's report, Gómez suffered a fatal "convulsion" while in the sheriff's car in the early afternoon of August 5, 1943. The hospital attributed the death to acute mania, exhaustion, and shock. Five days after the bracero's death, the official death report determined that there was "no dereliction on the part of the employer."[52] When notified of her son's death, Josefa C. de Gómez doubted the cause of death and asked the Mexican government to conduct an investigation. She demanded that the foreign minister investigate the cause of the death of her son.[53]

\* \* \*

There is little question that many braceros experienced extremely harsh living and working conditions. These unfortunate circumstances were compounded by the monotony and isolation of railroad work. Years before, seasoned nonbracero railroaders recognized this experience of loneliness as not too different from being in prison.[54] Factoring in cultural and social-psychological distance between the braceros and their communities in México, the occurrence of mental trauma becomes easier to comprehend. This may help to explain why mental disorders tend to appear more regularly in the War Manpower Commission records pertaining to such areas as the Pacific Northwest and less frequently in the Southwest, where established Mexican American communities were commonplace by the 1940s. The Mexican Ministry of Labor later concluded that during the wartime labor program, eighty-nine braceros experienced some type of mental illness. Although the Mexican government was unable to locate the majority of the afflicted men, the government did assess the mental health illnesses of the braceros. A study concluded that the braceros' lack of familiarity, or shock, with the work and cultural environment of the United States contributed to the onset of mental illness.[55]

When the bracero railroad program shut down in 1946, work-related and off-the-job accidents had taken their toll on the Mexican track laborers and their families back home. In the three-year period of the labor program, Southern Pacific, which employed the greatest number of braceros, had paid a total of twenty-three thousand dollars in funeral expenses and "donations" to beneficiaries for an estimated eighty-two men who had lost their lives. Settlement of personal injury and liability claims, which were more common than loss of life, amounted to between $150,000 and $200,000.[56] In contrast, the Northern Pacific Railway, which employed far fewer braceros and reported thirteen work-related deaths, paid out $2,240 in funeral expenses and death benefits.[57] México, however, reportedly accrued a total of 7.5 million pesos ($1.56 million) as a result of death claims and other claims or indemnities received from all U.S. railroad companies employing bracero track workers.[58]

# Chapter 8

# The Deception Further Exposed

O ver the course of the U.S.-Mexican railroad labor program, bracero
workers made it through the daily threats of injuries or death
on a daily basis. They were thrust into an unfamiliar social setting
and a different work culture, under the strict supervision of foremen. Not
all track crew supervisors disregarded the workers' rights as spelled out in
the bracero contract or trampled over their basic human rights. Some crew
foremen were compassionate supervisors. In some cases, they pushed the
railroad companies to provide adequate housing and did their best to see
that the workers had suitable and sufficient food. However, the dereliction
of other foremen, railroad companies, and the compounded failure of both
governments to live up to the spirit and guarantees spelled out in the braceros' contracts put these men in distressing situations.

With regard to the braceros' right to seek relief or redress from abuse,
the binational agreement between México and the United States gave workers the right to join together to elect their own spokesmen to deal with the
employer or with any duly authorized representative of the craft of employees or with other interested parties, concerning matters arising out of the
interpretation or application of their contract. According to the individual
work agreement, the braceros also had the right to join with other Mexican
laborers to negotiate with their employer. The language of the individual
work agreement and the binational covenant empowered the braceros with
the right to negotiate and seek arbitration over any violations of their rights
as contracted workers in the United States.

Moreover, since the Mexican railroaders technically belonged to the
class of track workers represented in the United States by the Brotherhood
of Maintenance of Way Employees (BMWE), they had some additional protection under the collective bargaining agreement negotiated with the rail-

roads and further strengthened by the National Railway Labor Act. It could be said, therefore, that the braceros had protections well beyond those enjoyed by some domestic track workers.[1] Yet, as described in chapter 7, the braceros experienced high levels of exploitation. Despite these seemingly ironclad protections, why did these employment and human rights violations occur? How did the Mexican and U.S. administrative officials react to these mistreatments and, more important, how did the braceros themselves respond? Even though many limitations were placed on these men (being in an alien political and social space), these men began to break down some of the ubiquitous racial assumptions regarding Mexican workers by marshaling their own inherent power to self-advocate.

Between May 1943 (the beginning of the bracero railroad program) and November 1944, the braceros lacked any dedicated Mexican official (outside of a few conscientious consulates who took the responsibility of protecting their citizens seriously) to investigate and resolve grievances or to ensure that employers complied with the provisions of the individual work agreement. The necessity for such a dedicated person to respond to the workers' grievances became evident just three months after the first bracero track worker arrived in the United States. The issue came to light at a August 1943 meeting, during which Rubén Gaxiola, speaking on behalf of the Los Angeles Mexican consulate, addressed representatives of the War Manpower Commission (WMC), the Brotherhood of Maintenance of Way Employees (BMWE), the Railroad Retirement Board (RRB), and the Southern Pacific and Santa Fe railroads. Gaxiola charged that many "railroad foremen used abusive, vulgar, and profane language to the Mexican Nationals." To start with, and hardly an original idea, he recommended that an interpreter should "be assigned to all camps where Mexican nationals are employed." The consul suggested that, whenever feasible, the workers should have access to telephone services as well as free transportation so they could report violations or poor conditions directly to the Mexican consulate.[2]

A representative of the BMWE gave credence to the Mexican consul's concerns. Perhaps being a union representative, he grounded his remarks by stating, "I hear all that no one else hears." He went on to accuse Southern Pacific of being "very backward" in providing facilities for the Mexican workers and requiring the men to put in ten-hour days, seven days a week. The extra gangs, he continued, were too large for one foreman and therefore the braceros were not being properly directed. All told, the workers' inability to understand English coupled with poor and insufficient food, unsanitary

conditions, little or no chance for recreation, and one in every two men ultimately deemed "unfit" for track work painted a pitiable picture of Southern
Pacific's bracero operation. The railroads, the WMC, and the RRB pledged
to take steps to correct these conditions, but México lacked a single official
in the United States assigned expressly to look out for the welfare of these
workers.[3]

Seventeen months passed after the first track workers reached the U.S.
before ten Mexican labor inspectors, assigned to the railroad program, arrived to ensure that the braceros' had adequate working and living conditions. Because the western railway companies employed the bulk of the braceros, four of the inspectors worked out of the WMC offices in San Francisco
with a single official placed in Chicago, Cleveland, Dallas, Denver, Kansas
City (Kansas), and New York City.[4] Such a small number of inspectors could
not possibly attend to all the workers' needs, especially since they were
spread across the country and quite often in very remote rural areas. Much
can be learned about character and effectiveness of these Mexican railroad
labor inspectors from communications between the U.S. Embassy in México
City and WMC officials. In agreeing to allow inspectors to enter the United
States, the U.S. agreed that the Mexican officials would "have free access to
places where Mexican laborers were working and that the Employer [the
U.S government] would ensure subcontractors [the railroads] cooperated
in every way to facilitate performance of their duties.[5] In reality, however,
the Mexican inspectors were hardly free to confer openly with the braceros
about anything. México's minister of labor appointed all the inspectors, but
the position carried no salary. This meant that once in the United States, the
Railroad Retirement Board not only paid all per diem and travel expenses
for the Mexican inspectors but also supervised them while they were stationed at WMC offices.

From the start, the U.S. Embassy and the WMC in México City expressed
considerable reservation about the capacity of the inspectors. The appoint-
ments, according to sources in México City, were made because the inspectors were personal friends of the minister of labor and not because of previous experience with labor issues. One official expressed his skepticism
about their role: "these collaborators would serve no useful purpose in this
country and their work performance has borne this out in the majority of
the cases." WMC officials did not want the inspectors interfering with their
railroad work at all. In fact, México had forced its inspectors on the WMC by
giving it an ultimatum. Either the WMC accepted the Mexican labor inspec-

tors or they risked the recruitment of additional Mexican workers. The U.S. ambassador in México City concurred with the WMC's reservations regarding the inspectors by warning: "I do not think we should expect too much of them and I only hope that they will not be more of a nuisance than of a help."[6]

Although quite dismissive of the capacity of the Mexican inspectors, U.S. officials were cautious about offending México. For this reason these communications did not go through open mail and were considered highly confidential. To avoid any suspicion that the United States would be shepherding the inspectors around, the WMC gave them the freedom to visit the railroad workers but only after receiving permission from the local program officials and the respective Mexican consulate. With these limitations, the WMC in México City reiterated its anxiety about the inspectors and recommended marshaling and escorting the Mexican officials while communicating with their own countrymen. The inspectors, the WMC warned, had to be guided in their visits to the bracero camps or risk exposure "to complaints of braceros in Portland and Sacramento" and "it is possible the inspectors might develop a disproportionate perspective."[7] In the end, the WMC had the authority to restrain or otherwise dismiss identified troublesome labor inspectors back to México.

Even if not under the close supervision of the WMC, it is highly unlikely that the Mexican labor inspectors were going to be effective in intervening on behalf of the braceros. Despite suffering from any humiliation on or off the job, the braceros were bound to progress economically and socially from their time in the United States. This was the point of view of the Mexican government. Architects of the bracero program, many of whom were upper class, held strongly to the supposition that derived from the prevailing class, racial, and ethnic prejudices toward the lower-class braceros. This belief that the bracero program could result in the social transformation of Mexican laborers filtered down from the highest administrative levels to the lowest bureaucrat in México involved with the labor program. Indeed, one of the biggest challenges workers in the U.S. faced was dealing with the attitude of the very representatives sent from México to protect them. But, of course, far greater issues existed beyond the small number of ineffectual officials impeding the ability of the Mexican labor inspectors to assist the braceros.

In 1944 the Mexican labor union, Confederation of Mexican Workers (CTM), sent a representative to the United States to examine the conditions facing railroad workers employed by railroads in the Midwest and the East.

In a highly critical report, the CTM accused the consulates and labor inspectors of dereliction. The labor union asserted that some railroad companies paid Mexican officials to avoid enforcing the workers' contract. According to the CTM, some of the consuls allegedly were reluctant to speak openly and raise objections in front of American officials on matters regarding the braceros. In one example, the CTM relayed that when a group of workers complained about poor food services, a Mexican official answered: "Why do you complain?" In México "you wear huaraches and eat tortillas with chile and in the U.S. you wear arrow shirts and eat ham and eggs?"[8] The complicity of some Mexican government officials is evident in other cases where men were upset over the lack of meat in their meals. Mexican officials urged the braceros to consider the shortage of meat because of the war and to be "tolerant of scarcity." This tacit siding with U.S. authorities prompted the WMC to issue propaganda posters defending the absence of meat dishes in the railroad camp kitchens.[9] In another instance of explicit cooperation between Mexican and U.S. officials, a labor inspector permitted the WMC to "disinfect" braceros in a U.S. railroad yard with DDT. Officials commonly sprayed braceros with DDT or other toxic chemicals, but in this case the WMC extoled and thanked the Mexican inspector for the "magnificent cooperation... given."[10]

According to the Confederation of Mexican Workers, the bracero railroaders faced exceedingly poor conditions to the point that a good number of the workers suffered emotionally, became ill leading to debilitation or grave respiratory sickness. Not only were the workers subjected to racial discrimination, they were also exploited by the railroad companies, oftentimes with the knowledge and cooperation of Mexican diplomats. The scathing report by the CTM investigator openly faulted the consuls for working to prevent demoralized braceros from returning to México before the end of their contractual period. The braceros often returned home suffering from dysentery, tuberculosis, dermatitis, venereal disease, and disabilities due to job-related accidents, lack of medical care, and poor nutrition.[11] The Confederation of Mexican Workers report closed by pointing out that although the braceros did not wear military uniforms, they were in fact Mexican soldiers working on the U.S. domestic front. Therefore, as industrial laborers, they were entitled to the same considerations and protections as other U.S. workers and soldiers. To make its point, CTM called attention to the patriotic speeches in which Mexican officials described the braceros and the "special trains" as elements in the global war for democracy. The CTM had other grounds for their assertions given that Southern Pacific, Union Pacific, and other railroads referred to the bracero workforce as "railroad soldiers."[12] In the end, however, the CTM investigative report did not have a significant effect on Mexican and U.S. labor officials or result in any major changes to the language of the binational agreement or the work contract.

Though it would appear that the Mexican railroaders were practically helpless to improve their working and living conditions in the United States, some men defied the odds by acting on their own behalf. By instructing each other, these men understood that they had the right to contest any violations of the work agreement through mediation. They recognized that they had the authority to present these grievances without fear of retaliation by being arbitrarily relocated, returned to México, or having their contract terminated. It did not take long for the Mexican railroaders to resist and challenge the imposed system of worker control. The inherent unfairness of it all compelled them to act, and in doing so they exposed the fault lines in the transnational labor agreement. As the braceros struggled, they exploded the stereotypic racial assumptions that Mexican contracted laborers bowed to authority and were gullible and compliant.

Some braceros took measure of the harsh reality of their situations as contract workers in the United States. Within days of entering the country, some simply deserted by jumping off the trains before reaching their place of employment. Others became recalcitrant. Just months into the railroad program, for example, a group of insubordinate AT&SF braceros shocked WMC officials by refusing to assemble for a patriotic publicity photograph. According to the workers, they "would have no part of such propaganda."[13] Considering they had not been long in the U.S., the men were already conscious of the empty promises associated with their work contract. This level of rebelliousness did not exactly catch Mexican officials by surprise. An official warned President Manuel Ávila Camacho about overexaggerating the spirit of patriotism because the men would rapidly contrast it with the "sad and dark reality of their poor existence as braceros."[14]

Other braceros did not assert themselves impulsively but instead carefully planned how to mount their subordination. In the fall of 1943, for instance, a crew of fourteen Southern Pacific braceros stationed in Valmont, New Mexico, went on strike three times in two weeks as a way to protest poor food services and treatment. During one of the days when they stopped work, the braceros left six hundred feet of rail "jacked up" and gathered in defiance in a nearby abandoned schoolhouse, where they remained for the day. In the end, and to avoid reassigning the workers to another location where they might organize another strike, the Southern Pacific wisely returned the strikers to México.[15]

North in Oregon, braceros in Section 1 of the Spokane, Portland and Seattle (SPS) Railroad were responsible for repairing the main track lines leading in and out of the Portland yard. Although the men had other objections, their main concern had to do with the food provided by the Addison-Miller Commissary. Day after day, the braceros sat down to eat the same monotonous and unvaried food. Aware of the issue, the company did not instruct the cook to change the menu. On April 26, 1945, Section 1 had enough of the bland lunch. The crew had carefully planned a work stoppage that day precisely at noon. They had orders to change rails leading into the yard. Once the worn rails were removed, the foreman told the braceros to stop for lunch, leaving the track unusable to all train traffic to and from the yard. At lunch the men caught the foreman off guard by refusing to eat unless the cook prepared a different meal. The crew let it be known that they would not finish laying the new rail unless the meal was changed. The workers wanted lunch that included "pork chops, green onions, and fresh sliced tomatoes," items near impossible to obtain in Portland at that time of year. The braceros' work stoppage had effectively paralyzed all switching and movement of yard traffic. After three hours of trying to coax the men to resume repairing the track, the railroad company offered to take the braceros to a local restaurant. Satisfied, the braceros ordered hamburger steak and called off the strike.

In the days following, company officials identified four of the main instigators who allegedly intimidated and cajoled the other members of Section 1 to lay down their tools. Three of the four "troublesome" braceros were subsequently separated from each other and transferred to two different locations. Regarding the fourth strike leader, the rail company canceled the man's contract and ordered him back to México.[16] The railroads did not actually have the authority to summarily cancel a worker's contract or reassign the person without notifying the Mexican consul, labor inspectors, and the Railroad Retirement Board. But employers learned that slowdowns or disruptions could be expeditiously quelled by transferring or terminating a bracero's contract. When an entire crew of SPS braceros assigned to Vancouver, Washington, protested food and living conditions, the company made an example of "one trouble maker" by rescinding his contract and shipping him home immediately.[17]

From the start of the bracero railroad program, some workers were un-willing to do the demanding track work and struck out on their own. Al-fonso Franco Manjarrez arrived in California with Southern Pacific on June 16, 1943. By September 12, he had seen enough, quit working, and asked to be released from the contract. Manjarrez claimed he would no longer work with Southern Pacific or "for any other railroad company in the United States." Mario Sosa-Baca, employed by the Chicago, Burlington and Quincy railroad in Wyoming, minced few words in his request to re-turn home. When asked the reason for terminating his contact, Sosa-Baca simply responded: "I don't like the work and refuse to do it."[18] Unhappy bra-ceros had other options besides striking or quitting work when they made up their mind about the horrendous working and living conditions. Some sought relief by simply deserting from the railroad company. When officials declined Ramón Mendoza Estrada's request to be released from his contract, he deserted from Southern Pacific that very day. The WMC required compa-nies to report any missing men after being absent from work for seven con-secutive days. In Estrada's case, however, weeks passed before the company notified the WMC that "division officials had not seen nor heard" Estrada since he went missing.

In another case, immigration agents arrested Gilberto T. Alfaro at his job with the Atchison, Topeka and Santa Fe Railway for being a deserter. Alfaro had left an agricultural employer and joined an AT&SF track crew. As punish-ment, officials ordered him to jail for thirty-nine days.[19] The braceros could also file a request for a thirty-day leave of absence from their employment in the U.S. as a form of relief from their situation. It did not take long for the railroad companies to realize that the braceros were clever in petitioning for temporary leave. Some workers simply wanted to return to México with no intention of returning. Apprehensive about the issue, an official with South-ern Pacific wrote to the WMC and Mexican consular offices: "While it is not the desire of this company to stop granting leaves of absence for short periods in cases of absolute necessity, such as serious sickness, death or other impor-tant reasons, [I] believe that you will agree with me that all Mexican Nationals requesting such leaves of absence should be questioned very closely as to the seriousness of the occasion requiring their return home." The leave concern arose after a six-week period during which Southern Pacific had granted two hundred men permission to return to México. The company subsequently concluded with little doubt that many of the men seeking leave "did not actu-ally have sufficient reason to return home."[20]

Some men had legitimate personal reasons to request a temporary leave of absence, but others gave questionable reasons raising suspicion. In October 13, 1943, José Carrillo Gutiérrez working in Illinois wrote to the San Francisco WMC. "I can't stand the cold weather," he explained, "and it is no use for me to be spending my time, furthermore I was notified from México that I have to be there for some important business. You know that the government gave us some land and, and I left that piece of land to another person. My wife wrote to me saying that that man is trying to make that land his own maybe will get in trouble. That's why I am asking of you that favor. It is not possible for me to stay any longer."[21] In their response, the WMC directed Gutiérrez to make the request to the local U.S. Employment Service office, where the reasons given to return to México could be verified and justified.

Other braceros had pressing reasons for wanting to return home besides discontent. In late summer of 1945, Ascensión Leal Galván received an urgent letter from his wife, Rosa, back in San Juan Del Río, Querétaro. "Your mother," she wrote, "is critically ill." She went on: "I don't believe the Doctor has much hope for her, so if you would like to see her you had better try to come as soon as possible." A few days later, another letter arrived from the attending physician in México advising Galván to "come if you can" as his mother was near death. With the correspondence as proof of the emergency in México, the WMC instructed the employer Pacific Fruit Express (PFE) to terminate Galván's contract and allow him to return home.[22] At times, entire groups of braceros asked to be relieved from their contracts and depart home. Such was the case in July 1945, near the end of the war, when Enrique Almaraz, Juan Escobedo, León Beltrán, Emilio Félix, and José Olvera working in Wyoming with the Chicago, Burlington and Quincy railroad asked to be terminated. The CB&Q granted their request. Earlier, at the height of the wartime labor shortages, the loss of five men would have moved the railroad to try and persuade them to reconsider, but by July 14 the five men were allowed to leave for the border.

The railroad companies certainly understood the ramifications of canceling a worker's contract. "Dissatisfaction among one or two persons in a gang rapidly spreads to the others. We found at least one instance where the desires of one man to return to México had caused a restlessness among the others. It would have been far better if this man had been promptly shipped out of the country."[23] The number of workers seeking leave or breaking their contract raised concern over the loss of labor, but mitigating circumstances existed. For one, the employer had to provide transportation to the men back to the point of recruitment. The granting of leave did not just deprive the company of the labor, it also set a precedent that once in place would be difficult to roll back. Some of the workers failed to return by the expiration date of the leave, forcing the company to cancel contracts and request replacements. To cut down on the number of requests, Southern Pacific urged foremen, division road masters, the WMC, and Mexican officials to reinforce to the braceros that their services were vital and any inappropriate use of personal leave violated the spirit of the Good Neighbor policy between the United States and México.[24]

Given the history of U.S.-México relations, official rhetoric notwithstanding, patriotism and the Good Neighbor policy meant little to both parties, the braceros and the railroad employers. The majority of braceros were working in the U.S. out of necessity and little else. The moment any bracero protested or filed a complaint, railroad companies across the industry were inclined to label the person as an agitator. Despite being entitled to an investigation and hearing of the specific grievance before the WMC, RRB or local federal labor officials, Mexican labor inspectors, or representatives of the Mexican consul, the braceros had little chance of resolving their concerns. Although the official labor agreement provided protections to workers from having their contracts nullified or from being reassigned and relocated to another location without their express consent and that of the Mexican government, the railroad companies used these means to deal with disgruntled braceros. When railroad companies reassigned workers, they did not just remove the "menace." By dispatching troublesome workers to less desirable locations, reassignment served as an effective warning to other would-be agitators. This method of reprimand worked exceedingly well. As a result, it was not uncommon for some men to rescind their criticisms for fear of being labeled an agitator, fear of being reassigned to another work location, or fear of having their contract canceled and having to return to México.

In some cases the railroad companies had local law enforcement officials at their disposal and relied on them to subdue labor unrest among the braceros. In 1945 thirty-six braceros at the New York Central Railroad Camp 201 in Ypsilanti, Michigan, contacted the Mexican consul, the local U.S. Employment Service office, as well as Ernesto Galarza of the Pan American Union in Washington, D.C., who had visited the camp, to complain of unsanitary conditions, poor food, and bullying from their foreman. In a letter signed by every one of the workers at the camp, the men described their situation as "desperate" and "terrible" as months had gone by without answer or action.

During the interim the camp foremen had on occasion threatened to call the police and warning the braceros that they might be returned to México. Two English-speaking Mexican Americans, one a cook and the other a woman employee of the State Welfare Association, were acting unofficially as the men's representatives at Camp 201. The woman had begun to organize social programs for the braceros during their off-hours. The cook, who interacted on a daily basis with the braceros, began to help them articulate their issues to the railroad company.

The presence of these two advocates at the camp angered railroad officials and exacerbated the rift between the braceros and the foreman. As a precaution, the railroad restricted visits by outsiders and summoned the Ypsilanti police to remove the cook from the camp. In subsequent statements to the Mexican consul, the railroad braceros expressed a sense of dire hopelessness as they no longer had anyone to "interpret their opinions" after the railroad banned the cook from the camp. Although the New York Central Railroad brought their own "Mexican" interpreters to Camp 201, the workers expressed no confidence in them as longtime faithful employees of the company. The interpreters, according to the braceros' testimony, took down the grievances but "sided" with the company. As one bracero put it: "Interpreting our needs and feelings does not interest them." Galarza, who visited Camp 201 as well as other work sites in California, Colorado, Illinois, Michigan, and New Mexico, agreed with the men's characterization of the interpreters. The braceros, he wrote, lack confidence in company interpreters, Mexican labor inspectors, and other railroad and government employees, who, "on the whole, line up against the workers."[25] To resolve the matter, the New York Central Railroad made improvements at the camp and contracted with a different commissary to provide meals to the men. In a final report on the workers' complaints, the WMC noted that the New York Central Railroad had responded to the men's grievances by upgrading living conditions at Camp 201. Interestingly, the report made no reference to the intervention by the local police at the behest of the railroad.[26]

In other instances, railroad companies marshaled the forces of local police authorities along with the Immigration and Naturalization Service to restrain the braceros. Two members of a Southern Pacific section crew at Saline, Utah, had enough of the poor food and living conditions, quit working, and filed a complaint with the WMC. Pending an investigation of the grievance, the local employment service office approved a temporary transfer of the two braceros to the nearby Ogden Union Railway and Depot Company.

When Southern Pacific learned of the transfer, it notified the Immigration and Naturalization Service that the men were in violation of immigration laws. The Mexican consul and the WMC arrived to look into the workers' complaints and found the braceros were in the Weber County jail. Immigration authorities had acted at the behest of Southern Pacific and ordered the men's arrest while they were working for the Ogden Union Railway. The consul, in Salt Lake City, interceded on behalf of the two braceros to force their immediate release from jail. Following their release, the employment service office learned that it had acted improperly: the WMC had the sole authority to reassign contract workers. Thus the two braceros remained under contract to Southern Pacific and were bitter toward the railroad, explicitly stating that "under no circumstances" would they return to work there. In the meantime, they stood idle without income, temporarily lodged at the Denver Hotel in Ogden pending return to México.[27]

When braceros were incapable of working, protests notwithstanding, they could always be returned to México for other reasons. Bracero J. H. Segura, traveling on a motor car on a normal work day, was involved in a severe accident when the car derailed after hitting a bar carelessly left lying across the tracks. The accident threw Segura into the air and he landed on his right hand. He suffered such a severe injury that doctors had to amputate his hand above the wrist. This unfortunate turn of events left him with only the use of his left arm, which prompted officials to cancel Segura's contract and order him back to México.[28] Although the history is unclear, Segura's experience as a bracero effectively ended when he returned to México permanently disabled and with no long-term compensation for his injury.

The leading reasons for missing work or having one's contract voided boiled down to desertions; requests for transfers; asking to return to México; or being involved in organizing strikes. These reasons reveal general worker disillusionment with the inequities of the bracero railroad program. The United States had anticipated some dissatisfaction among the bracero workforce and stipulated in the worker's agreement that braceros would not be released from their obligations within the first ninety days unless for breach of contract. Disappointment with their circumstances were wide-ranging among the railroad braceros. In October 1945, Félix Tapia Montaña, contracted to the Pennsylvania Railroad Company, Camp 20, located in Plainsboro, New Jersey, required emergency surgery for acute appendicitis. After the surgery, Tapia received a bill for $180 along with a request to authorize automatic monthly payroll deductions to clear the hospital charge. He initially refused to authorize the deduction but eventually agreed after being pressured by the hospital. Under the terms of the payroll deduction, the hospital would take $24 monthly from Tapia's paycheck. Considering his normal earnings amounted to $90 per month, minus the standard tax, food, medical, savings, and other miscellaneous deductions, Tapia stood to net very little in wages. And that is precisely what occurred.

In the next pay period, after authorizing the deduction to the hospital, Tapia's paycheck amounted to less than $10. Realizing that it would take more than seven months to clear the medical bill, and all the while he would have little income, Tapia contested the deduction, claiming the hospital had taken advantage of his inability to read English. When hospital and railroad officials did not accept his contention about not understanding the payroll agreement, Tapia refused to work. He went on strike on principle and stayed off work for over two months, until the WMC ordered him repatriated to México. Despite the contract between Tapia and the employer promising medical care, confusion surrounded emergency cases where braceros were treated by private physicians in private hospitals.

In truth, it is farfetched to think that Tapia, like many of his fellow braceros, could comprehend a legal document written in English. A clear violation was committed when officials coerced him into signing the document. Mexican bureaucrats, meanwhile, were ineffectual in protecting his interests. Tapia had reason to refuse to work, and the hospital should have made the Pennsylvania Railroad Company responsible for the hospital bill, because the work agreement guaranteed medical coverage for the railroad braceros. By the time Tapia became ill in October, however, Japan had already surrendered, bringing an end to the war. Braceros such as Tapia, once highly sought, were now an unwanted expense. By August 23, 1945, the WMC had officially terminated any further recruitment of braceros in México. Given these changing circumstances, it is reasonable to assume that Plainsboro hospital officials knew that Tapia, like all the other railroad braceros, would soon be returning to México and did not want to be left with unpaid medical charges. The WMC elected not to intervene on Tapia's behalf by pressuring the railroad to cover the medical expenses. Instead, the commission ordered Tapia back to México after he had stopped working in protest.[29]

At a meeting between Southern Pacific, the Railroad Retirement Board, the U.S. Employment Service, and the Mexican consul in San Francisco, the consul stated that foremen discriminated against braceros if they filed an official complaint against an employer. The consul went on to outline a case involving Ángel Herrera Monterubio working with Southern Pacific. Monterubio had filed a lawsuit for fifty thousand dollars for a job-related surgical procedure that required four months of hospitalization and left him impaired for the rest of his life. During the investigation of his claim, Monterubio learned he had signed a receipt for two hundred dollars that came from Southern Pacific as a gift. His signature on the "receipt" unknowingly released the railroad from any further responsibility or claim related to the injury and subsequent surgery.[30] The railroad industry objected to the "forcible interjection of consuls into the settlement of accident cases." The main objection concerned lawyers retained on a percentage basis by the consul, which the railroads characterized as "ambulance chasing." The industry's unspoken apprehension was that an organization or individual outside of the RRB and the WMC would begin to intrude in workers' claims for damages. The railroad companies feared "that if they agree that Mexican cases must have the intervention of the consul, domestic workers will cook up something that all domestic cases must have the intervention of a union or some other powerful organization."[31]

* * *

The Mexican braceros experienced the powerful effect of the intersection of race and status at the hands of their job supervisors. The braceros did not necessarily ignite racism in the railroad industry by their presence. Well before the braceros entered the country, the League of United Latin American Citizens (LULAC) advised the Mexican and the U.S. governments that the importation of Mexican workers would result in heightened "racial hatred, intolerance, segregation and discriminations."[32] Indeed, LULAC's warning simply affirmed what the State Department and WMC officials already knew about deeply rooted racism about Mexicans and nonwhites in general many sectors of the United States. Exclusionary racial segregation in Portland, Oregon, and Vancouver, Washington, prompted one African American man to write to the U.S. Secretary of Labor. Both of these areas had benefited greatly from war-related expansion. The letter pointed out that eligible African Americans found it impossible to obtain employment in the area's shipbuilding industries. When Black workers are hired, he continued, employers enjoy an "unrestricted freedom" to fire them. He asked: "Has it become a practice of the USES to deny Negroes employment in the shipyards? Is slavery returning to the United States of America?"[33]

Top to bottom, the WMC understood that racial discrimination was pervasive throughout many sectors of employment. Instead of taking steps to address the issue, however, the U.S. Employment Service encouraged the practice by suggesting to the secretary of labor that Mexicans be kept separate from African Americans. Local officials went further by recommending complete separation of Jamaican and Mexican bracero farmworkers. In their estimation, segregation seemed to be the most desirable arrangement to avoid disagreement between the working groups. These same officials were particularly apprehensive about the braceros' culture, which they considered "intolerant and very excitable."[34] Perhaps this degrading assumption encouraged WMC officials to instruct supervisors not to make any remarks or insinuate that Mexican braceros were not of "white origin."[35]

As the recruitment of braceros moved away from México City to San Luis Potosí and other parts of the Mexican Republic, WMC officials, already keenly cognizant of imaginary racial differences, observed changes in the pool of potential workers. They took note that outside of México City, "indigenous mestizos" considered "unsatisfactory" were more inclusive among the assembly of workers. The obsession with the racial typology of the braceros continued among WMC personnel in the United States. At Lake Pinot near Watsonville, California, the War Manpower Commission, despite its intention to racially segregate contract workers, placed Jamaican and Mexican braceros in close proximity. To their surprise, the WMC concluded that when compared with other Mexicans, ethnic indigenous braceros, previously thought to be "unsatisfactory" were better suited for assignment to racially diverse groups. They surmised that Oaxacan workers, in particular, were more apt to exhibit greater "tolerance and patience with the Jamaicans thus averting friction."[36]

In light of this preoccupation with setting racial boundaries and studying ethnic differences, in 1942 the Fair Employment Practices Committee (FEPC) suggested holding public hearings to address discrimination against Mexican and Mexican Americans in Phoenix, Arizona, and El Paso, Texas. The proposal immediately caught the attention of State Department officials, who objected to the meetings on the grounds that raising the issue of racial discrimination would only impair relations with México and seriously jeopardize the bracero agreement. In a "strictly confidential" communication, one State Department official, stationed in Ciudad Juárez, México, took issue with the FEPC. In his opinion these hearings were not necessary and would only add to the detriment of the Good Neighbor policy. In defense of his position, the official revealed his own ignorance and ethnocentric view of Mexican people: "I know of no disturbing case of [racism] serious enough to warrant the outlay of government expenditures or which is endangering the happy and contented life everyone on the American border who has a desire to work is enjoying. The Mexicans are paid, in fact, very much so, in proportion to the wages received just across the border in Mexico."[37]

The U.S. ambassador in México City held similar condescending views and reproached the FEPC for wanting to "kick a sleeping dog" if it went ahead with the hearings. The ambassador believed

> that fundamentally the attitude of our Mexican government remains the same and the less said about discrimination except in the most constructive way, the better for the relations of the two countries. I feel it necessary to inject a realistic note into this discussion by stating frankly and bluntly that the holding of hearings by the Committee on Fair Employment Practices with respect to Mexican workers in the Southwest may merely lead to the raising of all sorts of questions, the repercussions of which will be such in Mexico that the Mexican government will not be able ... to send workers to the United States.[38]

As a result of the State Department's intervention, the FEPC backed away and canceled the hearings. The cancelation failed to address discriminatory employment practices against workers of Mexican descent; but perhaps no one else experienced the immediate outcome the FEPC's judgment worse than the braceros.[39] Later, Eleanor Roosevelt reflected on the discrimination of the braceros: "I was ashamed to read some of the things which México felt it had to write in our labor contracts in order to protect those of its citizens who came to work on our farms and ranches."[40]

Despite the action of the FEPC and President Roosevelt's proclamation of a Good Neighbor policy between the two nations, most Mexicans were well aware of virulent animosity toward Mexican-descent residents in the United States. Some Mexicans had experienced racism firsthand as victims of the U.S. deportation drives in the 1930s, and many others living in México learned of discrimination from relatives living north of the border. The Mexican government understood the level of prejudice toward its former compatriots and therefore attempted to safeguard the braceros from social and economic discrimination. The Mexican press periodically reminded the government and the public that racism toward Mexican laborers remained unabated and prevalent in the United States. *El nacional* and other newspapers carried stories describing ubiquitous racial discrimination toward Mexicans. In September 1945 the paper *Novedades* carried a story describing how workers returning from Detroit had experienced discriminatory racial practices and wage discrimination. According to the paper, braceros earned thirteen dollars per week, while U.S. citizens received two hundred dollars for comparable work. Regardless if such a large disparity in wages existed between the braceros and domestic railroad workers, the newspapers kept the Mexican public keenly aware of racial animosity toward the bracero workforce.[41]

On October 30, 1945, the newspaper *Excelsior* carried a story describing how authorities had jailed eighty Chicago, Milwaukee and St. Paul Railroad braceros for protesting undetermined deductions, including deductions taken during days when the braceros were unable to work because of inclement weather.[42] These articles kept Mexicans informed about the incessant specter of racial animosity toward Mexicans in the United States. Hence, when forty-two American students from Texas registered for classes at the University of Puebla in June 1945, the university student body called a strike in protest. The students demanded the university cancel the registration of the visiting students in an effort to call attention to widespread racial discrimination against Mexicans in Texas.[43]

As the war dragged on and the euphoria of a common goal to win the war wore off, discriminatory treatment of the Mexican workers hardened. The blatant racist mistreatment of the braceros was so commonplace that the State Department became concerned with damage to the labor program. According to the State Department, white citizens of Sweetwater and San Angelo, Texas, were particularly opposed to permitting Mexican railroaders to enter barbershops, theaters, restaurants, and other businesses.[44] Yet, unlike the case of Jamaican workers (who because of systemic racism against them were not contracted to employers south of the Mason-Dixon Line), federal government officials did little to protect the braceros from commonplace racism throughout the Southwest.[45] This racism did not confine itself to Texas. By 1944 the Mexican government heightened its protest of discrimination against braceros throughout the larger U.S. West. México noted how residents of Grand Junction, Colorado, acted in a vexatious manner toward the contracted workers. Whites similarly refused to allow braceros to enter public spaces in Wheatland, Wyoming. In Torrington, Wyoming, theaters set aside "special seats" for braceros. In Syracuse, Kansas, where theaters were segregated, locals stoned Mexican workers as they left the movie theater. In a separate reinterpretation of the binational bracero agreement, the War Food Administration (WFA) claimed it was not under any legal obligation to act against societal racial discrimination: the contract only addressed racial and social discrimination in *employment*.[46]

The racialization of the bracero farmworkers extended to the Mexican trackmen. Like African Americans, braceros were shunned and not welcomed in many public places. In 1945 the Mexican government observed that railroad company hospitals segregated ill braceros alongside African American patients, separate from whites.[47] During a cold day in December 1945, a group of Atchison, Topeka and Santa Fe Railway braceros working at Quenemo in eastern Kansas decided to seek temporary shelter in a nearby train depot from the bitter winter cold and snow. When the ticket agent noticed the Mexican men inside the AT&SF building, he ordered them to "get out" immediately, back into the cold, using vile language.[48]

The braceros encountered disparaging mistreatment in many places. In June 1943, Southern Pacific braceros assigned to the San Joaquin Division in Delano, California, called on Eugenio Aza, the Mexican consul in Fresno, regarding their inability to tolerate their crew foreman. According to the workers, the foreman consistently swore at the men and in frustration threatened to "strike" them. The crew described the supervisor as a slightly built man of Greek descent with a rather nervous disposition and very "exacting in his requirements." Added to his bothersome edgy and tense personality, the crew had difficulty following instructions. When the consul called for an inquiry, he learned that the foreman claimed to be able to speak "Mexican fluently." The braceros disputed the fact. They simply could not follow directions because the foreman could not actually speak Spanish. As the consul pointed out in his report, the problem with the Southern Pacific crew in Delano developed from the language divide between the braceros and the foreman. "Naturally," he noted, "nobody will expect the workers to learn in a few days a foreign language." The foreman's threats to resort to violence had also precipitated the complaint. When questioned, the foreman vehemently denied being abusive or ever striking any of the crew members. He did concede, however, that at times his manner of supervision and instructing the braceros "might have been somewhat sharp." Under further questioning by the

WMC and the consul, the foreman finally laid bare his insensitivity toward the Mexican culture. The overall problem, he surmised, had little to do with language or his personality. Instead, it merely stemmed from his refusal to allow the braceros to take their "siestas during their working hours."[49]

Added to the foreman's offensive mannerisms, the crew had other pressing issues. They did not comprehend the numerous deductions taken from their payroll checks. Upon inquiry there were numerous and varying deductions, including a 10 percent deduction to the personal savings accounts in México, a 5 percent victory tax, a 3.2 percent RRB tax, a charge of $1.03 per day from the commissary, as well as medical hospitalization and emergencies charges. The medical deduction varied among the men and had nothing to do with the actual use of medical services but were instead pegged to their earnings. If a bracero earned a check for less than one hundred dollars, the deduction amounted to one dollar. Workers with earnings ranging between one hundred and six hundred dollars could expect to see $1.75 for medical deductions.[50] The issue grew from there. The crew claimed it preferred to purchase food and work clothing on the open market, but the foreman pressured them to purchase at higher prices through the Threlkeld Commissary Company. Whether the braceros agreed or not, the commissary made regular shipments of individual food boxes to each worker at a cost of fifteen dollars per delivery. Again, the foreman deflected the allegations by maintaining he had only the workers' best interests in mind.[51]

Inconsiderate foremen were in many bracero railroad camps. Railroaders assigned to the Northern Pacific Camp 8 at Kennewick, Washington, complained to Mexican officials about the terrible treatment they received from their supervisor.[52] Not too far away, another group of Northern Pacific braceros in Spokane requested help in coping with abusive treatment from Mario Ragucini, a former Italian naval captain and prisoner of war, who was assigned to oversee the Mexican laborers.[53] In another case, bracero Braulio A. Gómez requested in July 1945 to be returned to México from Laramie, Wyoming. He could no longer endure the repeated invective, racial insults, and dismissive responses to his requests to see a doctor at the hands of a Pacific Fruit Express (PFE) assistant foreman and crew interpreter. In his complaint, Gómez wrote feeling "more like a slave than a worker." According to him, his relationship with the crew foreman, Henry West, had gradually deteriorated over the summer. Assigned to a loading crew at a PFE ice plant in Laramie, the situation reached a crisis point when Gómez and four others had completed loading a refrigerated car with ice. As they stood waiting to see what would be required of them next, West insulted the braceros by calling them "mules," asking in Spanish, "What are you doing loafing?" Gómez returned the insult by shouting that West was "more of a mule."

This provoked a long string of profane shouting between the two men that did not end until West invoked Gómez's "mother." Gómez stood up to the foreman and refused to take any further orders. He refused to continue working at all and thereafter filed a complaint against the foreman. In the investigation that followed, Gómez arranged for his own interpreter but arrived fifteen minutes late to the inquiry. Unwilling to wait, PFE and WMC officials conducted the hearing without him. Unable to present his testimony, Gómez found that the WMC had sided with the foreman. "I do not mistreat any of the Mexican workers and show them the same consideration I show Americans," West had testified. Another PFE employee present at the hearing leveled a more serious charge against Gómez by painting him as a saboteur: "This man has been a nuisance and an agitator ever since he came, and I believe he has a touch of sabotage in his blood." Another PFE employee substantiated the allegation by describing how he had caught Gómez repeatedly shutting down the ice line to disrupt icing the railroad cars. In the end, because of the critical wartime rail effort, the WMC agreed to send Gómez back to México but set aside the more serious charge of vandalism.[54]

Representatives of the Mexican railroad labor program intermittently expressed sincere compassion for the plight of the braceros. Acting on their behalf, an escort traveling with a group of workers called for an investigation. According to his report, the train had two diner cars with a capacity for thirty-six persons. The braceros were not permitted to take their meals at the dining car tables. At breakfast they had to file into the dining car, grab a paper plate with a "few scrambled eggs, and quite often only one link of sausage, a few pieces of potatoes and two slices of bread," then return to their passenger cars to eat. The kitchen provided a small wooden spoon and a paper cup filled to about three-quarters' capacity with coffee. By the time the men worked their way back to their seats, the coffee had "sloshed" out, and some of the braceros had lost the majority of food from their plates. For this the workers paid one dollar, the cost of a "regular military meal." The escort made note that the usual fruit juice, cereal, salt, pepper, cream, sugar, and other commodities as well as water were missing from the braceros' meals.[55]

Other fissures in the bracero railroad agreement surfaced. The Mexican and U.S. architects of the bracero railroad program had failed to reflect on the lives of the braceros in other ways than as laborers. Faced with the understandable reality of workers dying, the WMC and individual employers addressed the death of a worker if for no other reason than the loss of labor and investment in the deceased. Braceros who survived harsh conditions and escaped death or injury experienced other traumatic psychiatric disorders. At the outset of the bracero program, the Congress of Industrial Organizations (CIO) blamed the WMC for being blind to the social and psychological needs of the braceros. The union pointed out that "humane consideration of these workers was not in evidence. Many of these workers had families and could not and did not contemplate the extreme distances of separation the work required when they originally applied for employment."[56] Section 8 of the individual work agreement required that the U.S. government "shall arrange for the transportation of the worker and his family named in this agreement." In its self-serving reading, however, the WMC interpreted this requirement to mean that because no members of the family were named in the agreement, "workers are not, therefore, entitled to have members of their families brought into this country at the expense of the railroad."[57] In effect, while the braceros were in the United States, the worker's family members and vital social support networks remained in México.

The braceros, many of them young men, lived more isolated than their counterparts that had been contracted in the U.S. agriculture industry. Outside of the minority of men assigned to roundhouses, car shops, stores, and section crews, most of the braceros worked in remote areas. Telephone service in México was limited at the time, and the workers in the United States lacked telephone access in any case. While postal service or news carried by arriving and departing workers could be communication tools with family members back home, mail itself presented problems. With the use of Spanish translators, the postal service routinely intercepted and censored mail between the braceros and persons in México for various reasons. The U.S. Naval secret service, working with the embassy in México City, surveyed correspondence to apprehend Mexican communist or fascist sympathizers before they could enter the United States.[58]

The State Department also kept an eye out for suspected unauthorized border-crossers. In México, Japanese Mexicans identified as alleged pro-Nazi sympathizers, were under close scrutiny particularly from Sinaloa to San Luis Potosí.[59] The U.S. consulates created "blacklists" containing the names of Mexicans who were members of the fascist party Partido Nacional Socialista Mexicano and members of the Mexican Communist party. Once in place, the censorship of mail and careful observation of border crossers into the United States continued long after the war and into the Cold War era between the Soviet Union and the U.S. In fact, testifying before the House Committee on Agriculture in 1951, H. L. Mitchell of the National Farm Labor Union proposed screening foreign workers to keep out "communist agents" from entering the United States.[60] This sophisticated level of surveillance, for instance, identified twenty-six-year-old Manuel Maldonado among hundreds of braceros as a member of the Mexican Fascist party from a 1939 photograph. Once identified, the secret service instructed border immigration service inspectors to issue a "stop card" to prevent Maldonado from entering the United States.[61] After the braceros had entered the country, district postal censors intercepted the content of outgoing letters to take note of any complaints and "unusual features" in the correspondence.[62] All of this censorship significantly and unlawfully delayed or prevented mail from reaching the workers, resulting in enormous anxiety in cases where emergencies were occurring in workers' families in México.

Difficulties with keeping in touch with loved ones extended far beyond the issue of postal censorship. The braceros did not always know their physical location other than the camp number. When braceros did know their address, they struggled to correctly affix the return address in English. Men at Arbuckle, California, wrote the name down phonetically as "arbule" and "arbolie." The name Brentwood, the braceros heard as "brenlrvoo." Postal officials remarked that the braceros often just "scribbled something utterly illegible" on an envelope in place of the correct name of the location. Confronted with trying to decipher "gayserville" for Geyserville, "ijeoldebrag" for Healdsburg, "rogz" for Rogers, "whiach" for Ukiah, and "watzorbille" for Watsonville, postal workers simply assumed the braceros were largely "a semi-literate class of people."[63]

# Chapter 9

# Split Families

## Repercussions at Home and Away

A lone and separated from their families and communities, the braceros, many of them young and married, experienced serious psychological and social challenges adjusting to an unfamiliar environment. Some railroad companies historically kept domestic track workers, including Mexican Americans, content and strengthened employee loyalty by providing recreational activities. When the bracero railroad workers arrived in 1943, the Southern Pacific Railroad had for years already been supporting and providing uniforms for local "Mexican" American baseball teams as well as attire and instruments for musical bands. These activities not only boosted worker morale and company loyalty; they provided a welcome escape from the drudgery of everyday work. The absence of meaningful leisure-time activities for the bracero track laborers (other than patriotic celebrations organized on Mexican national holidays) stood in marked contrast to the recreational events that had been made available to other domestic Mexican Americans in earlier years.

The Railroad Retirement Board recognized the value of recreational facilities for trackmen but could not always convince railroad companies to extend these activities to braceros. It advised employers to furnish small inexpensive items like playing cards, checkers, radios, baseball equipment, and horse shoes as valuable activities for maintenance-of-way employees.[1] This disregard for the free time needs of the railroad braceros and the absence of their social and psychological networks precipitated other problems. In some cases, being young adults, the men gravitated toward the worst parts of towns, where they frequented bars and brothels. Taking advantage of a well-intended train pass to Eugene, Oregon, to wire money to his family back home, one bracero took an ill-advised turn into a house of prostitution. Upon return to the camp, he realized he had contracted a sexually transmitted disease. Since his foreman did not speak Spanish, the man did not receive medical attention until eight days later. At that point a doctor informed him that the treatment would take ten to twenty days. In the meantime, his fellow workers and foreman made life impossible as they harassed the infected man, wanting nothing to do with him. The man had to pay the cost of the medical services, working to pay for the medical treatment, medicines, and food. The treatment escalated until the regretful man could no longer cope with the stigma of being ostracized. He finally wrote to the War Manpower Commission seeking an expedited pass back to México.[2]

Another bracero, married and with a child in México, contracted a venereal disease in Sacramento, California, while traveling to his work assignment in Corvallis, Oregon. When Southern Pacific medical doctors examined him, they determined he had contracted syphilis and nothing could be done for him. The railroad company canceled his contract and returned him to México.[3] In other cases where a bracero contracted syphilis, physicians prescribed treatment allowing the individual to continue working. Doctors monitored their "patients" closely to check if a bracero receiving treatment "will become active [infectious] and dangerous to the public and the men in his crew."[4] In many places prostitutes aggressively worked to draw the braceros' attention. Out of shame, language barriers, and limited access to medical services, infected men often did not quickly treat sexually transmitted diseases, but waited until the infection incapacitated them. In one instance a Southern Pacific crew in southern Oregon returned from Salinas, California, claiming to have contracted venereal disease while using a privy. A medical inspector later determined the men had contracted the disease after frequenting a local brothel. The frequency of such cases contributed to the prevailing American view of the braceros as hypersexual Mexican men. This stereotypical cultural view had already been expressed by Manuel Gamio, one of the architects of the bracero railroad program, when he described immigrants in the United States as having "experienced many difficulties owing to their Latin temperament, drinking and their fondness for undesirable women."[5]

One thing is certain, however: braceros often sought out female companionship but not always with "undesirable women." In Sacramento, for example, a large group of Southern Pacific women from the company's upholstery department organized a party to celebrate the wedding of a female Mexican American coworker to a Mexican man from the machine shop. The *Southern Pacific Bulletin* carried an interesting and telling photograph of the wedding celebration at the company upholstery shop. The lone groom dressed in work overalls stands next to his bride. The couple is surrounded by an all-female wedding party. In the background are piles of fabric-like materials. The accompanying celebrants are all dressed in their work clothes, bib overalls and head scarfs, standing next to a table used to cut patterns, with plates and what appear to be home-baked cakes. The photograph reflects a joyful day in an otherwise routine wartime workday.[6]

Another young bracero working for the Pacific Fruit Express (PFE) in Laramie, Wyoming, became infatuated with an unmarried office worker. He ultimately asked her for a date. After being rejected on several occasions, the young and foolish man had a fellow worker pen a letter to her. It is not certain if the bracero understood the content and implications of the sloppily written letter, but he delivered it while the young woman worked alone in the office. The letter expressed his affection: "Dearest and best of girl I have personally have been thinking of you I have no right to even talk to about this But if you will forgive me and it will be this Will you give me the right to company in a nice bed and I know you will never regret this and will pleas ans me favorably Yours Truly." The young woman reported the incident immediately to the PFE, who called for an investigation for fear the young man "might cause her injury." Such investigations generally included the worker or workers, a railroad company representative, the WMC, and sometime the Railroad Retirement Board and Mexican consul. In the investigative hearing that followed, the bracero admitted he had brought the letter to the office. In light of the worker's testimony, the WMC determined to cancel his contract and return him to México. In many respects, the young and unsuspecting bracero narrowly escaped more serious repercussions. Unknown to him, the other office workers had already determined that the situation had escalated to a point where police might be called to "take action" against the impertinent and persistent young man.[7]

In a state of near social segregation, and faced with the reality of being in an all-male work environment, some braceros crossed local social norms, putting themselves in precarious situations such as approaching white women. But the braceros were not completely alone. Women back home in México stood as some of the strongest advocates for their well-being. Most historians have overlooked the manner in which women in México acted on behalf of their loved ones working temporarily in the United States. Unlike the case of Bahamian and Newfoundlander women and children who were permitted to accompany contracted workers to the U.S., the WMC never considered allowing Mexican spouses or female members to accompany the braceros.[8] Brothers and sons, however, did serve as braceros, and in some instances they were assigned to work together.[9] The role of women in México in support of the braceros and the war deserves to be highlighted.

From the start of the bracero railroad program in México City, the WMC made note of the scores of women eagerly volunteering with the hope of joining the labor force soon leaving for the United States.[10] They were not attempting to take advantage of the opportunity for employment, as that opportunity rested with men, but they stepped forward wanting to do their part in the war effort. This level of gender consciousness prevailed in México stretching back before the Revolution of 1910, the Cristero Wars, and through the Great Depression of the 1930s. During the Depression, women organized the Frente Único Pro Derechos de la Mujer to represent the economic and political concerns of working-, middle-, and upper-class women in México. With the outbreak of World War II, the Frente Único Pro Derechos de la Mujer became the Coordinating Committee of Women in Defense of the Fatherland (Comité Coordinador Femenino para la Defensa de la Patria).[11] The role of women in national defense stretched far beyond this one organization. The Central Committee for the Civil Defense of México City and the Defense League of Women organized women to come to the defense of the city during the war. Nurses volunteered to act as first responders in case of Japanese or German attacks, while other women trained to enforce emergency blackouts, manning search lights in case of aerial attacks. Women, as they did in the United States during the way, prepared to respond to any wartime emergency and do their part in the overall national war effort.[12]

The national campaign to send braceros to the United States had tremendous implications for Mexican women. Theoretically, women were eligible for the bracero program, but the WMC for various reasons considered their presence in the U.S. an insurmountable obstacle. Women could accompany their men north at government expense if their name appeared in the worker's contract, but during the life of the transnational bracero labor program, no women boarded a train carrying braceros to the United States. The fascinating interplay between the women left behind in México and the braceros in the U.S. reveals much about the Mexican spirit of womanhood.

In early 1944, María Asunción Juárez's husband, intending to land a bracero contract, left her and their children behind in Valle de Salamanca, Guanajuato. He met all the qualifications and was assigned by the WMC to work as a railroader in Washington State. In the beginning, all went well for him but in July and nearing the end of the contract period doctors hospitalized him in Vancouver after he suffered a serious foot fracture. Five months later, María Asunción's husband remained in the hospital unable to work. This situation caused great hardship for the Juárez family in Valle de Salamanca. In letters from her husband, María Asunción learned that the foot would not heal until March, eight months after the accident.

As the New Year began in 1945, María Asunción took action by writing to Mexican president Manuel Ávila Camacho. Her letter described her husband's situation, but it also stressed her own misfortune, grief, and suffering. She made a simple request to the president: she begged for his empathy and to arrange for her to travel to Ciudad Juárez. Once there, she planned to cross into Texas and contact the Mexican consul. In closing, she asserts her claim: "I believe I have the right to reach my husband wherever he is." With the assistance of the consul, María Asunción intended to proceed north to Vancouver to reach her husband. The historical record establishes that the president received the letter, but any response to the request is unknown. The president's response notwithstanding, María Asunción's letter demonstrated that women, although left at home, considered themselves very much an integral part of the international labor program.[13]

María Asunción joined many other women seeking information about their husbands, sons, and brothers. Most of the letters from individuals in México to the U.S. railroad companies typically came from women and relatives inquiring about the whereabouts of a particular bracero after losing contact, doing everything possible to trace the location and learn about the well-being of their loved ones. Consuelo Méndez de Ávila had not heard from her husband Jesús Enrique Ávila for some time, but she knew the WMC had assigned him to the Northern Pacific Railway. She wrote to the company in Saint Paul, Minnesota, and located him in 1944 after months of trying. Justina Bárcenas de Pérez wrote to Northern Pacific from San Luis Potosí on October 1944, seeking information regarding her husband, Margarito Pérez.[14] Often letters from the family described the poignant anguish felt by the women. Esperanza Fernández Bautista expressed her emotional state in a letter addressed, "To Whom It May Concern." The last communication from her husband, Fausto Fernández Ramírez, had come from Tacoma, Washington, but she had not heard from him in some time. Esperanza's inquiry was simple and direct: "Is he sick or been in an accident."[15] For similar reasons, Esperanza Hernández de Alfaro, living in Zamora, Michoacán, wrote and finally located her husband Francisco Alfaro Ramírez, an SPS employee working in Portland, Oregon.[16]

The women lost track of their husbands for several reasons. As the WMC explained when a company contracted a bracero, the railroad worker could be placed and reassigned anywhere along the vast network of track lines. That meant that a bracero with Northern Pacific, for instance, could be working at any time anywhere from Minnesota to Washington State. Also, men in rural areas and away from lines of communication—even when they knew how to write—had little access to postal or other common communication services. Sometimes a man enlisted for the initial six-month period, then opted to renew for a second or third contract without returning home. For the most part the braceros managed to stay in touch and connected to their waiting, dependent families. Yet there were the others who chose to ignore the pleas from their spouses in México. Northern Pacific reported one case in particular, where a woman tracked her husband to the company. When company officials instructed the individual to contact his wife, the man rebuffed the well-meant intentions. He told the company to mind their "own business and that he would write to his wife whenever he felt like it and did not need anyone to inform him when he should do it."[17] Such instances were not uncommon, and one can only imagine how it increased the anguish of the women left at home.

Ignacio García Téllez, who served as minister of labor and who helped to frame the bracero program, concluded years later that there were some cases in which braceros chose not to return to their hometowns and simply abandoned their families.[18] More often than not, the braceros remained faithful and committed to their wives and families. One can argue that familial commitment may have grown during the six months or more that the workers were away from their families. The following examples illustrate the continuity of spousal affection and devotion between a railroad worker, his wife, and the family. In one case, José Ledesma Hernández, contracted to the Western Pacific in Elko, Nevada, received news from his eighteen-year-old married daughter Carmen about the death of his wife. Ledesma had four other children, ranging from one-and-a-half to fourteen years of age. The unedited letter read:

Mi muy estimado papa pues le mando estas cortes ringlones para saludarte
ye después de saludarlo no le puedo suplicar el pesar que llo tengo porque
mi mama lla fallesio ye agame el favor de que sebenga lomas pornto que
se pueda paque vega a recoger su familia porque mi mama tacha llano
contamos con ella no a podido ser buena desde que usted sefue a sido uan
gran atribiulacion papa begase lo mas pronto que sepueda aber quien quita
ila alcansara pero ella esta mui grabe.

Translated by the WMC, the letter read:

I send you this few lines to greet you and after that I cannot explain the
sorrow I have for my mother passed away and please come back as soon as
you can so you can come and take care of your family because my mother
Anastasia, we can't count on my mother. She has been sick ever since you
left. Please come back and you may get here because she is very grave and it
is a great sorrow for every one of us, especially the little ones so come back
to take care of them. I cannot do it myself as I have my own obligations. You
can take care of the little ones.[19]

In 1945, Hipólito Robles Mendoza contracted to work with the Atchison,
Topeka and Santa Fe (AT&SF) railroad. While traveling from New Mexico to
Colorado to a new work site, the railroad reported that Mendoza had been
involved in a serious accident. As AT&SF reported the mishap, Mendoza allegedly got drunk in a local saloon during a train stop in La Junta, Colorado. Later on, an army truck driver struck Mendoza as he ran carelessly
into the street attempting to retrieve a hat. As a consequence of being hit
by the truck, Mendoza suffered a severe skull fracture and bone breaks at
both ankles. While confined to a nearby AT&SF hospital, doctors diagnosed
and treated Mendoza as being "disoriented" and "disturbed mentally." During his hospital stay, a fellow bracero preparing to return to México visited
Mendoza.

Perhaps assuming that that there was little hope for recovery, the ac-
quaintance took possession of all of Mendoza's personal documents, including his work contract, identification card, ration book, and social security
account number. When this bracero arrived in México, he visited Mendoza's wife and turned over all of the documents. Three months after the accident, Mendoza remained hospitalized, however; he was still considered
disoriented. With little hope of retuning to México soon, he wrote to his wife,

Carmen Cervantes de Robles. The letter, on official AT&SF stationery, begged her to pray for his return, adding she should "not believe them, I still live. I am still alive." Reassured but alarmed by the tone of the letter, Mrs. Robles contacted México's minister of labor to inquire about her husband's mental health, details about the accident, and any possibility of repatriation. Four months after the accident, Mendoza's documents were on their way back to the United States, permitting the WMC and AT&SF doctors to make arrangements for his return to México.[20]

Women acted with resiliency in other ways. When Josefa C. de Gómez learned of the death and burial of her son in California, she acted forcefully. Not satisfied with the local coroner's, the WMC's, and the Mexican government's explanations of the cause of death, she demanded a full investigation. Mourning but determined to learn more, she rejected the $150 entitlement and proceeded to press for the return of her son's body to México at her own expense.[21] In a separate case in Albert Lea, Minnesota, a bus struck a truck carrying braceros, killing one of the men. Although the WMC attempted to mitigate responsibility, both the bus company and the employer rejected any liability in the mishap. The Mexican consul contacted the deceased man's spouse and arranged for his burial in Albert Lea. When the man's wife learned of her husband's death, she traveled to Minnesota and consulted with local attorneys. In the end the lawyers persuaded the WMC to disinter the body and return it to México at U.S. government expense. Speaking on behalf of their client, the lawyers took the position that the government had "induced" the man to come to the United States and "common courtesy" called for burial in México.[22]

*  *  *

World War II affected everyone in México as it did in the United States. Early in the bracero railroad program, México acknowledged that families in small rural and larger urban communities were being profoundly affected by the departure of the workers. Aware of the social distress, the Mexican government mobilized the Investigative Office of the Situation of Women and Minor Workers to intercede with the WMC on behalf of women and other dependents of the braceros.[23]

The war's effect went far beyond the psychosocial distress experienced by some women and families; it brought economic and political issues affecting women to the forefront of public discourse. A shortage of workers in some sectors of the Mexican economy led the Coordinating Committee of Women in Defense of the Fatherland to create a dramatic poster of an indigenous-looking woman holding the Mexican tricolor flag, cradling a child. The appeal to women exhorted them to join the war effort. Bold poster headlines carried the appeal: "Mexican Women, the Nation Calls You." The poster read: "Serve the nation working in industry, agriculture, home, wherever duty calls you."[24] Some women aware of potential labor shortages wrote to President Camacho suggesting that women of ill repute be obligated to replace the braceros who had left for U.S. farms.[25]

Although México instituted anti-inflationary economic measures similar to those already in place in the United States, the war destabilized an already disparate economy largely because of the monopoly of goods, hoarding, and the enormous exchange of raw materials for U.S. dollars. The resulting increase in the price of ordinary food commodities and other household necessities made life more difficult for the women left behind. Collaborating with labor unions and federal organizations, women began to report and organize protests against businesses suspected of hoarding or selling food at inflated prices. They had reason to protest. One legislator described how the miserable wages earned by the working classes and the "stratospheric" increase in basic food such as beans and corn resulted in widespread hunger. No one consumed meat as it was now a luxury. Instead, the legislator stated, "the families, and the women themselves, [eat] soup consisting mostly of water, beans, and one tortilla per person."[26]

On the morning of May 13, 1943, government officials were surprised when a group mostly of women protesting against the lack of corn (*masa*) to prepare tortillas forced open a corn mill in the Buenos Aires section of México City. This was one of many similar demonstrations throughout the nation against the food scarcity. At times carrying infant children in their arms, the women confronted government officials shouting, "We are hungry." México's exportation of agricultural products, according to the women, led to their hunger and that of their families. A shortage of corn dough provoked the riot. In other parts of the city, several women's organizations—including the CTM Feminist Sector, the Coalition of Revolutionary Women, and the Feminist Leagues of Tlapa—organized large demonstrations in front of government buildings. In México City alone, 150 out of 400 corn mills (necessary to process the basic element of the Mexican diet) closed for lack of corn to grind into *masa*. Throughout México City groups of women took to the streets in search of corn and other food items. Other rationed items, such as coal, milk, and meat, were difficult to obtain and sold at prices be-

yond the reach of the poor.[27] The press pushed the president to act: "Hear
the people who deserve to be heard. Promises cannot be eaten. Listen, Mr.
President, to the voices of the people who are suffering from hunger."[28] In
Iguala, Guanajuato, women protested the ongoing exportation of livestock;
meat, when available, could not be purchased except at very high prices.[29]

Elsewhere, in Pachuca, Hidalgo, women protested in front of the state
capitol. The protest was dramatic as the women arrived carrying empty bags
and their customary market baskets holding signs reading: "Our children
are hungry. Governor! We ask for your help to sell us corn, being held by
speculators."[30] The secretary of the economy rebutted that not one grain of
rice would be exported if needed by consumers. Unconvinced, the women
alleged that "livestock daily arrived from the interior and immediately left
by train for unknown destinations."[31] Despite government controls, the
wholesale price index had increased over 200 percent between 1939 and
1945. This led to a corresponding rise in the cost of living at a rate much
higher than the increase in the wholesale price index. Adding to the poor
domestic economy, Mexican export revenues began declining in 1945.[32]

It was not only the urban feminist groups that challenged the lack of
food. Women in rural communities understood the critical relationship between the departing contracted braceros and diminished farm production.
Well into the bracero program, Carmen Gallegos González, living in Tuitan,
Durango, finally wrote to President Camacho in April 1946. She outlined the
disruptive loss of labor and its effect on local corn and bean production,
criticizing the idea that these men were not necessary for local farm production. "There is no greater lie or worse farce, in Durango all you need is the
influence of any official." As a woman, she continued, "I understand little
about what motivates you to allow the departure of braceros to the United
States. Nothing will improve their situation or that of their families. Meanwhile our own farms will be abandoned."[33] These women were right in their
confrontations before civil authorities and private businesses. The war economy allowed some classes to take advantage of business opportunities; however, the bulk of the population consisting of peasants, municipal employees, and small shop owners remained impoverished. Despite government
controls, the wholesale price index had increased over 200 percent between
1939 and 1945.[34]

Years later, Ignacio García Téllez, minister of labor during the war, recognized and lamented the increasing level of class disparities caused by infla-

tion during these years. "Unfortunately, we must admit that despite official measures to curb monopoly and hoarding, war conditions have provided opportunities for easy gain and rapid riches among a reduced minority of grasping manipulators and profiteers—among those who have known how to capitalize upon the current inflation, how to exploit common poverty and helplessness to their own advantage. But the masses of peasants, of city workers, of salaried employees, of small tradesman—the bulk of the population—are suffering acute privation."[35]

Not surprisingly, some Mexicans sought to benefit from the war economy; some saw the flow of workers to the United States as an opportunity to make a handsome profit. In a routine censorship of mail addressed to the U.S., the Department of Justice intercepted a letter and halted a scheme to defraud Mexican laborers. The letter from Veracruz, México, addressed to a man in Los Angeles, outlined a simple business proposition. According to the scheme, laborers in Veracruz were earning fifty centavos (Mexican currency) working from dawn to darkness. Shipbuilding defense plants in Houston, Texas, paid a minimum of four dollars daily. The letter asked the man in Los Angeles to secure a labor contract with the local defense plants and in turn the letter writer would supply the workers from Veracruz by promising take-home pay at four dollars per day. Since defense plants in Los Angeles had higher salaries compared to industries in Houston, the business partnership stood to gain a handsome profit from everything above the four dollar per day salary promised to the recruits.[36]

Mexicans were not the only ones who sought to exploit the war effort. In a confidential note, the U.S. embassy reported that Elmer R. Jones, an employee with Wells Fargo Bank, had inquired about the railroad bracero program. According to the embassy, Jones had much experience and competence in railroads and transportation in México. He had acted as an intermediary facilitating the sale of a thousand obsolete freight cars owned by U.S. railroad companies to México's rail system. He had suggested that U.S. railway executives take over the administration of the Mexican railway system. U.S. Ambassador George S. Messersmith described Jones as an individual merely interested in selling to "make money." Jones, he went on, considered the bracero system as an opening to make "profit direct or indirect in our program." Messersmith continued: "Mr. Jones belongs to a generation which looked upon Mexico as a place for exploitation." Mincing few words about Jones's eagerness to profit, the ambassador added: "He has smelt blood and wants to be in on the killings, and if the Mexican railways need any equipment there is no necessity for any intermediaries, and in fact our effort is to keep intermediaries out of the picture."[37]

*  *  *

Inflation and profiteering brought on by the war cut like a double-edged sword across México, impacting women and the population at large. However, few in México felt the compounded stress and trauma experienced by many of the bracero railroaders. They had pinned their faith and family's hope for a better future by leaving for the United States and in many instances returned broken and with little to show.

# Chapter 10

# Victory and Going Home

The closing of the U.S.-México bracero railroad program in 1945 was as swift as the effort to begin it two years earlier. By early spring of 1945, the success of the military campaigns in Europe and the Pacific raised American hopes that the war would soon be over. Since the railroad bracero program emerged from war-related labor shortages and because the global conflict appeared to be winding down, the War Manpower Commission (WMC) now assessed how to bring closure to the labor contract program. With the efficiency of a well-timed military operation, the railroad program had successfully transferred a large pool of Mexican laborers to the U.S. railroad industry. By the end of April 1945, a total of 142 trains had left recruiting centers in México, carrying 109,461 bracero railroaders for employment in the U.S. industry.[1] Things changed abruptly in early summer, however, as returning soldiers and ebbing labor demands forced officials to begin to seriously consider closing recruitment centers in México and arranging for repatriation of the braceros in the United States.

Nonetheless, through the early summer of 1945, the WMC continued to enlist men in México. Braceros who were already in the U.S. had every reason to expect renewal of their contracts and to remain in the country until 1946. Suddenly, in June the WMC announced that contract renewals were now limited to ninety days instead of six months.[2] Officials were clearly moving closer to shutting down the bracero railroad program. The news of the looming repatriation did not sit well with some railroad employers. The Great Northern Railway opposed the thought of immediate repatriation because "most of the men in our track department are Mexican and unless we get authorization to extend their contracts we will, no doubt, lose most of them between now and the end of the year."[3]

When the day arrived for the official shutdown of the program, some repercussions of the wartime labor program immediately surfaced. Most notably, for years the braceros had endured tough socioeconomic issues as well as lingering personal ones while in the U.S. Still, when the braceros returned to México, they were confronted with a new set of issues related to the railroad program, and they received little support from either government. The unconditional surrender of Germany and Japan led the WMC to close its recruitment centers in México by late August 1945. Also prompting the sudden move was the stipulation in the original agreement between México and the U.S. stating that "no such person [railroad worker] shall be admitted for longer than the duration of the war in which the United States is presently engaged."[4] On September 19 the WMC ceased to operate, and without fanfare all responsibilities for the liquidation of the bracero railroad program moved to the Department of Labor. Just as suddenly as it had developed, the bracero railroad program abruptly ended.

A Mexican labor inspector working with the Department of Labor prepared the braceros for their return to México by telling them that the time to return home had arrived. "You may have to wait to return," he said, but "work up to the last day." Report all unsettled claims to the Mexican consul, he advised them, but under no circumstances should men "attempt to remain illegally."[5] Accordingly, the Great Northern Railway instructed its foremen at the Auburn and Tacoma, Washington, roundhouses that the company was obligated to free the braceros to return to México within fifteen days after the expiration of the worker's contracts.[6] So much had changed during the duration of the railroad program. Unlike the jubilation and the urgency that greeted the start of the bracero program, the announcement of the closure went largely unnoticed except among government employees and the braceros themselves. When the first contract workers arrived, the *Southern Pacific Bulletin* featured a front-cover photograph of a large group of bracero railroaders posing in front of large U.S. and Mexican flags. Asked to smile by the photographer, the men appear jubilant while flashing victory signs with their fingers. The image speaks to the pre-employment excitement and hopefulness of what was to come before the reality of their situation set in. So much had occurred in the three short years of the program that called into question the initial expectations of the WMC and the braceros themselves. By the war's end, the promise of the braceros railroad program had been so sullied that a celebratory image of jubilant braceros returning home after laboring for the war effort is hard to find.

In August 22, 1945, representatives of the WMC, the Brotherhood of Maintenance of Way Employees (BMWE), and the railroad industry met to discuss plans for closing the Mexican labor railroad program. Called together by the WMC, the government laid out its position regarding the future of the bracero track program. "It is the intent, at the end of the war, to immediately discontinue all recruitment, make no more contract renewals, repatriate workers as rapidly as their contracts expire and possibly transfer some Mexican Nationals from one carrier to another so as to utilize to the fullest extent all workers available and at the same time meet the requirements of the individual carriers involved."[7] The recruitment of braceros in México had ended on August 17, 1945. However, the men already on their way to the United States were allowed to continue. The WMC had canceled all bracero train departures from México to the U.S. The men already working in the U.S. and those who wanted to extend their stay were denied when the government stopped all further contract renewals after August 18. The WMC took these steps in response to indications of growing unemployment, predicted at six million and rising to eight million nationwide by year end.

The railroad industry rebutted the War Manpower Commission by arguing that closing the Mexican track labor program would precipitate an industrywide labor crisis. One after the other, the railroad companies responded negatively to the WMC's plans to stop contracting Mexican laborers. The Atchison, Topeka and Santa Fe Railray (AT&SF) stated that of thirteen thousand common laborers, 70 percent were Mexican. Among the fifty-five hundred skilled shop workers, the company employed twenty-two hundred Mexicans. According to the company, it would "be impossible to replace these 11,000 Mexican workers during the five months in which their contracts expire." The AT&SF added that it had routinely hired Mexicans going back as early as 1925 and that they could not be replaced by domestic labor. Moreover, its railroads were in need of repair, and lacking sufficient track workers, passenger and freight trains could not operate at peak efficiency, which would affect service for everyone. To avoid the interruption of service, the AT&SF urged the WMC to allow it to keep braceros working until the following year.[8]

Southern Pacific also responded to the WMC. Its maintenance-of-way department alone employed fourteen thousand Mexicans, and if more were available the company would hire an additional two thousand. If the braceros could no longer renew their contracts, Southern Pacific officials projected an "immediate rush of Mexicans back home in order to secure employment, thereby making the problem all the more serious." The Pacific Fruit Express (PFE) warned that Mexican workers were essential to load ice on their trains in order to avoid any loss of perishable food. A Western Pacific (WP) spokesperson pointed out that it saw no sign of sufficient domestic labor on its tracks. When local labor did take these jobs, the company experienced a 100 percent turnover among domestic workers. Unlike the other companies, 85 percent of the WP tracks were in isolated areas where sufficient domestic workers were nonexistent. If the end to contract renewals went into effect for braceros, the WP estimated it would immediately lose eighteen hundred Mexican workers, leaving approximately two hundred domestic workers in place. The Northern Pacific had thirty-three hundred braceros employed mostly maintaining tracks in remote areas of the Pacific Northwest. If it lost these workers, the company predicted a "heavy financial loss," due to lost operational revenue. In agreement with the other companies, the Chicago, Milwaukee, St. Paul and Pacific Railroad (CMStP&P) argued that it made every effort "to obtain other domestic workers, without success."[9]

The eastern railroads took a similar position by trying to stop the WMC from closing down the bracero track labor program so quickly. According to the Baltimore and Ohio Railroad, nineteen hundred of its nine thousand track workers were braceros. The supply of new rail and Mexican workers was critical to installing the new track. Domestic workers, according to the company, "appear to want some time off and are not interested in this type of work." Rather than taking railroad jobs, they seek better positions in the larger industrial centers. The New York Central pointed out that it had no desire and would not employ braceros if and when local workers were available. To date, however, the New York Central had no indication of local labor being available except in Detroit, where a few "colored workers" were employed recently. A Chicago and North Western Railway Company (CNW) official indicated that the company had resisted employing braceros until the lack of local labor forced it to employ Mexicans. Due to pending track repairs, the CNW had hired high school students during summer vacation but still came up short of meeting its labor needs. The company simply could not operate adequately "without Mexicans." Other employers presented a similar argument. "Mexican labor is absolutely essential," said the Chicago, Burlington and Quincy Railroad

The Florida East Coast Railway Company also considered braceros a "life saver" and was uncertain "what the company will do if Mexicans are cut off now." The New York, Chicago and St. Louis Railroad warned: "If Mexicans are withdrawn, the company will be nearly paralyzed between now and December." The Texas and Pacific Railway added that it was so dependent on Mexican laborers that if "withdrawn the Company will have section after section without a single man working."[10] The Association of American Railroads spoke in support of its members. The railroad companies, it pointed out, preferred domestic workers over Mexicans but had to keep braceros until local help became available. The association argued that the WMC's decision had serious repercussions outside the railroad industry, because if the manufacture of steel rails was slowed due a lack of track workers, the steel mills would lay off workers, causing more unemployment. The Western Association of Railroad Executives (WARE) put it simply: "Western railroads are dependent upon Mexican labor and cannot operate without it."[11]

The BMWE, however, sided with the WMC's decision not to extend the Mexican labor program beyond August 19 and wanted all railroad braceros out of the United States no later than December 15, 1945.[12] The union reminded the membership at its meeting:

> At the beginning of the program in the spring of 1943, the Railroads asked permission to bring in cheap Mexican labor because, due to the war, domestic labors were not available. The arguments used then do not hold today. There are between two and three million unemployed today but the railroads still say they cannot find native labor. It is not a labor problem but a wage problem. A minimum of 57 cents per hour is offered and 200,000 trackmen are receiving an average of 62 cents per hour. Workers with families cannot live on this amount and pay the present market prices, which have increased tremendously. No American can maintain a family in social decency on a 62-cent wage, yet thousands receive only 57 cents.[13]

The BMWE, like other labor unions, had made wage increases a centerpiece of their adaptation to the postwar economy and considered Mexican laborers as undermining the effort. In June 1945 the union tried to increase wages for track workers, and every railroad company refused because braceros were readily available. Now that the war had ended, the BMWE insisted: "If the railroads would pay a 75-cent wage, they could get all the labor needed at a cost less than the present over-all expense of importing Mexicans." Furthermore, the railroad companies could lower labor costs by employing domestic workers; Mexican track workers, they said, were less than "50 percent" as efficient as domestic employees. Therefore, the union argued,

"the quicker the Mexicans go home, the better it will be for the railroad industry itself." Besides, the union warned, the public did not favor the government continuing to support the bracero railroad program.[14] The Office
of Defense Transportation agreed with the BMWE by expressing fears that
"the presence of foreign workers in some localities may cause trouble," given
increasing unemployment and the end of the war.[15] Other unions, including
the Brotherhood of Railway and Steamship Clerks and the Railway Employees and Railway Labor Executives Association, supported the BMWE. They
stated the "employment of Mexicans has created dissension among domestic workers and had a demoralizing effect upon the efficiency of the entire
labor program." The Railway and Steam Clerks Union could not understand
why railroad companies had hired Mexicans, as they were believed to be
incapable of achieving "60 percent" of the efficiency of domestic labor.[16]

Already a separate informal agreement between the United States and
México stipulated the repatriation of the braceros would be orderly so
not to cause social, economic, or political problems in México. The agreement added complexity to the discussion of closing down the railroad labor program. The State Department, intent on honoring its commitment to
México, pushed for an orderly and systematic repatriation of the braceros.
The BMWE objected by insisting on the immediate termination of the employment of all railroad braceros. In their words, they wanted to "get the
Mexicans off the railroads" even if it meant holding them in camps while
awaiting transportation home.[17] In addition, the union accused the railroad
companies of purposefully slowing the repatriation of the braceros.

> We are aware of the fact that a railroad mission from the United States is, in
> effect, operating the Mexican railways, and we have reason to believe that
> the heads of that mission are officials of the United States railroads which
> desire to keep Mexican workers in this country as long as possible. We do
> not doubt that the Mexican railways have a capacity to return workers at
> the rate of 33,000, at least each month. If that were to be done, the Mexican
> workers now in this country could be returned to their homes before the
> end of next January.[18]

At the same time, the Office of Defense Transportation reported that
seven thousand veterans were arriving daily from overseas combat, and
even greater numbers of troops were arriving to eastern ports of the U.S.
This massive movement of military personnel across the breadth of the na-

tion necessitated sufficient labor to maintain the railroad tracks in good operating condition. In response, the Railroad Retirement Board (RRB) related that a survey of the federal regions in August 1945 found sufficient local labor to replace the bracero workforce if the railroads improved wages, working, and living conditions. The Association of American Railroads asked about the wisdom of trying to obtain immediate transportation for sixty-seven thousand railroad and sixty thousand agricultural workers. The association calculated that even if the government returned twelve thousand braceros monthly, it would take at least ten months to repatriate the entire combined Mexican contracted labor force. That being the case, the braceros would either have to keep working or be sent to a federal camp while awaiting transportation to México.

The WMC agreed and recognized that repatriating agricultural and railroad braceros simultaneously could create a potential transportation "bottleneck." To prevent the possibility of creating such a nightmare, the WMC suggested contract renewals could be considered if employers had evidence of a shortage of domestic workers and were willing to raise wages. The BMWE wanted no part of the compromise: "We want the Mexicans off the railroads." The union asked if the braceros continued working, what would compel the railroad companies to address the "social indecency" of paying fifty-seven cents per hour to domestic labor? The RRB also warned that fifteen thousand bracero contracts would expire in August, and in addition to congestion on U.S. trains, the Mexican railroads were ill prepared to accommodate the large number of braceros returning home. The BMWE did not alter its position, however, suggesting putting braceros "in camps or take them home by boats or buses, but get them out of railroad employment."[19] After an hour, the War Manpower Commission adjourned the meeting, without being any closer to finding a compromise between the BMWE and the railroads regarding the closure of the Mexican labor program. By September the government instructed railroad companies to keep the men working through the end of their contracts and beyond until transportation became available.[20]

Repatriating the braceros proved more difficult because both governments had other priorities for use of the trains than moving the discharged Mexican railroaders. In the United States, accommodating the returning soldiers took precedence. In México, the special trains that once raced workers to the border were likewise diverted to other purposes. The transportation issue worsened, prompting the U.S. embassy in México to suggest not waiting for trains to become available but shipping the braceros back by boat to the port of Tampico in Veracruz, México.[21] In organizing the repatriation, the U.S. government planned a regular monthly movement of men into México. The largest group of repatriates involved over fifteen thousand braceros in December 1945, followed by smaller groups until the last braceros departed in March 1946.[22]

Returning the contract workers back to México did not go as planned because of the ongoing problem of lack of transportation. One crew of sixty-seven track workers stationed at Markan, Washington, completed their contracts then traveled ninety miles to the Great Northern offices in Tacoma to protest having to wait to return to México. After they arrived in Tacoma, the men refused to return to work at Markan because they had received their final pay and had given all of their work clothes away.[23] After failing to persuade the men to continue working, the WMC decided to hold them in Tacoma until transportation became available. This arbitrary decision prompted one official to caution that holding braceros in "some kind of concentration camps until transportation is available obviously brings serious international repercussion."[24]

Elsewhere, family members of men contracted to the Chicago, Burlington and Quincy Railroad wired Mexican president Manuel Ávila Camacho, urging him to intervene and help get the workers home quickly. According to the telegram, the braceros stationed in Casper, Wyoming, had completed their contracts and were unable to return home because the company had "kidnapped" them and was holding them against their will.[25] Manuel Jiménez wrote a similar letter seeking the assistance of Mexican officials to help return workers assigned to the Baltimore and Ohio Railroad. According to Jiménez, the track crew had completed work in Ohio, but the company refused to allow them to return to México.[26] In December 1945 another group of nine PFE ice plant workers in Nampa, Idaho, refused to wait any longer and demanded payment in full so they could purchase their own tickets to El Paso. Despite pleas from the ice plant manager for the laborers to continue working until arrangements for their return could be scheduled, the braceros refused. Not willing to work or wait any longer, they deserted and set out on their own for México on December 5.[27] Braceros in other parts of the country were not eager to wait for transportation back to México, so they left earlier on their own accord. Aquilino Ramírez Gamboa did just that. Employed by the Reading Railroad Company, Gamboa departed for México five days after his contract expired without waiting for transportation for his group.[28]

The railroad workers were not the only ones being detained. Agricultural braceros in Yakima, Washington, faced a similar predicament and complained to President Camacho. Aquileo Bravo, spokesperson for the group, wrote to the Mexican president explaining that for weeks he and others were being "held in this concentration camp coping with a severe winter" without taking into consideration our willingness to "cooperate with this nation." "Our capricious detainment," the letter continued, "has caused us and our families very serious economic problems since we have not received a salary of any kind for four weeks." Without a doubt, the men had not worked since their contracts expired in October. They asked President Camacho to intervene immediately on their behalf, arrange for their return to México, and demand compensation for the weeks they were held in Yakima.

The president acted on the complaint by sending Manuel Amézquita, the Mexican labor inspector from Portland, to investigate. Once in Yakima, Amézquita assured the president that all men had been paid through the end of their contacts. However, they were not and would not be paid after the expiration of the work contract because technically they were in transit and therefore not eligible for compensation. Amézquita determined the U.S. government did not act capriciously or in an arbitrary manner in deciding to hold the men at Yakima. The main problem, according to the inspector, had to do with the fact that that trains normally available to move the braceros were now reserved for military troops, which were considered a higher priority. Amezquita guaranteed the president that, despite the complaint, the braceros were being fed at no expense to the workers. Given the labor inspectors' report, the president did nothing else while the braceros endured harsh conditions in Yakima. During the eight weeks they remained in the Yakima camp, northwestern winter temperatures dropped to near zero degrees Fahrenheit. Finally, on December 3, 1945, the last group of extremely disillusioned and bitter men boarded a train for their journey back to their families in México. In the years that followed, they undoubtedly shared their story of despair and involuntary confinement many times over.[29]

\* \* \*

During the winter of 1945, the Mexican ambassador Espinoza de los Monteros repeatedly informed President Camacho that many braceros, having completed their contracts and awaiting transportation in the United States, were impatient. They refused to work any longer and would not purchase winter clothing as it was too costly and of little use in México.[30] As the braceros waited, the stress among the men worsened appreciably. Acting on information received from the labor inspectors, consulates, and presumably the men themselves, the ambassador described the situation as "grave."[31] On November 11, 1945, the ambassador contacted the president to suggest that Mexican military convoys or private vehicles be used to pick up the braceros at the border and return them quicker to México.

Two days later, de los Monteros followed up with a more detailed memorandum on the emerging crisis. The ambassador delivered a perceptive appraisal of the problem to the president. Even though the workers cannot renew their contracts, railroad companies expected them to continue working without any protected rights. In the meantime, the winter cold had begun and the men required wool clothing and shoes to guard against the elements. This clothing, according to the report, should be provided by the railroad if the braceros are expected to remain working under adverse conditions. The ambassador noted that railroad companies were taking complete advantage of the fact that the work contract is no longer in force and medical, food services, and living conditions were bound to deteriorate.[32]

De los Monteros complained that company foremen and supervisors, with few exceptions, were unsympathetic to the braceros' predicament. They readily overlooked the important war contributions the workers had made, he wrote, and now simply wanted cheap malleable labor. With regard to the BMWE, the ambassador reminded the president that the union had never accepted the braceros and only grudgingly tolerated them because of the necessities of the war. The BMWE had done everything to stop the renewal of contracts and insisted that all of the braceros leave by spring 1946. The ambassador added that yellow journalism, together with entrenched prejudice toward Mexicans, inflamed other parties in the United States. This, he added, had the potential to destroy everything México had accomplished through the Good Neighbor policy and binational wartime agreement. The ambassador urged the president to do everything possible to secure transportation quickly for the workers back to México.[33] A week later, de los Monteros sent another memorandum to President Camacho. Even though the braceros were expected to continue working without a contract, he stressed, the idea seemed quite impractical as the men preferred to return to their homeland. He had another concern: unless the U.S. had assurances that México could pick up the workers at El Paso, Nogales, and Laredo, the U.S. government would not move them from their work sites to the border. The ambassador felt that the use of Mexican military vehicles to carry the braceros to México City or other recruitment centers now seemed impractical because of the lack of tires and other parts.[34]

During the winter of 1945, U.S. secretary of labor Lewis B. Schwellenbach also heard from various organizations urging him to accelerate the repatriation of the braceros. The National Farm Labor Union expressed concern over the plight of the agricultural and railroad braceros.[35] Other community and social organizations expressed a similar concern and urged returning the braceros at the "earliest possible moment." The Philadelphia Council of the Railroad Workers of America demanded prompt action after describing the braceros as suffering from the cold and enduring improper clothing and inadequate housing.[36] Letters expressing concern over the workers continued to arrive at the secretary of labor's desk. The American Federation of Labor mentioned the "dangerous plight of the braceros if detained in the U.S. beyond the end of their contacts." It urged that "drastic steps be taken to keep faith with these men and provide promised transportation home."[37] The National Secretary of the Women's International League joined the protests, calling the detention of the braceros "utterly shocking."[38] The National Association for the Advancement of Colored People (NAACP) advised the secretary "that every effort be made to supply them with suitable and adequate transportation" to México.[39] Not unexpectedly, however, the railroad industry criticized the WMC for being too quick to return the braceros home. In its view those in favor of hastily deporting the braceros should question the wisdom of ignoring the railroad industry's advice that all passenger trains and other equipment would be delegated to get veterans home for the holidays.[40]

Once the workers actually departed for El Paso, they had to carry their personal belongings in bags limited to seventy-seven pounds. WMC officials thought too much confusion and trouble would follow if the braceros were permitted to check excessive baggage. Instead, the men had the option to arrange for large trunks and similar heavy items to be shipped at their expense to México before their departure. Few did and, as a consequence, México's expectation that the returning braceros would bring back modern farming equipment and tools to their hometowns failed to materialize.[41] Aboard the southbound trains, the braceros experienced the all-too-familiar strain of indifference and disregard to their needs and comfort. Special agents on the trains guarded the braceros, wiring ahead to alert officials at the next stop to watch for potential deserters and to be ready for "near riotous feeding problems" or, as guards mocked, "lunchie" time. Among the regular train stops, Denver, Colorado, had the notorious reputation for taking advantage of the braceros. Officials warned the men to safeguard their earnings by not to patronizing "Jew stores," "second hand stores," and "Mexican dives."[42] At other stops along the way, the trains collected additional braceros being held in county and city jails for criminal offenses, desertion, or on orders of immigration officials.

Circumstances worsened for the braceros upon arriving in El Paso. By December 1945 the town's train depot overflowed with trains arriving packed with braceros from various railroad lines across the nation. Hundreds of railroad braceros in transit to México entered the city, joining thousands of other former contracted agricultural workers. This prompted El Paso officials to express concern about the problems caused by the multitude of returning braceros congregating in town. Out of concern for the city and its infrastructure, and given the time required by immigration officials to clear so many men, the War Manpower Commission considered using military bases as temporary bracero holding centers. At one point, officials thought about using Fort Lupton, Colorado—a point along the route and distant from El Paso. Officials also considered using Lordsburg Internment Camp in eastern New Mexico, constructed by the military to house Japanese aliens considered suspicious or dangerous as well as German and Italian prisoners of war. Lordsburg was one and a half miles from a Southern Pacific track that led directly to El Paso. The former internment camp was situated on thirteen hundred acres with ample room to hold hundreds of braceros and double-wire fence to guard against anyone attempting to leave without authority.[43] The camp, although empty by now, remained well equipped except for food and other supplies. Southern Pacific train engineers were willing to stop and idle their locomotives for fifteen minutes to allow the braceros to detrain. The braceros had to walk from the tracks carrying their baggage to the camp. Officials did not consider this a major drawback, as the Japanese and Japanese Americans and other detainees had walked the distance without difficulty. The WMC was more concerned about the potential "acute" problems that might develop when local residents learned of the government's intention to use the camp to house the Mexican laborers.[44]

Officials also deliberated about housing the returning braceros at Fort Bliss, Texas, a camp closer to El Paso that had been used to hold German and Italian Americans as well as Japanese from Hawaii during the war. This army base had more advantages than Lordsburg as it was fully functional in the fall of 1945 with a railroad connecting directly to El Paso. The army could provide security at Fort Bliss to prevent any braceros from leaving on their own for México or deserting into the local Mexican American population. Labor officials ultimately decided to use both Lordsburg and Fort Bliss to hold the braceros to ease the pressure on El Paso. By November 1945 the government had confined 590 railroad braceros at Lordsburg and another 601 at Fort Bliss.[45] The camps had a mixed population of thousands of agricultural and railroad braceros. Fort Bliss held 3,000 agricultural braceros, with 260 coming from Okanagan, Washington, and 75 from Chelan, Washington.[46]

When transportation became available, officials eventually moved the braceros out of the military camps aboard trains to El Paso. Upon arrival, the men encountered long delays before U.S. and Mexican officials allowed them to cross the border into Juárez. In some cases, braceros arrived at El Paso after several days of travel but waited on board the trains for hours before being allowed to transfer to México's National Railroad trains and continue the journey across the border. Unable to resist detraining, the men got off to relieve themselves or tossed their garbage from the long trip onto the tracks. A year before the end of the bracero program, El Paso city officials had expressed concerns over sanitation issues associated with the bracero trains. Sanitary engineers complained that garbage and sewage from the trains waiting to enter the city's Union Depot created unsightly and unhealthy conditions, violating local ordinances. The complaint arose when men began throwing refuse from railcar windows as trains stood idle on tracks waiting to enter the depot. The absence of proper lavatory facilities and sanitation cans aboard the cars raised more serious health concerns. To address the issue, city officials recommended that arriving bracero trains be staggered and prohibited from stopping briefly before proceeding into the depot, where sanitation facilities were available.

With so many workers returning in the fall of 1945, the Union Depot could not cope with failing sanitation conditions at the station. The situation grew worse because of the number of men arriving and the time required to check paperwork before allowing them to proceed to México. In the meantime, trains remained inside the station as men exchanged currency, immigration agents checked documents, and a local commissary company provided food. This tedious process took five hours or more. Since the station also handled regular passenger, freight, and postal traffic from across the country, it became congested. Train monitors found it impossible to prevent the braceros from disembarking if only to stretch their legs. As congestion

and sanitation conditions worsened, a local newspaper described the cha-
otic situation as a "health menace."

To alleviate the problems at the depot, the WMC and depot officials decided to stop the arrival of bracero trains and redirect them to nearby freight
yards, where immigration inspection, feeding, and currency exchange could
take place before allowing the trains to proceed to the Union Depot and
eventual transfer to the Mexican Railways. In preparation, workers placed
sanitary cans, with access to water and disinfectant in the freight yards to
prevent any health problems. Using the freight yards resulted in other unintended consequences, however. Trains and railcars were constantly moving
in and out of the yards, raising the potential that some of the men could be
accidently killed. To prevent any accidents, officials escorted braceros to a
nearby open exercise space free from the hazard of moving trains and away
from the residential areas.[47]

When the braceros finally crossed into México, corrupt Mexican officials often extorted money by demanding bribes to allow the men to bring
along their personal belongings.[48] At one point a group of six hundred braceros telegraphed President Camacho to complain about Mexican officials
who promised transportation to México City but then threatened to drop
the braceros "off at different locations," demanding payment for travel from
the U.S.-México border.[49] Unfortunately, such incidents were a harbinger of
worse things to come for the returning workers. When the men departed
from the United States, the Railroad Retirement Board gave them information about the total amount of their 10 percent savings that had been deposited with the Nationals Savings Bank in México City. With that information
and each man's own records justifying the same, the braceros had every expectation of receiving their full wage contribution. According to U.S. officials, however, the RRB savings totals were regularly disputed by Mexican
banks when men attempted to withdraw funds from their accounts.[50]

It became clear that mistakes could have occurred in the wage withhold-
ing system. The railroad companies, even after reporting to the RRB, did
not always deposit the correct amount with Wells Fargo Bank and Union
Trust Company in San Francisco for transfer to the National Savings Bank
of México. The international interbank transfer involving the conversion of
dollars into pesos could well have resulted in innocent or deliberate errors.
To add to the complexity, the corruption in the Mexican banks, as alluded
to by the WMC, prohibited the braceros from receiving the full value of their
wage savings. The mishandling of the workers' contributions to their sav-

ings ranged from simple to more serious errors at the expense of the braceros. In one case, the WMC mistakenly assigned an identical contract number
to two different railroad workers with the last name González. Despite working for two different railroad companies and being stationed in different
states, the two workers' deductions went into one account at the National
Savings Bank. Left uncorrected, the men had no idea of the gross error until
they entered the bank in México City. The first bracero to arrive at the bank
presented his contract number and withdrew all of the savings credited to
both workers. Later, when the second bracero tried to withdraw his savings,
he learned the account had already been paid out. Despite pleading his case,
the bank refused to make any restitution to the empty-handed bracero. According to the bank, it could not be held accountable as the WMC had committed the error and therefore it was fully responsible for any discrepancies.[51]

These bureaucratic mistakes were not everyday occurrences but grew
out of a variety of common factors. In July 1944, for instance, Ramón Trejo
Hernández and Higinio Trejo Ángeles contracted with the Western Pacific
Railroad in Lassen County, California. Neither of the men could read or
write; they had signed their contracts by affixing a fingerprint. In October,
Higinio Trejo Ángeles requested to return to México because he was not accustomed to the cold winter of northern California. Company officials con-
fused the two names and erroneously made out the termination papers for
Ramón Trejo Hernández. Since Ramón Trejo Hernández could not read, he
signed "Ramón Trejo Ernandes" and mistakenly terminated his own employment. The mix-up left Higinio Trejo Ángeles in California and Ramón
Trejo Hernández without an official contract and on his way to México.[52] In
another case, the WMC could not locate information for Hersamo González
Martínez, who claimed two days' back pay from the Atchison, Topeka and
Santa Fe Railway. Initially, officials could not find any records for Hersamo
González Martínez but later located his file under the name Erasmo Marinez Gonzales. The error became more complicated because the contract
number recorded for Erasmo Marinez Gonzales had also been assigned to a
different bracero named Ambrosio Porte Andrade.[53] These errors had critical repercussions, especially when the men returned to México, each expect-
ing to cash in a nonexistent savings account. Unfortunately, in many cases
the braceros only learned of these discrepancies after returning to México.

In 1944, for instance, Luciano Espinoza Martínez enlisted in the railroad
labor program while living on the former Guanamé hacienda near Venado,

San Luis Potosí. Although the people in the area had benefited from the breakup of the old landed haciendas during the country's land reforms in the 1930s, they continued to struggle to eke out a living, particularly during the Great Depression. When news of the bracero program arrived, many young unemployed men left for México City to enlist. Despite watching others go, Martínez hesitated until early 1944. The WMC ultimately assigned him to the Northern Pacific Railway in Washington State. After completing the six-month contract, Martínez continued working for two more weeks before returning to México on August 18, 1944. Back in San Luis Potosí, Martínez learned that after nearly seven months of hard labor, his total savings contribution amounted to $130.47. He had calculated that his savings were higher and wrote to the WMC to dispute the discrepancy. His letter explained how other braceros had spent less time working in Washington State had already received their reimbursements. From Martínez's calculations, and compared to those of other workers, his total savings could not be correct. He complained that he had not been able to make a withdrawal because the bank just kept sending one form after another.[54]

Martínez's problems were shared by others. Juan Ríos Balades worked with the Northern Pacific in Washington State in 1944. In a short but detailed letter to the WMC, he tried to get help with his savings account. He explained his first job had been with extra gang 11 at Tenino, before being transferred to Olympia, Washington. After three months, because of family illness, he returned to La Piedad, Michoacán. Balades explained that Northern Pacific withheld 10 percent of his earnings during the ninety-day period. Back in Michoacán, he learned that Northern Pacific had not made any deposits into his work contribution savings. While his letter carried a tone of humility, Balades pressed officials to respond to his inquiry as soon as possible. "Too much time has passed," he wrote "and please do not forget my address, Number 42 Calle Ramón Corona, La Piedad, Michoacán."[55]

Braceros wrote inquiring how to collect their savings accounts so often that the WMC considered these letters second only to the number of those from women seeking information about their husbands.[56] Regrettably, the historical records do not indicate the outcome of most of these cases, but it is likely that the returning braceros stood little chance of receiving accurate and full monetary compensation. Consider the case of twenty-nine-year-old Silvino Rosas Gutiérrez from México City, who had similar problems with his savings. On December 11, 1945, he wrote to the Southern Pacific office in San Francisco asking about his savings account. Apparently aware of the problems experienced by other braceros, Gutiérrez provided a full explanation of his work record, including birthplace, work contract, social security number, and dates when he entered and departed the United States, along with information about his workplace at Crescent Lake, Oregon. To ensure that Southern Pacific would not question his identity and entitlement, Gutiérrez affixed a photograph to the letter as if to say "this is who I am."[57]

The braceros' difficulties with their savings accounts stemmed from rampant corruption and fraud that plagued the program from the beginning. Early in 1943, the State Department in México City noted the appearance of street individuals called "usurers" taking advantage of braceros coming the bank to withdraw their savings. The scam involved approaching the braceros and convincing them to sell key identification documents to get to their savings. When Mexican officials jailed two of these offenders, the State Department expected the swindling of the braceros would end, but as more workers began to return, the scam only grew.[58] By the end of the war, the "usurers" (now referred to as *coyotes* by the State Department) were still actively swindling innocent workers at the bank's doors.[59] State Department personnel described how this illicit street business operated with the complicity of bank officials:

> Juan Gomez who has, let us say, cumulative savings of up to $35.00 or $40.00 or more comes to México from his home in Oaxaca and goes to the bank to collect. On arrival there, he is given a very definite runaround. This goes on for several days during the course of which Juan, who has been sleeping on a bench in the Alameda, eats or drinks up the money he brought with him. He therefore finds himself on the spot with no money in pocket, no way to eat, no place to sleep and the prospect of having to return to Oaxaca and then make another trip to México at a later date at which time he would, in all probability, get the same treatment. When he is in this malleable state and it is easy to so determine, he may be offered a chance by one of the bank tellers or some individual outside to discount his savings at say anywhere from 25 to 50 percent. He is only too glad to accept, gives clearance, takes his share and goes back to Oaxaca, while the coyotes start to clean up. If as we think, this traffic has reached sizeable proportions, you can imagine the amount of money involved when total savings come to $10,000,000.00. It really gets into big business.[60]

The State Department noted that coyotes "permeates the entire bank and goes right up to the President." The department alleged "that the Ministry of Labor is completely familiar with the situation in the bank and has done nothing about it."[61]

Considering the collusion between the street hustlers, the bank, and Mexican government officials, the braceros had little chance of collecting their savings in full. The WMC was just as disinterested in the plight of the men. Espiridión Ambriz Cruz found this out when he sought help from the WMC in México City. Cruz made several withdrawals from wage deposits forwarded to the bank by the AT&SF but needed to know the balance of his savings account. After the bank ignored his requests, Cruz wrote to U.S. officials with the WMC to please protect him and other workers from the bank, which was "openly robbing the braceros."[62] The WMC replied it could do little as it had no right to interfere with the business of the Mexican bank. Instead, the commission advised Cruz to write to the AT&SF and ask for the total of all the credits, along with the dates of each deposit. Even if the AT&SF provided that information, however, Cruz likely would not have been able to retrieve all his savings because of the corrupt culture at México's National Savings Bank.[63]

The braceros' difficulties with their savings accounts went beyond dishonesty among bank officials, the government, and the street coyotes. In some instances, railroad companies forwarded large numbers of checks to México for repatriated or missing braceros. Most of these checks were for retroactive wage adjustments owed to railroad braceros who had been employed in the United States before January 1944.[64] According to U.S. officials, the number and amount of these backdated checks were "substantial."[65] In April 1946, for example, Northern Pacific sent fifteen thousand dollars in checks to México's National Savings Bank for wage adjustments to four hundred braceros.[66] The majority of these braceros were unaware of back wages as the U.S. State Department arranged for these payments to be made directly through the Mexican savings bank for disbursement to the workers already residing in México.[67] Unless the bank notified them personally, the braceros unfortunately remained unaware of their entitlement to retroactive earnings.

Also, the War Manpower Commission withheld 3.25 percent from the braceros' wages to meet the federal RRB retirement program. The men resented the obligatory contribution to this program because they could not understand how it would serve them. Because some men experienced difficulties accessing their savings, what hope did they have in México to claim entitlement to the U.S. RRB retirement fund years later? Ernesto Galarza adroitly articulated why the men objected making contributions to the RRB pension plan. "The enjoyment of retirement benefits through the operation of a foreign agency, the character of which they do not understand, twenty-five or thirty years hence is a prospect too remote to arouse their enthusiasm," he wrote. "If, in addition, the Nationals themselves will have to take the initiative in applying for benefits under the law on reaching the retirement age, the probabilities of eventually enjoying the benefits of deductions from current payrolls will be even further reduced."[68]

Braceros had other reasons to feel bitter about paying into the railroad retirement system, as employers already took deductions for medical services, commissary charges, and the workers' savings account. Some companies mistakenly subtracted taxes, such as the 5 percent "victory" and income taxes, which were not applicable to the braceros. Awareness of diminishing income, and knowing they would not recover these deductions, led to much discontent among the braceros. These erroneous income tax subtractions were enough to persuade eighty Chicago, Milwaukee, and Saint Paul braceros to strike, willing to go to jail in protest of the income tax deduction.[69] In other cases railroad companies attempted to collect funds owed by braceros already in México for overpayment of wages, commissary charges, and other unpaid services. In one example, Northern Pacific wrote to México's National Savings Bank to collect $8.10 and $7.07 from the savings account of two braceros to cover unpaid meal charges.[70]

Given that railroad companies had posted a five-hundred-dollar bond guaranteeing the return to México of each bracero contracted for employment in the United States, the railroad industry had a substantial amount of capital invested in the workforce. To cancel the bond, railroad companies had to present proof that absent braceros were not residing in the U.S. but had returned to México. Many braceros left for México on their own without notifying their employer. Others simply walked away from the program and integrated into the local Mexican American community. When workers went missing, the railroad companies had to determine their whereabouts in México or in the United States. Between 1943 and 1945 the Southern Pacific Railroad reported 2,457 braceros missing from company work gangs.[71] When the war ended, the Western Association of Railway Executives stated that in 1945 an industrywide twenty-three hundred contract railroaders had absconded from their contracts, leaving individual companies holding the outstanding bonds.[72]

Because the railroad companies stood to forfeit their surety bonds if the missing workers could not be located in the United States or México, their response was straightforward and predictable. The employers tried to track down lost braceros in the U.S. by enlisting their own police along with the assistance from local, county, and state police units as well as U.S. immigration authorities. When police officers apprehended braceros, they booked them in city and county jails until the immigration authorities could take custody and return them to México. Railroad companies also relied on the Mexican consulates and labor inspectors to join the hunt for missing braceros. Although the railroad companies and the WMC had once considered the Mexican labor inspectors more of a nuisance than a help, they now heavily relied on inspectors to help locate missing braceros. Although they never garnered much respect, U.S. officials depended on the labor inspectors until March 1946, when the inspectors returned to México and the majority of the braceros were back home.[73]

One month after the labor inspectors left for México, Northern Pacific still could not account for one hundred missing braceros. Concerned with fifty thousand dollars in outstanding bonds, the company urged the U.S. State Department in México to help in the "roundup" of their former workers. As a last resort, Northern Pacific contemplated using Mexican newspapers to publish the names of every deserter and offering a reward for anyone who could locate the men. In the United States, Northern Pacific took a different approach by printing what amounted to large public "wanted posters" to apprehend the missing braceros. Each black-and-white poster featured six men identified by their immigration card, listing full name, date of entry, and photograph. At the foot of the poster appeared the statement: "If any one of these men are located please notify a representative of the Northern Pacific Railway Company." The name of the "special agent" for the company was also included.[74]

Although authorities located and jailed some men, including Teófilo Jacobo Gaytán, who had deserted from extra gang number 3 in Tacoma, Washington (found working on a farm in Toppenish, Washington), the poster campaign had limited success in the Pacific Northwest. In contrast to the Southwest, where Mexican American communities offered a welcome sanctuary to deserting braceros, similar communities in the Pacific Northwest were almost nonexistent at this time. As a result, many of the missing men left the Pacific Northwest for Mexican American communities in the Southwest or simply set out for México without notifying the employer.

Railroad officials, Mexican consuls, and the Railroad Retirement Board saw communities with sizable Mexican American populations as fertile grounds to find missing braceros. Spontaneous inspections were organized with the hope of apprehending braceros among the Mexican American population. The inspections had a profound psychological effect on Mexican families living in the small rural and urban search areas. Despite the concentrated energy to locate missing men after the war wound down, railroad companies maintained lists of unaccounted-for braceros.

The areas of México where the braceros had originated now became the focus in the search for unaccountable men. The Western Association of Railway Executives reasoned that if the braceros who had not officially terminated their contracts could not be located in the United States, then many of them were already back in México. To gather evidence to support their assumption that close to five thousand men were no longer in the United States, WARE, the RRB, and the U.S. Foreign Service, along with the National Savings Bank of México, designed an elaborate strategy to avoid forfeiting the bracero departure bonds.[75] Of course, the interplay among these entities is interesting: these same organizations never provided this level of assistance to the braceros' efforts to obtain their earned work-related savings.

Because braceros could only draw from their work compensation after clearing immigration and returning to their home communities, officials decided to take advantage of the moment the men sought reimbursement by mail or in person to verify the braceros were back in México. Many of them residing outside México City avoided the cost of travel and asked for their savings by mail. To match the identity of the person making the request with the bank account, braceros had to complete a form verifying their identity. The bank would then forward a check after comparing signatures on the completed form with their own records. All information simultaneously went to WARE so it could follow up with a letter to the person making the inquiry with a request to verify a correct address. In case the bracero or his family failed to respond, a WARE representative attempted to contact the person at the address provided.

In trying to locate the braceros, WARE also sent official inspectors with photographs and identification cards of the men to conduct house-to-house canvassing in various states in México. Upon discovery, the men were taken to the nearest U.S. consulate to verify their residency in México. To be thorough, WARE questioned family members of missing braceros for possible leads about addresses in the United States where the person might be working. Any information about workers in the U.S. went directly to the immigration service office nearest where the bracero was reportedly living, so the worker could be apprehended.[76] Travel to México's rural areas to track down braceros took a physical toll on the WARE search personnel. In some instances, to reach a worker's family, the railroad representatives had to travel on horseback through rough terrain to some of the most remote villages. They often encountered difficult living and complained often of not finding any accommodations, having to contend with "an almost intolerable condition of flies, insects, and other vermin, as well as unsanitary water and toilet facilities."[77]

Of course, confirming a missing bracero's residency in México was less difficult when men showed up in person to claim their work savings. An intricate process went into effect to preclude a worker who had not cleared his departure with U.S. immigration from drawing his account until verifying his residency in México. When a bracero entered the bank, he received a form ascertaining his name and identification number. The worker then took the form to the WARE office in México City for a final review. If records matched, WARE directed the person to the U.S. embassy to notarize and record the form. At the embassy, the bracero finally received a copy of the completed document permitting him to withdraw his own funds.[78] Given the high level of illiteracy among the braceros, it is hard to imagine that all of them would be able to follow this complicated bureaucratic procedure, which often lasted for days. This process functioned only to satisfy the interests and obligations of the U.S railroad companies holding outstanding worker bonds.

The actual success rate of the efforts to identify missing braceros in México or the United States is unknown; however, companies did maintain active lists of unaccounted-for men. Three years after the war, Southern Pacific had pared its list of missing contracted railroaders to just 173.[79] Despite some cooperation from other railroad companies operating in the Southwest, Northern Pacific could still not account for 163 men by 1956.[80] One year later, in August, the RRB magnanimously canceled all outstanding Northern Pacific bonds. Eventually the impossibility of locating the whereabouts of all the missing men became evident, and the government began to set aside the remaining departure bonds. In 1957 the Railroad Retirement Board also voided all departure bonds held against Great Northern, thus closing the book on the Mexican contracted railroad labor program in the Pacific Northwest.[81] By July of 1947, WARE and the RRB had realized that tracking the unaccounted-for men through their savings was ineffective, and the two organizations closed their offices in México City. Some workers would never be found; individuals could have become ill and died before they could request their work savings. In these cases, relatives may well have been unaware of the deceased's savings deposit and made no attempt to contact México's National Savings Bank. Other braceros perhaps did not know that they were entitled to unpaid wages.[82]

*  *  *

When WARE shut its office in México, the binational railroad program began to fade into oblivion. By the time it wound down, ample evidence already suggested a wide gulf between the program's promise and actual outcomes. When the last incoming Southern Pacific track bracero entered the United States at El Paso on August 13, 1945, the echoes of patriotic euphoria that had accompanied the first groups arriving at the border in the summer of 1943 were long forgotten.[83] No "special trains" burned the track racing to the border, much less sped the returning men home. In the end, Manuel Gamio's vision of Mexican labor transformed through the industrial railroad program had little credence. The savings deduction plan that proposed to ensure that the railroaders would not return penniless worked for some but not for the majority of braceros. At a time when both countries had pledged to be good neighbors and to cooperate to win the war, some of the contract railroaders came home physically and emotionally abused by their employers and officials, both Mexican and U.S.—all of whom had pledged to protect the braceros' health, civil rights, and dignity as laborers.

# Chapter 11

# Forgotten Railroad Soldiers

According to the War Manpower Commission (WMC), Mexican government officials were not very concerned with the return of the braceros at the end of World War II. On August 14, 1945, the WMC office in México City reported that it "contacted many officials of the Mexican Government in an effort to ascertain what plans, if any have been made for the returning braceros." The WMC found that, "unfortunately, no plans whatever appear to have been made, although a number of proposals have been advanced such as the colonization of virgin land on the west coast, cooperative colonies, etc." Other than that, Mexican officials had met and agreed to study the needs of the braceros but, at the time of the report, no social workers had been assigned the task of interviewing the arriving workers.[1]

In many respects the braceros were returning to a homeland that had also been changed by the war. Although the bracero railroaders had not earned much in the United States, their earnings were above the norm in México. On average, rural Mexican workers earned twenty cents a day, with those working in México City earning seventy cents a day. The high rate of inflation pushed higher the cost of food and housing until it approximated the cost of living in the United States. Some items, such as clothing, actually cost more in México than in the U.S.[2] Given inflation and food scarcities, a week's income meant that Mexican families couldn't make their money stretch as far as previously and purchased less food.[3] A year before the war ended, the U.S. Embassy in México City took note of the effects of the high inflation on the arriving braceros.[4] In a 1945, U.S. officials found that the cost of living had increased more than 100 percent since 1939. Their analysis concluded that the inflationary pressure fell most heavily among the lower classes and was "reaching a point where political stability may be endangered."[5]

While some Mexican officials had anticipated that braceros working in the United States would affect unemployment in México, the return of the contracted labor challenged the idea. Once in México, many of the men realized that jobs, particularly in the rural areas where the majority of the population resided at the time, were hard to find. Guadalupe Montoya Gonzales, for example, wrote a short simple letter to his former Northern Pacific foreman, D. S. Colby, in Spokane, Washington. He requested a letter of recommendation so he could get a job with the Mexican railroads in Torreón, Coahuila. Gonzales began the letter with a greeting, "Say hello to all the employees of the company." He explained that he had moved to Torreón because work was unavailable in Zacatecas. "I hope you will not disappoint me," he wrote. The letter closed with an entreating but hard to decipher phrase: "pls send mi li capi, la contestacion, pronto."[6] Herminio Ramírez also wrote to the Northern Pacific, asking for a similar letter of recommendation to apply for railroad work in the U.S. He had worked with the Northern Pacific in 1945, returned to México, and then immigrated to Washington State for farm work. With his Northern Pacific experience and the letter of recommendation, Ramírez hoped to get hired for a railroad job.[7] The requests for these letters of recommendation were common, prompting Northern Pacific to prepare a generic letter of recommendation in Spanish with places for the railroad superintendent to complete the dates of a bracero's employment and add his signature.[8]

Gonzales and Ramírez were among many railroad braceros unemployed in México after the war. The majority of them had acquired very few useful skills while in the United States. Some men did acquire limited skills working in the railroad shops, stores, constructing bridges, and similar structures. But even they found it difficult to find employment outside of working in agriculture or doing menial jobs. After one year working in the United States in a railroad car shop, Francisco González García returned home with the intention of withdrawing his savings and applying his experience to establish a repair shop. His business plan fell through, however, when he learned that the railroad company made no deposits in his name at the National Savings Bank.[9]

As the end of the war approached, the problem of unemployed braceros gathering in the streets of México City came to the attention of President Camacho. In June 1945 officials asked the president to encourage the Ministry of Labor to address the multitude of jobless braceros.[10] The concern of the Mexican government over the adjustment of recent returnees was perplexing, as it did little to assist the braceros. Out of self-interest, however, the Mexican government became very involved settling bracero wage-related issues. In 1944 the United States and México agreed on a three-hundred-thousand-dollar payment to settle all prevailing back wage issues.[11] This amount reached México in 1945, and the government assigned a trustee to pay all qualifying workers. At the end of one year, the president assumed the right to take the balance and invest it as he deemed appropriate.[12]

Most wage issues were centered on retroactive wage increases that had been won by the Brotherhood of Maintenance of Way Employees (BMWE) in 1944 and payable to braceros still in the United States as well as to those back in México. Repaying the braceros their back wages continued for several years after the war. In 1946 some railroad companies owed retroactive earnings but failed to notify the workers until two years later and well after many of the braceros had returned to México.[13] In practice, railroad companies determined the amount due in back wages and then forwarded a check in the worker's name to México's National Savings Bank. Because the men were not always aware of the arrival of this money or they were simply unable to make a withdrawal because of the underhandedness and inefficiency of bank officials, officials in México became concerned. The concern had less do with the men's benefit and more to do with the fact that the railroad checks had to be redeemed by the workers within eleven months of the date of issue. México dreaded the possibility that checks not cashed for reasons of death, missing heirs, or failure to locate the workers would have to be returned to the U.S. railroad companies. To avoid returning the wages, the government declared that all unclaimed residual back pay issued by U.S. railroad companies, held after eleven months by the National Savings Bank, belonged to the Mexican government.

When some WMC and Mexican government officials questioned the right of México to claim personal income belonging to the braceros and paid by a private entity, the government announced that retroactive wages were available to eligible braceros. From the point of view of the U.S. railroads, companies hoped that the public notice of back wages would serve to lure out some of the bracero deserters believed to be residing in México and avoid forfeiting the five-hundred-dollar departure bond per bracero.[14] Although the WMC gave the impression that it opposed the Mexican government's claim to the braceros' back wages, it failed to intercede. Reflecting on the issue, an official wrote: "It is all too apparent why they would prefer global payments. Somebody should clean up in a big way, but I suppose that is one of the prices we must pay and close our eyes in order to make a final settlement in so far as the railways themselves and the Department and Embassy are concerned."[15]

In the meantime, the braceros and their survivors continued to experience difficulty receiving their back pay. In 1945, for example, Catalina Moreno de Salazar attempted to draw the savings account held by the National Savings Bank under her husband's name, Jesús Salazar Flores. Her husband had worked as a bracero for the Atchison, Topeka, and Santa Fe Railway (AT&SF), but he died without taking out his railroad savings. For months, Mrs. Salazar attempted to draw from her deceased husband's account without success. A year later, she wrote to U.S. officials seeking help: "I am widowed and with the little work that I can find is insufficient for my family. I have been asking for a refund since last year but to date have received nothing." The WMC did little to assist Mrs. Salazar other than suggest she contact AT&SF directly.[16]

A few years later, in 1949, an interesting case regarding wages involved a naturalized U.S. citizen from Milwaukee, Wisconsin, who had married a bracero formerly employed by the Chicago, Milwaukee, Saint Paul, and Pacific Railroad. When the woman tried to obtain her husband's back pay, she got caught up in the bureaucratic runaround familiar to Catalina Moreno de Salazar and countless braceros. Her attempt to withdraw the earned wages began when she wrote to the National Savings Bank and got nowhere. Next, she contacted to the railroad company office in Chicago and verified that the funds were indeed forwarded to the bank in México City. Another letter to the Mexican consul seeking help on behalf of her husband yielded nothing. Despite these futile attempts, the woman persisted by writing to the U.S. Department of State in México City, asserting her U.S. citizenship in seeking for assistance for her husband. The historical record does not provide the outcome of the case, but if Mexican braceros were met with dead ends at the National Savings Bank, what chance would this foreign woman receive writing from Milwaukee?[17]

The bracero railroad retirement fund administered by the Railroad Retirement Board (RRB) offers another view into the Mexican government's interest in claiming funds that had been set aside for the braceros. Because of the amount of retirement money involved, this issue became even more contentious than back wages. Under the terms of the bracero railroad workers' agreement and the U.S. Railroad Retirement Act, the RRB deducted 3.25 percent from workers' earnings to cover unemployment compensation and retirement benefits. From the inception of the program, México had sternly opposed these deductions. México felt that the amount of unemployment compensation payments would be insignificant to benefit the workers. Regarding the retirement program, México believed it would be near impossible to locate the workers two or three decades after they returned from the United States, when they would become eligible for retirement.[18]

Over the life of the labor program, braceros had contributed approximately five million dollars, with the same amount matched by their employers, to the RRB general retirement fund. Because the braceros were mostly young and far from retirement, they would have to wait a long time to benefit from their contributions. American railroad workers, however, after many years of being employed, received retirement benefits from the RRB from a combination of the bracero and domestic worker general funds. At the end of the war, Mexican officials contended that the entire amount drawn for retirement from the braceros' income should be "refunded as quickly as possible" to México and paid in one lump sum.[19] Considering the amount of money involved, México purposefully eyed the retirement monies, as well as other deductions taken from the braceros' earnings, as a quick way of cutting into the ballooning economic deficit that had resulted from the unfavorable balance of trade with the United States.[20] Understandably, the RRB resisted releasing any of the braceros' contributions to the Mexican government. As a rationale for this position, the RRB argued the individual amounts were insignificant and of little good to the contracted laborers; and, besides, braceros, unlike domestic workers, were already entitled to a payment of $150 upon an accidental work-related death. More important, the RRB became concerned that by allowing México to take the braceros' contributions, it would encourage other short-term workers employed during the war to want their deductions returned.[21]

Because of mounting economic concerns, México persisted in claiming the braceros' share of the RRB pension fund. In addition to the unfavorable balance of trade, México owed the United States approximately seven million dollars for military supplies and equipment obtained under President Franklin Roosevelt's World War II Lend Lease program. México became more forceful in its claim of the bracero retirement funds by hinting that not turning over the entire sum of the bracero retirement fund might jeopardize its ability to continue to service the outstanding war-related debt. Citing that the transfer of the retirement fund would "greatly help México's present exchange situation" and that further delays might cause damage to newly improved binational relations, the U.S. supported México's entitlement to the bracero portion of the RRB trust.[22] In an exchange of notes signed on November 11, 1946, the United States formally agreed to push for the refund and subsequently endorsed several unsuccessful congressional bids to authorize sending monies to México.[23] All the while, México remained unwavering in its claim to the bracero RRB fund, and at one point the country even asserted that the matching sums paid by the railroads be turned over as well.[24]

In response to questions about what México intended to do with the bracero retirement funds, the government disclosed that if it recovered the five million dollars from the RRB, the amount would be devoted to serve a larger public good. Specifically, officials proposed using the money to establish the Instituto Mexicano del Seguro Social (Mexican National Institute of Social Security) for the benefit of all workers. Without a clear definition of the purpose of the institute, the idea proposed starting a hospital or an institution to rehabilitate workers incapacitated by occupational diseases.[25] President Camacho questioned the proposal, however.[26] Although the U.S. State Department had already approved transferring returning the funds to México, it denounced the idea of building the institute with RRB funds. According to interdepartmental correspondence, rejection of the idea was unequivocal: "If the Mexican Foreign Office instructs their Embassy in Washington to present a plan which involves using the money for the purpose of establishing some kind institution to the benefit of workers, the answer of the United States will be no."[27] In January 1952, Senator Dennis Chávez from New Mexico, a longtime advocate for workers' rights and social equality, introduced Senate Bill 215 during the first session of the 82nd Congress. The language of Senate Bill 215 read: "Directs the Railroad Retirement Board to refund the taxes deducted from wages of Mexican workers on United States railroads under the United States–Mexican agreement of April 29, 1943. Payment shall be made to the Mexican National Institute of Social Security."

After Congress failed repeatedly to enact legislation compelling the RRB to transfer the bracero retirement funds to México, the two governments negotiated a compromise. If no resolution could be reached by 1957, the United States would forgive México's Lend Lease debt and the RRB retained the bracero retirement monies. In the settlement México agreed not to present any future claims on its own behalf or in the interest of individual braceros for refund of the retirement contributions or earned wages. The record is not entirely clear on this matter, but since the RRB never returned any part of the retirement funds to México, the agreement presumably went into effect and the issue faded from official commentary.[28]

* * *

The closure of the bracero railroad program brought other issues to the forefront. During the short time the railroad labor program lasted, more than 136,000 braceros worked in the United States to keep the trains moving. When this number of railroaders is considered together with almost a quarter million wartime agricultural braceros, the total number of braceros represents a significant employment use of México's human capital. But many more men traveled to the recruitment centers in México than the number that qualified as braceros, stimulating migration across regions as well as rural and urban spaces. The demographic shifts, especially among indigenous and rural poor, caught the attention of WMC and State Department officials. U.S. government personnel described how large numbers of indigenous peoples and the country poor were uprooted after being lured to the recruitment centers in México City, San Luis Potosí, and Querétaro. One official wrote at length:

> It is interesting to note that a substantial number of the braceros sent to the United States have not been Spanish-speaking Mexicans. Approximately 30 percent of the Mexican people speak little or no Spanish and remain virtually autonomous Indian races. For example, considerable numbers of Zapotecs, Mixtecs, and Tarascans have gone to the United States as braceros: and it has frequently been necessary in order to deal with them, not only to have Spanish interpreters but also interpreters to translate from their Indian language to Spanish. At first it was quite difficult to persuade these shy people to leave for the United States as braceros, but as the first contingents returned, migration to the United States became increasingly popular and in our last recruitment among the Otomis it would have been possible to have secured the labor of almost the entire race.[29]

A few Mexicans observed the same phenomenon noted by the United States, including Antonio Toledo Martínez, who wrote to President Camacho expressing concern. The men most eager to go to the U.S., he explained, came primarily from rural areas. The men left adobe shacks or *jacales*, journeyed barefooted or wearing *huaraches* to the recruitment centers, and arrived suffering from malnutrition.[30] Martínez pointed out that indigenous men from Nahuatzen and Cherán, Michoacán, had sold everything to come to México City. Unable to secure bracero contracts, a good number these men were now desperate and in complete misery in an unfamiliar urban environment.[31] In all probability, the indigenous braceros men described by Martínez endured the most hardship during their employment in the United States and after their return to México. From the moment they left the comfort of their immediate vicinities and social spaces, they entered an environment with unfamiliar standards of social equality and culture. In the United States the psychological and social challenges must have been enormous, as these racially mixed and indigenous braceros adjusted to dissimilar mores and attitudes. Their supervisors expected them to learn to repair track lines quite often in extreme work situations and distant from their homes.

At the time, few Mexican social scientists had any interest in the indigenous and rural poor who had been uprooted by the bracero program. In 1944, Manuel Gamio, perhaps wanting to update his earlier 1920s study, proposed a new six- to seven-month study of immigrants and braceros in the United States. Instead of testing his earlier assertion that the bracero program would serve to uplift and otherwise modernize the underclasses of Mexican society, Gamio sought to quantify, locate the population, and measure remittances and earned wages.[32] Two years later, the director of the Ministry of Labor and Social Welfare undertook the first wide-ranging study of the wartime braceros. The report drew from government documents and personal interviews with returning braceros. When completed, the study was critical of some aspects of the program but overall, and as would be expected, the official assessment was positive.

There was very little public and official awareness of the railroad bracero program in the United States as well. The lack of awareness resulted in part from the obscure nature of railroad track maintenance work. Maintenance crews, it must be kept in mind, worked in a particular locality for one or two days then quickly moved to a different section of the track. For this reason local newspapers seldom devoted attention to the track workers unless the news involved accidents, criminal activity, or similar sensational incidents. Still, some American communities expressed their gratitude for the braceros. In Barberton, Ohio, for example, the community and the chamber of commerce acknowledged the eighty braceros who had been employed by Erie Railroad. When the braceros readied to leave Barberton for México on the afternoon of January 9, 1946, people came to wish them well. A writer stated: "The service of the men from Mexico in keeping our trains rolling deserves the special gratitude of both the Mexicans and Americans." The writer vividly described the sounds of the approaching trains in the distance, the locomotive whistle, and apprehension building among the crowd at the town's depot.

> During a minute or two of good wishes, the train appeared and halted for a
> brief time. On board were other Mexicans from other camps who were also
> on their way home. Many of these left the waiting cars to shake hands with
> the friends in Barberton who stood in the sidelines. Soon, the engine began
> to move and the faces inside the cars pressed close to windows for a last
> glimpse as the train rolled on and out of sight. We cannot forget the labors
> of these men whose backs bent for long hours over pick and shovel and who
> braced themselves against the gnawing cold in order to help us fight a war.[33]

The railroad companies, the BMWE, and the RRB repeatedly ran articles about the imported railroaders. Some railroads printed articles in company newsletters. Most of the them overflowed with adulation to the point of being condescending toward the Mexican workers, yet they offer valuable insights into the men's lives that is otherwise available. The New York Central Railroad ran an article titled "Trabajadores Mexicanos prestan su ayuda para ganar La Guerruna trabajando por el New York Central System" in the August 1944 edition its newsletter, *Central Headlight*. Written in Spanish, the eight-page article was descriptive of the braceros' work and featured photographs of the work crews identified by name.[34] In 1944 the Pan American Union commissioned Robert C. Jones to write an official summary of the bracero programs titled, *Mexican War Workers in the United States*. Published in 1945, the study outlined the purpose and function of the railroad and agricultural labor programs. Jones, who served in the administration of wartime labor programs, outlined the function of the labor programs without referencing the unpleasant aspects. Despite this shortcoming, the study served as a useful introduction to the bracero programs. Ernesto Galarza, also employed by the Pan American Union, found much to fault after visiting some of the bracero railroad camps during the war; his reports were exclusively addressed to U.S. and Mexican administrators. Years later after leaving the Pan American Union, he published two significant exposés of the agricultural bracero program, unfortunately without reference to the railroad track workers.[35]

Table 11.1 Distribution of Mexican railroad workers, August 1945

| State | No. | Percentage | State | No. | Percentage |
|-------|-----|------------|-------|-----|------------|
| CA | 5,122 | 22.46 | CT | 297 | 1.31 |
| OH | 1,987 | 8.71 | ID | 257 | 1.13 |
| PA | 1,692 | 7.41 | OK | 224 | 0.99 |
| KN | 1,407 | 6.17 | NE | 214 | 0.94 |
| IL | 1,387 | 6.08 | MA | 151 | 0.67 |
| NY | 1,283 | 5.62 | MT | 144 | 0.64 |
| AZ | 1,025 | 4.49 | IA | 113 | 0.50 |
| OR | 896 | 3.92 | WY | 102 | 0.45 |
| NV | 833 | 3.87 | CO | 100 | 0.44 |
| WA | 833 | 3.87 | ME | 100 | 0.44 |
| NM | 792 | 3.47 | WI | 100 | 0.44 |
| IN | 731 | 3.20 | FL | 95 | 0.42 |
| TX | 670 | 2.93 | DE | 85 | 0.38 |
| NJ | 631 | 2.76 | MN | 84 | 0.37 |
| MS | 378 | 1.65 | ND | 74 | 0.33 |
| MI | 371 | 1.62 | RI | 35 | 0.15 |
| MD | 317 | 1.40 | LA | 10 | 0.42 |

Source: *Boletín del Archivo General de la Nación*, México, D.F., third series, 4, no. 4 (October–December 1980). Fondo Gobernación, Departamento Administrativo, Oficina Documentadora de Braceros, VI/100 (724)/3, AGN.

Over the course of three years, the bracero railroad program delivered 136,090 workers to U.S. railroad companies. The number of railroad braceros represented approximately 61 percent of the combined total of farm and track workers contracted to U.S. employers during World War II. At the end of the war, in 1945, braceros worked in thirty-five states across the nation. It is hard to understand the scant recognition paid to the nationwide presence of the Mexican railroad braceros. The railroads, however, did not overlook the importance of this large number of braceros. Conscious of labor cost, they maintained detailed expense records that offer much information about the Mexican railroad workforce. The Southern Pacific Railroad, which employed the most braceros in the industry, reported a little over $3 million in costs between 1943 and 1945 to recruit, feed, and return the braceros to México. Burial and funeral expenses totaled $23,000, and accidents and liability cost Southern Pacific between $150,000 and $200,000. In wages alone, the company paid more than $48 million to the bracero workers.[36]

Operating with fewer braceros, the Northern Pacific Railway calculated it paid $5.36 million in wages to its bracero employees from 1943 through 1947. During the same period, the company reported losing money by providing housing and food services to the braceros because the cost exceeded the revenue collected from the men. The expense for recruiting the braceros, transporting them north on other railroads, and returning them to México totaled approximately $359,230. Other related expenses included $2,138.25 for Spanish-language periodicals, and $2,240.75 for funeral expenses and death benefits.[37] By 1947, Northern Pacific's total expenditures on the bracero employees, excluding wages, amounted to a little over $5.8 million.[38] In three years of the Temporary Migration of Mexican Non-agricultural Workers program, the 136,090 railroad workers earned $161.4 million (U.S.), and $16.1 million of this amount represented the savings deductions deposited in the National Savings Bank.[39] These amounts represented essential capital flowing from the United States into the revenue-deficient Mexican economy.

\* \* \*

Yet the experiences of the wartime railroad soldiers quickly faded from the Mexican memory, except among the braceros, as all attention shifted to the bracero agricultural program, which continued to supply workers to U.S. farms through 1964. A few surviving period songs, such as "El Corrido de los Trenes Especiales," written by Enrique García during the World War II, relayed the men's experiences or were sung to lighten the burden of hard labor.[40] Composed as *corridos* and recorded in the oral tradition popular in México, these important testimonies express the thoughts of the braceros as well as critics of the wartime labor program. "El Regreso de los braceros," written by Sabino Casarrubia in 1943, faulted the men who left México for the United States and criticized the Department of State language translators in México City. Its lyrics warned the men that "for earning one penny or peso no one needs to go so far" and that those who left for work often came back months later complaining they had been robbed, "after crossing the border / They were simply 'cleaned out.'"[41]

The railroad industry's reliance on Mexican labor, especially in the U.S. Southwest and West, did not cease when the bracero railroad program ended. In fact, war or no war, railroad companies continued to be dependent on Mexican track workers. Some braceros married U.S. citizens and never went home, while others reunited with their families without having to return to México. Being able to immigrate to the United States legally or in violation of immigration laws after the war marked a significant change in labor flows across the U.S.-México border. In the decade of the Great Depression, Mexican immigration had practically stopped and did not resume until the beginning of the World War II with the bracero labor programs. Some U.S. citizens, deported to México during the repatriation drives of the 1930s, found it near impossible to return to the United States except as braceros.

Consider, twenty-three-year-old Rogelio Briceño Regalado, a U.S. citizen deported as a child to México during the Great Depression. Regalado joined the bracero program without disclosing his citizenship in order to return to the United States. As a result, the WMC mistakenly assumed he was a Mexican national and assigned him to work with the Southern Pacific Railroad in California. His U.S. citizenship surfaced when Los Angeles police officers arrested him for fighting and possessing marijuana on November 14, 1944. Three days after the arrest, a court sentenced Regalado to serve three months in the Los Angeles County jail. Coincidently, his work contract with Southern Pacific expired while he was still in jail. Knowing this, Regalado feared the Southern Pacific and the WMC would return him to México. To avoid being sent back, Regalado claimed he was born in Pasadena, California, in 1923 and therefore a U.S. citizen. In the days that followed, U.S. immigration officials located Regalado's birth certificate under the name "Rojillo Regoolods" and thus confirmed his rightful citizenship.

Regalado's family, like thousands of other Mexicans, had been repatriated to México during the 1930s. He had taken advantage of the bracero program to return to the United States, and when arrested, he renewed his contact twice. In an interview with immigration officials, Regalado explained why he deceived the WMC. He always "wanted to come to the United States," he said, "and had no other way to come" except as a railroad bracero. Since Regalado's work contract had expired, Southern Pacific stated he was in the country illegally, that he should be repatriated, and that the company was relieved of "any and all contractual obligations." The railroad was mainly worried that if Regalado remained in the United States and did not return to México, the company would forfeit the five-hundred-dollar departure bond. Immigration officials had already confirmed Regalado's U.S. citizenship and that he had every right to remain in the country. But the WMC viewed his case much differently: as far as the WMC was concerned, Southern Pacific had ruled correctly that Regalado remained a bracero and therefore a Mexican national. He was residing illegally in the United States without a work contract. The WMC advised Southern Pacific to request an extension of the work contract until Regalado's "alleged citizenship" could be verified. In the meantime, he remained in the Los Angeles County jail.[42]

In a separate case involving another U.S. citizen, twenty-five-year-old Guadalupe Ayala Cardona entered the United States as a Southern Pacific bracero assigned to the Sacramento Division.[43] For the next twelve months, Cardona worked repairing track until two days before Christmas 1944, when he reported to the local draft board with a baptismal document and U.S. birth certificate. The draft board accepted his U.S. citizenship, classified him fit for military duty, and scheduled his induction for January 1945. Because U.S. citizens could not serve as braceros, the railroad company canceled Cardona's work contract. The WMC, however, reinstated the contract, overruling the draft board's decision and disputing his U.S. citizenship. The WMC explained that it refused to relinquish Cardona to the military: "It is the policy of the War Manpower Commission to treat all workers recruited in México and transported to the United States for employment as Mexican Nationals. This position would hold regardless of any statements made or evidence submitted by a worker to the War Manpower Commission or the employer alleging United States citizenship."[44] In the opinion of the WMC, immigration officials—not the draft board—had to determine if Cardona was a U.S. citizen or not. Until immigration ruled, the WMC ordered Cardona to rejoin Southern Pacific and instructed the railroad company to "consider and treat this worker as a Mexican National."[45]

Determined to join the army, Cardona reported for induction; however, the military rejected him for an unknown reason. A week after the rejection, Southern Pacific complied with the WMC and assigned him to bracero section crew 37 in Nelson, California. Back at work with his old company, Cardona now had twenty-five dollars per month of his wages withheld by Southern Pacific for unpaid income taxes required of all U.S. citizens. Immigration officers reported that Cardona had not presented his case for review or applied for citizenship. One official warned that even if Cardona's documents were validated, U.S. citizenship could not be assured. The official thought that "if [Cardona] had been born in Texas and returned to México during his childhood days, there is a possibility that he has lost all of his rights to American citizenship."[46]

These two cases were not atypical. The historical records show that similar situations involving U.S. citizens who used the railroad bracero program to return to their place of birth did in fact occur among the bracero workforce in Idaho, Oregon, and other states. Regardless of citizenship issues and whether they were contracted as braceros or not, workers entered the United States from México in unprecedented numbers after World War II. They immigrated because the ongoing recruitment of braceros for the U.S. farm industry functioned as a "help wanted" sign in México. Immigration also occurred in response to job availability with the railroads. Simply stated, the postwar economic boom meant that many domestic workers turned away from low-salaried and tough jobs, including railroad track maintenance.

Consider Northern Pacific's workforce in Seattle in 1946. Despite hiring 608 new extra gang employees between February and March, 622 men quit, offsetting any gain. The retention of better paid section laborers was slightly better. In this case, the company added 139 new workers, and only 120 left for higher-paying jobs in lumber and logging camps.[47] In the coming year, the availability of maintenance-of-way workers deteriorated to the point that track superintendents warned the company president that recruiting labor had become "serious," particularly on extra gang crews.[48] For this reason, Northern Pacific lobbied Congress in the hopes of having the bracero railroad worker program continue after the war.[49] Other companies struggled with the same issues. On D-Day in 1944, "Mexicans," many of them braceros, held 78 percent of all Southern Pacific track jobs in western railroads. With the braceros gone by 1946, the company struggled to find replacements. The federal government had similar concerns filling critical low-wage railroad jobs in the event of a national emergency. In 1950 federal labor analysts looked at the railroad bracero program and noted that, if necessary, three hundred thousand to four hundred thousand railroad and farm braceros could be contracted from México.[50]

Although the railroad companies introduced more efficient track repair equipment after the war to make better use of fewer laborers, the demand for track workers remained constant. Confronted with finding sufficient workers, railroad companies returned to hiring domestic Mexican and Mexican American laborers. Despite improved wages, finding able workers proved challenging. In 1947 the Association of American Railroads reported that gang workers earned $173.26 and section crews $181.10 per month, compared with farm laborers, who were paid $106 per month.[51] However, crew foremen became selective in hiring, passing over many ex-bracero and Mexican American track workers because they had minimal skills. The railroad work culture had functioned to keep workers of Mexican descent from becoming skilled workers. In the case of the braceros, the program was designed with that same intent and prevented them from attaining any job

seniority over domestic workers. For these reasons Mexican American domestic and ex-bracero railroaders remained unemployed for longer periods
of time than other track workers.

Despite having a harder time securing employment with the railroads,
important postwar Mexican American track communities grew in Pasco,
Washington; Salem, Oregon; Pocatello, Idaho; Sacramento, California; and
elsewhere. Mexican Americans ushered in a new era in railroad track labor history but not because they replaced the braceros. In one generation,
Mexican American railroaders had taken advantage of the benefits that
came with BMWE membership, accumulated job seniority and better jobs,
and in time retired with RRB pensions. In contrast, bracero railroaders may
have hoped for similar job rewards, but the labor program functioned to
deny them these opportunities. In the United States the era of the Mexican
railroad braceros was over. In Washington State the last bracero employed
by Northern Pacific departed from Tacoma on February 10, 1946, starting a
six-day train journey back to México.[52] When the bracero railroad program
began, the New York *Herald Tribune* described the labor program this way:
"What did this brasero [sic] business have that their old jobs lacked? It had
adventure for one thing—a day-coach ride for four days and nights with Un-
cle Sam paying the transportation, a chance to see the wonderful land of the
Gringos, where the poorest peon might possibly become rich."[53]

Despite the absurdity of the *Herald Tribune*'s piece, however, the majority of braceros returned to México with little for their sacrifice for the U.S.
war effort. Some went back maimed, physically and psychologically, and
most with few material gains. At times, U.S. officials consented as railroad
companies violated basic rules of human decency and considered braceros as little more than commodities to be used and replaced as needed. In
a telling example of how braceros were considered differentiated workers,
U.S. officials in 1945 gave the equipment used to fumigate Mexican contract
workers with toxic insecticide to México. The move suggested that the WMC
no longer had any use for the sprayers because the bracero railroad program
had ended.[54] The United States betrayed the railroad workers in their efforts
to recover earned income held by the National Savings Bank in México by
allowing the Mexican government to apply wages and other earned funds to
ends very different from the original intent.

But México had the prime responsibility to protect its own citizen braceros. The Mexican government was well aware of their employment and
living conditions, but in numerous cases it declined to act on their behalf.

The failure to defend the braceros is perplexing, even if México was not in a political position to do anything about it. The failure to act at all was harder to defend. In the years that followed the braceros' return to México, officials responsible for the administration of the labor program gave no indication that it had experienced a crisis of conscience for its role in many of the workers' harsh and disagreeable experiences. In fact, until 1964, Mexican officials continued to permit agricultural braceros to endure many of the same, if not worse, conditions. Although México eventually acknowledged the World War II bracero program, it tailored the official report to tell a story of the program's benefits to the workers and the nation. Looking back, the bracero program failed in many of its original intentions, especially the goal of delivering on México's postrevolutionary dream of placing the country among the world's modern nations. Nonetheless, the railroad braceros command respect. Their work was arduous and made worse as each passing and heavily loaded war train wore out the track. Yet at the cost of human fortitude, and by working in unison, the braceros replaced tie after tie and spike after spike to keep the war trains rolling. As a testimony to their value, U.S. employers across the country agreed that the majority of the bracero railroad workers were excellent and reliable men.

* * *

The bracero program was little more than a labor system of control that extracted the maximum labor from the contracted Mexican workers. Party to a written contract they had no part in negotiating, and often ignored by both governments, the men nevertheless challenged the railroad companies' abuses. For years the railroad braceros, similar to the Japanese Americans who were forcibly removed from their communities and incarcerated during World War II, remained largely silent about their wretched experiences toiling on U.S. track lines during wartime. Regardless of how México contrived the narrative, the men and their families did not forget the injustices experienced in the United States. It is hoped that this book brings some long overdue recognition and remembrance of these Mexican railroad soldiers.

# Epilogue

After more than a half century, México and the United States have missed an opportunity to offer reparations to World War II railroad braceros who never collected their 10 percent wage deductions and compulsory contributions to the Railroad Retirement Board (RRB). Beginning in the late 1990s, activist braceros in México and the United States began to organize, calling public attention to the Mexican government's failure to return all money owed to the braceros. By early 2001 groups of braceros filed several federal lawsuits against the U.S. and Mexican governments, Wells Fargo Bank, and the two Mexican banks entrusted with the braceros' wages.[1] Filed in the Ninth and Fourth U.S. District Courts on behalf of surviving braceros and their heirs, the lawsuit sought to recover all unpaid earnings assigned to the Mexican government. Later, in 2002, these cases were consolidated and reassigned to the Ninth U.S. District Court in California.

Both governments immediately opposed the braceros' claims and asked the court to dismiss the allegations. Notwithstanding the historical record discussed throughout this book, México initially denied any knowledge of lost earnings and claimed immunity from foreign courts. The United States, in turn, argued that the Mexican judicial system was the proper venue for the lawsuit. In 2002 the court dismissed the braceros' lawsuit without examining the merits of the case. The judge's ruling was based on two legal points. Although U.S. law after 1952 rescinded immunity to foreign governments from legal claims, the revocation was not retroactive to the 1940s. The court also ruled that the braceros had failed to file legal claims for the unpaid earnings within six years after they became aware of their lost income. In effect, the court ruled that México was immune and the braceros had missed the deadline for filing their claims. The court also threw out claims against the United States and Wells Fargo Bank, claiming the government and the bank had not violated the braceros' rights.

Although the court's ruling was a disappointment to many, the back pay issue did not end there. In a way, the ruling vindicated the braceros' claims and strengthened their determination to continue to recoup their lost income. The *San Francisco Chronicle* reported that the presiding judge had little doubt "many braceros never received savings fund withholdings to which they were entitled." The judge expressed some compassion for the aged workers: "The court is sympathetic to the braceros' situation. However, just as a court's power to correct injustice is derived from the law, a court's power is circumscribed by the law as well."[2] The legal and political effort to keep the issue of lost bracero earnings alive persisted beyond 2002. Section 354.7 of the California Code of Civil Procedure ("Braceros, heirs, beneficiaries of braceros, right of action for recovery of savings fund amounts; limitations; severability of provisions") allowed former braceros, their heirs, and other benefactors to bring legal action to recover any unpaid wages. This law, which was effective September 2002 through December 2005, applied to braceros contracted to the United States between January 1942 and January 1950.

In 2004, after México's repeated denials of any wrongdoing, hundreds of braceros protested at President Vicente Fox's ranch in Guanajuato, demanding the return of their earnings. This public incident was effective in convincing México to agree to pay approximately thirty-five hundred dollars (U.S.) to each bracero or descendants able to prove employment in the United States between 1942 and 1946.[3] Considering that interest accrued over fifty-plus years, and the fact that some braceros renewed their contracts more than once, the payment was more symbolic than an official atonement. Although México offered compensation to the World War II braceros, it refused to acknowledge or accept any responsibility for the mishandling of the men's earnings. Contrary to documents in México's national archives, the Mexican government initially maintained that there was no documentation supporting the braceros' claim.

However, in 2002 the head of México's National Archives acknowledged that the two national banks in México received in excess of 168 million pesos in bracero savings contributions but only paid out 149.2 million pesos. As has been pointed out, the actual owners of the savings accounts did not always receive their share of the 149.2 million pesos paid by the banks. The director of the National Archives stated: "It is also unclear what, if anything, was ultimately done with the funds that remained unclaimed as of 1946 in the two government-owned savings banks." Regarding the railroad braceros, the director added that as late as 1948, the Mexican government publically announced that nine thousand savings accounts remained in the National Savings Bank. "However, there is no subsequent record of how many of these individuals responded to this notice, or what happened to those amounts, the archives contain no further information on this subject with respect to either the railroad or agricultural braceros."[4]

The U.S. lawsuit and México's offer of compensation represent another disappointing chapter in the long overdue redress of unjust treatment and swindling of World War II braceros. To qualify for payment, México required each petitioner to present original documents in a matter of weeks proving their employment in the United States, along with apostille copies of personal records. Almost sixty years after the bracero program began, the majority of the men and their heirs found it impossible to locate authentic documentation, leaving them empty-handed. The failure of the majority to meet the requirements outlined by México was too reminiscent of the 1940s, when braceros first began experiencing difficulties withdrawing their saved earnings from the national savings banks. The braceros' legal and political maneuverings to win decades-old back pay served to lay bare the unjust treatment and inconvenient truths of the World War II bracero labor programs. Sadly, the men who began to organize in México for the return of their lost income—and the braceros who filed the lawsuit in 2001—have aged and will probably never receive full monetary compensation for their sacrifice working in U.S. farms and on the railroads. Still, it is hoped that someday their successors may be able to finally bring closure to this historical controversy and settle their grievances against the United States and in particular México.

# Notes

## Preface and Acknowledgments

1 These statistics are from *Railway Age* 118 (April 28, 1945): 747.

## Introduction

1 México was not the sole supplier of contracted foreign labor to the United States during World War II; Costa Rica, Jamaica, Bahamas, Barbados, Honduras, and Canada had similar labor agreements. Puerto Ricans also traveled to the mainland as contracted laborers under similar conditions, but not as foreign workers.

2 Ana Elizabeth Rosas, *Abrazando el Espíritu: Bracero Families Confront the US-Mexico Border* (Oakland: University of California Press, 2014), 28–29.

3 Kitty Calavita, *Inside the State: The Bracero Program, Immigration, and the INS* (New York: Routledge, 1992), 181.

4 Rosas, *Abrazando el Espíritu*, 38.

5 Natalia Molina, *How Race Is Made in America: Immigration, Citizenship, and the Historical Power of Racial Scripts* (Oakland: University of California Press, 2014), 6–11.

6 Historians are challenged in constructing the history of the railroad braceros because few survivors remain and firsthand accounts of the wartime braceros are limited. Where the official records of the labor program exist, they are primarily administrative. This is not necessarily an issue regarding the postwar bracero years.

## Chapter 1. Labor and the Railroad Industry before World War II

1 Thomas G. Edwards and Carlos A. Schwantes, *Experiences in a Promised Land: Essays in Pacific Northwest History* (Seattle: University of Washington Press, 1986), 100.

2 Ibid., 10–16.

3 Carlos A. Schwantes, *Railroad Signatures across the Pacific Northwest* (Seattle: University of Washington Press, 1993), 96.

4 Ibid., 22, 8.

5 Sucheng Chan, *Asian Americans: An Interpretive History* (Boston: Twayne Publishers, 1991), 38.

6 Earl Pomeroy, *The Pacific Slope: A History of California, Oregon, Washington, Idaho, and Nevada* (Seattle: University of Washington Press, 1973), 269.

7 William Thomas White, "A History of Railroad Workers in the Pacific Northwest, 1882–1934" (PhD dissertation, University of Washington, 1980), 173.

8 Ibid., 167.

9 Ibid., 184.

10 U.S. Congress, House of Representatives, Hearings before the Committee on Im-

migration and Naturalization, "To Limit the Immigration of Aliens to the United States, and for Other Purposes," 71st Congress, 2nd session, 1930, 347.

11 White, "History of Railroad Workers," 215.

12 Ibid., 216.

13 Herbert R. Northrup, *Organized Labor and the Negro* (New York: Harper and Brothers, 1944), 261n.

14 Ibid., 261.

15 U.S. Congress, House, Hearings before the Committee on Immigration and Naturalization, 1928, p. 402.

16 U.S. Congress, House of Representatives, Hearings before the Committee on Immigration and Naturalization, "Immigration from Countries of the Western Hemisphere," 70th Congress, 1st session, 1928, p. 391.

17 U.S. Immigration Commission, "Immigrants in Industries," Part 25, Immigration Hearings, Reports of the Immigration Commission (Washington, D.C.: Government Printing Office, 1911), 31.

18 U.S. Congress, House, Hearings before the Committee on Immigration and Naturalization, 1928, p. 406.

19 Michael M. Smith, *The Mexicans in Oklahoma* (Norman: University of Oklahoma Press, 1980), 25.

20 Ibid., 35.

21 U.S. Congress, House, Hearings before the Committee on Immigration and Naturalization, 1930, pp. 104, 113.

22 Mark Reisler, "The Mexican Immigrant in the Chicago Area during the 1920s," *Journal of the Illinois State Historical Society* 66 (193): 144–58; 147.

23 Dionicio Nodin Valdez, *Barrios Norteños: St. Paul and Midwestern Mexican Communities in the Twentieth Century* (Austin: University of Texas Press, 2000), 28.

24 *Railway Age* 115, no. 9 (August 28, 1943): 356. The term *bracero* is used to refer to Mexican contracted laborers recruited in México for employment in the U.S. The term is derived from the word *brazo* ("arm").

25 U.S. Congress, House, Hearings before the Committee on Immigration and Naturalization, 1930, p. 355.

26 Ibid., 113.

27 Charles Soto Sánchez, "Alien's Personal History and Statement," June 11, 1942, Selective Service System, Washington State Headquarters, Tacoma, Washington, Folder: Yakima County Local Board No., 1, Sunnyside, Box, 10, NARA Region 12, Selective Service System, RG 147, NARA.

28 Ibid.

29 Ibid.

30 Paul S. Taylor, *Mexican Labor in the United States: Bethlehem, Pennsylvania* (Berkeley: University of California Press, 1931), 257–63.

31 Ibid., 82.

32 U.S. Congress, House, Hearings before the Committee on Immigration and Naturalization, 1930, p. 350.

33 As quoted in Erasmo Gamboa, *Voces Hispanas / Hispanic Voices of Idaho: Excerpts from the Idaho Hispanic Oral History Project* (Boise: Idaho Humanities Council, 1992), 12.

34 Patricia K. Ourada, *Migrant Workers in Idaho* (Boise: Boise State University: 1979), 17.

35  Sánchez, "Alien's Personal History and Statement."
36  Pomeroy, *Pacific Slope*, 281.
37  U.S. Congress, House, Hearings before the Committee on Immigration and Naturalization, 1928, p. 410.
38  U.S. Congress, House, Hearings before the Committee on Immigration and Naturalization, 1930, p. 371.
39  Ibid., 371.
40  Ibid., 119.

## Chapter 2. The Great Depression, Deportations, and Recovery

1   Joseph R. Rose, *American Wartime Transportation* (New York: Thomas Y. Crowell Company, 1953), 31.
2   Ibid., 33–35.
3   Ibid., 21, 143.
4   David Goldfield, Carl Abbott, Virginia D. Anderson, Jo Ann E. Argensinger, Peter H. Argensinger, William L. Barney, Robert M. Weir, *The American Journey*, second edition (Upper Saddle River: Prentice Hall, 2000), 762.
5   Gregory L. Thompson, "The Interwar Response of the Southern Pacific Company and the Atchison, Topeka, and Santa Fe Railway to Passenger Road Competition," *Business and Economic History* 25, no. 1 (Fall 1996): 288.
6   Northrup, *Organized Labor and the Negro*, 51.
7   D. W. Hertel, *History of the Brotherhood of Maintenance of Way Employees: Its Birth and Growth* (Washington, D.C.: Ransdell, 1955), 137.
8   Rose, *American Wartime Transportation*, 37.
9   Northrup, *Organized Labor and the Negro*, 51.
10  Hertel, *History of the Brotherhood*, 146.
11  Ibid., 7, 57.
12  Ibid., 11, 120.
13  Kevin Stan, *Endangered Dreams: The Great Depression in California* (New York: Oxford University Press, 1996), 64.
14  The federal census only counted persons born in México. The federal count placed all other persons of Mexican descent in the Pacific Northwest in an amorphous category called "other."
15  Paul H. Landis, "Rural Population Trends in Washington," *Washington State College of Agriculture Experimental Station Bulletin* (Pullman, Washington), no. 333 (July 1936): 62.
16  See Juanita Zazueta Huerta, "World War I and the Making of the Mexican American Community in Eastern Idaho" in *Voces Hispanas / Hispanic Voices of Idaho: Excerpts from the Idaho Hispanic Oral History Project*, edited by Erasmo Gamboa (Boise: Idaho Humanities Council, 1992), 13.
17  Erasmo Gamboa, "Mexican American Railroaders in an American City: Pocatello, Idaho," in *Latinos in Idaho Celebrando Cultura*, edited by Robert McCarl, 35–43 (Boise: Idaho Humanities Council, 2003), 38–39.
18  Ibid., 11, 120.
19  Barbara Driscoll, *The Tracks North: The Railroad Bracero Program of World War II* (Austin: University of Texas Press, 1999), 47.
20  Ibid., 18, 155; see also Abraham Hoffman, *Unwanted Mexican Americans in the*

*Great Depression: Repatriation Pressures, 1929–1939* (Tucson: University of Arizona Press, 1974), 87.

21 U.S. Congress, House of Representatives, Hearings before the Committee on Immigration and Naturalization, 1930, p. 369.
22 One writer states that Mexicans accounted for 45.5 percent of all deportees between 1933 and 1937. Luisa Moreno, "Caravans of Sorrow: Noncitizen Americans of the Southwest," in David G. Gutierrez ed., *Between Two Worlds: Mexican Immigrants in the United States* (Wilmington: Scholarly Resources, 1996), 121–24.
23 Hoffman, *Unwanted Mexican Americans*, 148–50.
24 Thomas E. Sheridan, "La Crisis," in *U.S.-Mexico Borderlands: Historical and Contemporary Perspectives*, edited by Oscar J. Martínez (Wilmington: Scholarly Resources, 1996), 163.
25 Rose, *American Wartime Transportation*, 37.
26 Don L. Hofsommer, *The Southern Pacific, 1901–1985* (College Station: Texas A&M University Press, 1986), 148.
27 Ibid., 40, 150.
28 Ibid.
29 Ibid., 48–49, 150.
30 Ibid., 41, 150.
31 Ibid., 11, 126.
32 Ibid., 11, 201.
33 Ibid., 112.
34 Ibid., 11, 201.
35 Ibid., 112.

## Chapter 3. We Will Need the Mexicans Back

1 Blanca Torres, *Historia de la Revolución Mexicana, 1940–1952: México en la segunda guerra mundial* (México City: El Colegio de México, 1979), 69.
2 Michael Mathes, "The Two Californias during World War II," *California Historical Quarterly* 44, no.4 (1965): 325.
3 Alfonso Taracena, *La vida en México bajo Ávila Camacho* (México City: Editorial Jus, 1976), 204.
4 Torres, *Historia de la Revolución Mexicana*, 136.
5 Lyndon I. Daly, "A History of the [United States] Railroad Mission in México, 1942–1946" (MS thesis, Texas College of Arts and Industries, 1965), 4.
6 Ibid., 25.
7 Daly, "History of the [United States] Railroad Mission," 17–19.
8 Sandra Kuntz Ficker and Paolo Riguzzi, *Ferrocarriles y vida económica en México* (1850–1950) (Austin: University of Texas Press, 1999), 224.
9 Daly, "History of the [United States] Railroad Mission," 25.
10 Ibid., 59.
11 Ficker and Riguzzi, *Ferrocarriles y vida económica*, 85.
12 Ibid., 70.
13 Ibid., 75.
14 Daly, "History of the [United States] Railroad Mission," 113.
15 Ibid., 120.
16 Ficker and Riguzzi, *Ferrocarriles y vida económica*, 297.

17  Driscoll, *Tracks North*, 97.
18  Daly, "History of the [United States] Railroad Mission," 116.
19  Congress largely closed Asian immigration to the United States by World War I. Likewise, Filipino emigration to the United States was limited to a mere 150 persons a year by 1935.
20  "Ng Ah Foo, June 10, 1911," Document No. 101, Chinese Exclusion Files, Oregon District, Records of the District Courts of the U.S., 1839–1992, National Archives Administration Records, Region 12, Seattle.
21  Linda C. Majka and Theo J. Majka, *Farmworkers and the State* (Temple University: Philadelphia, 1982), 138.

## Chapter 4. Railroad Track Workers Needed; Where Are the Domestic Laborers?

1   S. Kip Farrington Jr., *Railroads at War* (New York: Samuel Curl, 1944), 5.
2   Ibid., 142.
3   Ibid., 7.
4   Ibid., 201.
5   Ibid., 112.
6   Driscoll, *Tracks North*, 61.
7   Ibid., 21, 174.
8   Ibid., 30, 111.
9   Ibid., 20, 159.
10  Farrington, *Railroads at War*, 90, 149.
11  Ibid., 121,134.
12  Ibid., 7, 38.
13  Ibid., 38
14  U.S. Congress, House of Representatives, Hearings before the Committee on Immigration and Naturalization, 1928.
15  Hofsommer, *Southern Pacific*, 201.
16  Interview with Arnulfo Álvarez, October 28, 2000, Pocatello, Idaho.
17  See Frances Wadsworth Valentine, "Women's Emergency Farm Service on the Pacific Coast in 1943," *Bulletin of the Women's Bureau*, no. 204 (1945): 1–35.
18  *Southern Pacific Bulletin* (April 1943): 6.
19  George B. Harrington to E. J. Connors, January 5, 1945, Folder: General, Box 63, RG 219, Records of Defense Transportation, NARA.
20  "Historical Data in Connection with Employment of Mexican National Laborers Imported From Mexico," California State Railroad Museum Library, 2, 41.
21  Jonas A. McBride to A. E. Lyon, May 18, 1944, Folder: Lyon A.E., Box 11, RG 211, Records of the WMC, NARA.
22  "Historical Data in Connection with Employment of Mexican National Laborers Imported From Mexico," 2.
23  Ibid., 3.
24  Carey McWilliams, "Report on Importation of Negro Labor to California," Folder: RR Workers, Box 20, Entry 89, RG 211, Records of the WMC, NARA.
25  Fair Employment Practices Committee, Folder: Discrimination, Box 4, Entry 23, RG 211, Records of the WMC, NARA.
26  "The Railroad Manpower Situation," Folder: RR Workers, Box 20, RG 211, Records of the WMC, NARA.

### Chapter 5. Bracero Railroaders, "Soldiers of Democracy"

1   As mentioned in *Southern Pacific Bulletin* (August 1943), 2.
2   W. L. Mitchell to John J. Corson, July 23, 1942, Folder: RRB 1942, Box 8, Entry 191, RG 211, Records of the WMC, NARA.
3   T. J. Finneran to E. E. Milliman, August 1, 1942, Folder: RRB 1942, Box 8, Entry 191, RG 211, Records of the WMC, NARA.
4   Ibid.
5   George S. Messersmith to His Excellency, April 29, 1943, Box 38884, RG 59, General Records of the Department of State, NARA.
6   "Mexican Nationals Brought in for Railroad Track-Labor: A Temporary War-Emergency Measure 1943–1946, June 1946," Records of the Reports and Analysis Service, Box 3, RG 211, Records of the WMC, NARA.
7   "Summer Brings the Mexican," *Commonwealth* 48 (July 2, 1948): 277.
8   Gamio discusses how Mexicans can improve themselves through immigration in Manuel Gamio, *Mexican Immigration to the United States* (Chicago: University of Chicago Press, 1930).
9   David A. Pfeiffer, "Riding the Rails Up Paper Mountain: Researching Railroad Records in the National Archives Part Two," *Prologue* 29, no. 1 (Spring 1997): 2.
10  Secretaría del Trabajo y Previsión Social, *Los braceros* (México: Dirección de Previsión Social, 1946), 61, in AGN, México, D.F.
11  Gabriel Ward Lasker, "Environmental Growth and Selective Migration," *Human Biology: An International Record of Human Biology* 24, no. 4 (December 1952): 262–89; 264.
12  Memorandum, Harry F. Brown to Robert McGregor, June 10, 1943, Foreign Service Posts of the Department of State, México City Embassy, General Records, RG 84.
13  Gurría as quoted in *Southern Pacific Bulletin* (June 1943): 7.
14  *El popular*, October 21, 1944.
15  Ibid.
16  Robert G. McGregor to Joseph F. McGurk, August 12, 1943, Foreign Service Posts of the Department of State, México City Embassy, General Records, 1937–1949, RG 84.
17  Ibid., translation by the U.S. government.

### Chapter 6. Contractual Promises to Keep

1   See Erasmo Gamboa, *Mexican Labor and World War II: Braceros in the Pacific Northwest, 1942–1947* (Austin: University of Texas Press, 1990).
2   Luis Fernández, *Los Braceros* (México: Secretaría del Trabajo y Previsión Social, 1946), 75.
3   "Pacific Fruit Express Company, Roseville, California," Folder: Railroad Retirement Board Complaints, 1945, Box 8, Entry 191, Records of the WMC, RG 211, NARA.
4   "Exhibit 15," Folder: Mexican Track Labor, Box 3, Records of the WMC, RG 211, NARA.
5   The complaint by Armando Suárez Rodríguez is cited in this 1943 letter: Robert L. Clark to J. F. McGurk, November 3, 1943, Folder: Mexican Labor 859.4, Box 489, México General Records, RG 84, NARA.

6 Mexican Importation Committee "Region XII," Series 269, Box 31, Records of the WMC, RG 211, NARA.

7 Michael F. Potter, "The History or Bedbug Management," *Thermal Remediation, Pest Control Technology* (August 2008): 3–6.

8 Regional director to Chicago Burlington and Quincy Railroad, September 27, 1944, Folder: RRB Complaints, 1944, Box 8, Records of the WMC, RG 211, NARA.

9 RRB Inspection Reports 1943, Box 8, Records of the WMC, RG 211, NARA.

10 John F. Alexander, December 28, 1944, Folder: Mexican Track Workers, General, Box 2965, Records of the WMC, RG 211, NARA.

11 W. J. Macklin to B. M. Brown, October 31, 1944, Folder: RRB Complaints, Entry 191, Box 8, Records of the WMC, RG 211, NARA.

12 Folder: RRB Complaints, Mexican Track Labor Program, 1943–1946, Box 3, Entry 119, Records of the WMC, RG 211, NARA.

13 Folder: "Gangs" Miscellaneous Reports, 1943, Region XII Regional/Central Files, 1942–1945, Box 2964, Series 269, Records of the WMC, RG 211, NARA.

14 W. J. Macklin to E. E. McCarty, August 13, 1943, Region XII, Box 38, Records of the WMC, RG 211, NARA.

15 García Sebastián Pérez, *Rostros y rastros: Entrevistas a trabajadores migrantes en Estados Unidos* (San Luis Potosí: El Colegio de San Luis, 2002), 35.

16 "Hoja de Instrucciones para los Mexicanos bajo Contrato con la War Manpower Administration," Folder: OPA Instructions, Box 7, Records of the WMC, RG 211, NARA.

17 Sidney R. Macklin to WMC, November 16, 1943, Folder: Rationing Mexicans, Threlkeld Commissary Company 1943, Box 2972, Records of the WMC, RG 211, NARA.

18 R. J. Gammie to WMC, September 16, 1943, Region XII Mexican Importation Committee, Box 31, Records of the WMC, RG 211, NARA.

19 RRB Inspection Reports 1943, Box 8, Records of the WMC, RG 211, NARA.

20 Memorandum, John P. Gifford and George E. Bodle to W. K. Hopkins, July 30, 1943, Folder: "Mexican Workers, General Correspondence," 1943, Region XII, Box 37, Records of the WMC, RG 211, NARA.

21 Ibid.; RRB Inspection Reports 1943, Box 8, Records of the WMC, RG 211, NARA.

22 Memorandum, John P. Gifford and George E. Bodle to W. K. Hopkins, July 30, 1943, Folder: "Mexican Workers, General Correspondence," 1943, Region XII, Box 37, Records of the WMC, RG 211, NARA.

23 Ibid.

24 Dirección de Previsión Social, Expediente 6, Office Files of the WMC in México, 1943–46, Box 5 Entry 196, Records of the WMC, RG 211, NARA.

25 Minutes of Meeting of Committee on Mexican Importation Program, August 4, 1943, File: Mexican Nationals, Box 2916, Series 2916, Records of the WMC, RG 211, NARA.

26 William K. Hopkins to H. R. Harnish, June 22, 1943, Folder: Mexican Complaints, Box 2964. Mexican Track Labor Program, Folder: Commissary Charges, Box 20.Both in Records of the WMC, RG 211, NARA.

27 Memorandum, John P. Gifford and George E. Bodle to W.K. Hopkins, July 30, 1943, Folder: "Mexican Workers, General Correspondence," 1943, Region XII, Box 37, Records of the WMC, RG 211, NARA.

28 *W. K.* Hopkins to Lawrence A. Appley, Aug., 23, 1943, Folder: Individual Persons, Box 2968, Records of the WMC, RG 211, NARA.

29  Pérez, *Rostros y rastros*, 23.
30  Eugenio Aza, Consul, to War Manpower Commission, June 18, 1943, Folder: "Mexican Complaints, etc.," Box 2964, Series 269, Records of the WMC, RG 211, NARA.
31  *W. F. Northway to Claude L. Kemp, June 29, 1943, Folder: Various, Box 2967, Series 269, Region XII,* Records of the WMC, RG 211, NARA.
32  H. L. Carter to John D. Coates, October 17, 1945, Folder: RRB Complaints 1945, Box 8, Records of the WMC, RG 211, NARA.
33  E. W. Engle to W. E. MacLean, March 23, 1944, Box 3885, General Records of the Department of State, RG 59, NARA.
34  M. Parks, "A New Pattern in International Wartime Collaboration," *State Department Bulletin* (August 13, 1944): 160–65; 163.
35  Office Files of the WMC Representative in México, 1943–1946, Entry 196, Box 5, Records of the WMC, RG 211, NARA.
36  Gamio as quoted in his report *Boletín del Archivo General de la Nacion* (México D.F.) third series, 4, no. 4 (1980): 38–40.
37  Memorandum, "Handling of Mexican Nationals Employed by Southern Pacific Lines," August 27, 1943, Folder: RRB Complaints, Entry 191, Box 8, Records of the WMC, RG 211, NARA, p. 3.
38  Memorandum, July 13, 1943, Folder: Chinese Laborers for the U.S., Box 350, General Records of the Embassy in México City, RG 84, NARA.
39  Zach L. Cobb to Mr. Hughes, February 25, 1944, Box 3885, General Records of the Department of State, RG 59, NARA.
40  M. C. Threlkeld Jr. to American Ambassador, July 15, 1943, Folder: Chinese Laborers for the U.S., Box 350, General Records of the Embassy in México City, RG 84, NARA.
41  Decimal File 1940–44, Box 3887, General Records of the Department of State, RG 59, NARA.
42  M.C. Threlkeld Jr., to American Ambassador, July 15, 1943, General Records of the Embassy in México City, RG 84, NARA.
43  Zach L. Cobb to Mr. Hughes, February 25, 1944, Box 3885, General Records of the Department of State, RG 59, NARA.
44  Gamboa, *Voces Hispanas / Hispanic Voices*, 10.

## Chapter 7. The Perils of Being a Bracero

1   George E. Bodle to W. K. Hopkins July 31, 1943, Folder: Agencies, Housing, and Transportation, Region XII, Box 22, Records of the WMC, RG 211, NARA.
2   "Individual Work Agreement," Records of the War Manpower Administration, Folder: Foreign Workers, Entry 155, Box 22, Records of the WMC, RG 211, NARA.
3   Torres, *Historia de la Revolución Mexicana*, 261.
4   John P. Gifford to W. K. Hopkins July 30, 1943, Mexican Importation 1943, Box 37, Series 269, Records of the WMC, RG 211, NARA.
5   Luis Fernández, *Los Braceros* (México City: Secretaría del Trabajo y Previsión Social, 1946), 61.
6   Lasker, "Environmental Growth and Selective Migration," 264.
7   Nathan L. Whetten, *Rural Mexico* (Chicago: University of Chicago Press, 1948), 363–64.
8   Manuel Barajas, *The Xaripu Community: Across Borders: Labor Migration, Com-*

*munity, and Family* (Notre Dame: University of Notre Dame Press, 2009), 80.

9   Manuel Gamio, *Hacia un México nuevo: Problemas sociales* (México City: Instituto Indigenista Nacional, 1935), 53–54.

10  Whetten, *Rural Mexico*, 364.

11  See Lynn Stephen, *Transborder Lives: Indigenous Oaxacans in México, California, and Oregon* (Durham: Duke University Press, 2007), 57.

12  Directive 21, September 3, 1943, Farm Labor, Folder: Discrimination Records of Executive Director, April 42–January 46, CIO, Box 4, Records of the WMC, RG 211, NARA.

13  Hofsommer, *Southern Pacific*, 202.

14  Labor Research Association, *Labor and the War: Labor Fact Book* (New York: International Publishers, 1943), 64.

15  Al Henry to M. C. LaBerteu, January 10, 1942, File Aliens, Box 137 G 6.7.LB, NPR Chief of Labor Relations Records, MHS, Saint Paul, Minnesota.

16  C. O. Jenks to F. J. Gavin, March 9, 1942, Presidents Subject File, 137.E6. (F) NPR President Files, MHS, Saint Paul, Minnesota.

17  W. T. Kennelly to M. V. Wicks, December 12, 1945, File Aliens, Box 136 B.14.5–137, NPR Chief of Labor Relations Records, MHS, Saint Paul Minnesota.

18  "Final Accountability, Topaz Japanese American Relocation Center Digital Collection," Digital Collections, Utah State University Library, Logan, Utah, p. 195.

19  Presidential Subject File No. 367–20, Folder 2, NPR President Files, MHS, Saint Paul, Minnesota.

20  Torres, *Historia de la Revolución Mexicana*, 255.

21  E. H. Price to W. J. Macklin, August 31, 1943, Folder: RRB Complaints, Box 8, Entry 191, Records of the WMC, RG 211, NARA.

22  Mexican Civic Committee of the West Side of Chicago to President Camacho, January 17, 1944, "El Problema de los braceros en el periodo de 1942 a 1946," *Boletín del archivo de la nación*, (México) third series, 4, no. 4 (October–December 1980), 28.

23  Charles Taft to Mr. Kelly, February 16, 1944, Decimal File 1940–44, Box 3885, General Records of the Department of the State, RG 59, NARA.

24  W. J. Macklin to Director of Employment and Claims, September 7, 1943, Folder: Region XII Mexican Importation Committee 1943, Box 31, Series 269, Records of the WMC, RG 211, NARA.

25  M. C. Berton to C. E. Denny, October 8, 1942, File 1389A-7 N.P. Presidents Subject File, NPR President Files, MHS, Saint Paul, Minnesota.

26  See, for instance, the cases of Salvador Vásquez Huante, who died of heat prostration in Ligurta, Arizona, on June 20, 1943; Antonio Osorio Amaro, who succumbed to heat in Growler, Arizona, on July 27, 1943; Hipólito C. Carrillo, who suffered a sunstroke in Edom, California, on August 3 1943; Salvador S. Ramírez's death was attributed to heat in Araby, Arizona, on July 27, 1943; and Juan Sánchez Muñoz, who perished due to heat prostration on July 28, 1943, in Emporia, Kansas. Samuel B. Hough to Silvestre Navarro, August 6, 1943, Office File of the WMC Representative in México, 1943–1946, Entry 196, Box 5, Records of the WMC, RG 211, NARA.

27  "Pacific Lines," *Southern Pacific Bulletin*, August 1944, 13.

28  "Instrucciones de seguridad para trabajadores Mexicanos," Northern Pacific Railway, 1943, author's collection.

29  "Pacific Lines," *Southern Pacific Bulletin*, November 1944, 10.

30  "Historical Data in Connection with Employment of Mexican National Laborers Imported From Mexico," Southern Pacific Railroad, California State Railroad Museum Library, Sacramento, California, p. 68.

31  Southern Pacific to Alfredo Elías Calles, March 20, 1944, Folder: Mexican Track Workers, Box 2965, Records of the WMC, RG 211, NARA.

32  L. P. Hopkins to James H. Bagan, April 9, 1945, Folder: Mexican Track Workers General, Box 2965, Records of the WMC, RG 211, NARA.

33  The reports of these and other deaths can be found in Folder: Mexican Track Workers, Box 2965, WMC Series 269, Records of the WMC, RG 211, NARA. Similar reports can be found in Folder: Death of Mexican Nationals 1943–1945, Box 3, Entry 196, Records of the WMC, RG 211, NARA.

34  C. E. Denny to Carlos Grimm, January 1, 1946, Folder 2: President's Subject File No. 368, NPR President Files, MHS, Saint Paul, Minnesota.

35  Southern Pacific to WMC México, Telegram, March 1944, Folder: Daily File, March 1944, Box 8, Entry 190, Records of the WMC, RG 211, NARA.

36  Meeting with Lumber and Lumber Products Division, April 7, 1945, Office of Deputy Director, Folder Cross Tie Campaign, Box 11, RG 219, NARA.

37  "Historical Data in Connection with Employment of Mexican National Laborers Imported From Mexico," 32.

38  A. F. Whitney, *Wartime Wages and Railroad Labor: A Report on the 1942–43 Wage Movement of the Transportation Brotherhoods* (Cleveland: Brotherhood of Railroad Trainmen, 1944), 109.

39  WMC México to Secretaría del Trabajo y Previsión Social, June 18, 1945, Folder: Daily File June 1945, Box 3, Entry 196, Records of the WMC, RG 211, NARA.

40  Inventory of Hernández's possessions can be found in the folder Mexican Track Worker Deaths, Division Office Files, Box 2695, Records of the WMC, RG 211, NARA.

41  F. W. Hunter to Charles M. Hay December 11, 1944, Folder: Mexican Track Worker Deaths, Series 296, Records of the WMC, RG 211, NARA. William A. Anglin to William R. Buie, August 23, 1946, Folder: Mexican Labor, Box 38, entry 8, RG 224, NARA.

42  Samuel B. Hough to Silvestre Navarro, August 6, 1943, Office File of the WMC Representative in México 1943–1946, Entry 196, Box 5, Records of the WMC, RG 211, NARA.

43  Southern Pacific to Alfredo Elías Calles, March 20, 1944, Folder: Mexican Track Workers, Box 2965, WMC Series 269, Records of the WMC, RG 211, NARA.

44  Elpidia Macías de Casas to Consul de México Kansas City, August 28, 1943, Office Files of WMC Representative in México 1943–1946, Entry 196, Box 5, Records of the WMC, RG 211, NARA.

45  WMC México to Secretaría del Trabajo y Previsión Social, June 1945, Folder: Daily File, June 1945, Entry 196, Box 3, Records of the WMC, RG 211, NARA.

46  H. G. Pett to Churchill Murray, December 11, 1945, Folder: Northern Pacific RR, entry 196, Box 6, Records of the WMC, RG 211, NARA.

47  WMC México to RRB, September 4, 1945, Folder Daily File, September 1945, Box 8, Entry 190, Records of the WMC, RG 211, NARA.

48  Telegram WMC to WMC México, December 11, 1945, Folder: Daily File, December 1945, Box 6, Entry 196, Records of the WMC, RG 211, NARA.

49 Churchill Murray to Luis Fernández del Capo, January 27, 1945, Folder: Daily File, January 1945, Box 2, Entry 196, Records of the WMC, RG 211, NARA.

50 WMC to Director Previsión Social, June 25, 1945, Folder: Daily File, June 1945, Box 3, Entry 196, Records of the WMC, RG 211, NARA.

51 Chief of Special Agents to H.W.M., Telegram 11/26/45, Folder: Files of Mexican Nationals Correspondence and Records, December 1945, Presidents Subject File, 137.E6. (F) NPR President Files, MHS, Saint Paul, Minnesota.

52 Thelma Bender to George H. Kilborn, August 10, 1943, Folder: Mexican Railroad Worker Deaths, Division Files, Box 2964, Records of the WMC, RG 211, NARA.

53 *Josefa C. de Gómez to Secretaría de Relaciones Exteriores*, August 10, 1943, Folder: Atchison, Topeka, Santa Fe Claims, Entry 196, Box 1, Records of the WMC, RG 211, NARA.

54 Taylor, *Mexican Labor in the United States*, 183.

55 Fernández, *Los Braceros*, 119–20.

56 "Historical Data in Connection with Employment of Mexican National Laborers Imported From Mexico," 68.

57 "Various Expenses Incurred in Connection with the Recruiting, Transportation, and Employment of Mexicans, August 1943-February 1946," March 12, 1947, Folder 1, N.P. Presidents Subject File, Mo. 367–20, NPR President Files, MHS, Saint Paul, Minnesota.

58 Paul J. Revely to Guy Ray, September 4, 1946, Mexican Labor, Box 730, México City Embassy, General Records, RG 84, NARA.

## Chapter 8. The Deception Further Exposed

1 For instance, the binational agreement stipulated that the U.S. government was required to pay Mexican track workers when work was not available. Domestic unionized track workers had no such stipulation in their contract with the railroad companies.

2 Meeting, August 19, 1943, in Los Angeles, Relative to Mexicans Nationals in Railroad Employment, Series 269, Mexican Importation Committee Meetings, Box 2901, Records of the WMC, RG 211, NARA.

3 Ibid.

4 Ibid.

5 Luis Fernández, *Los Braceros* (México D.F.: Secretaría del Trabajo y Previsión Social, 1946), 23.

6 These dispatches are found in Robert G. McGregor Jr. to William G. MacLean, August 10, 1943, Box 3883, General Records Department of State, RG 59, NARA. And in William A. Anglin to Philip G. Burton, August, 26, 1944, Entry 6, Box 18, Office of Labor, RG 224, NARA.

7 Churchill Murray to John D. Coates, January 9, 1945, 1945 Daily File Feb 1945, Office Files of WMC Representative in México, 1943–46, Box 2, Records of the WMC, RG 211, NARA.

8 Enrique A. Lozano to C. Fidel Velásquez, "El problema de los braceros," *El boletín*, October 3, 1944, p. 28.

9 Expediente 73–101/662–1, Folder: RRB Complaints 1944, Records of the WMC, RG 211, NARA.

10 Churchill Murray to Jorge L. Medellín Feb. 11, 1945 Daily File Feb 1945, Office Files

of WMC Representative in México, 1943–46, Box 2, Records of the WMC, RG 211, NARA.

11   Lozano and Velásquez, "El problema de los braceros," 29.

12   *Southern Pacific Bulletin*, October, 1943, 6.

13   W. J. Macklin RRB to E. E. McCarty, Atchison, Topeka and Santa Fe Railway, August 13, 1943, Records of the WMC, RG 211, NARA.

14   Memorándum Para El SR. Presidente De La República, November 2, 1944, 546.6/120, Camacho Manuel Ávila (187), Archivo General de la Nación (AGN).

15   Regional Director Report, October 26, 1944, Folder: Railroad Workers, Box 20, Records of the WMC, RG 211, NARA.

16   G. C. Peterson to E. B. Miller, May 3, 1945, Folder: RRB Complaints, Box 8, Records of the WMC, RG 211, NARA.

17   Inspection Report SPSRR, November 11, 1944, Folder: RRB Complaints, SPSRR, Box 8, Records of the WMC, RG 211, NARA.

18   W. L. Hack to W. J. Macklin, October 1, 1943, Region XII Regional/Central Files, Box 2964, Records of the WMC, RG 211, NARA. R. B. David to W. T. Williamson, May 16, 1945, Regional Central Files, 1942–1945, Records of the Region XI Office Denver, Colorado, Entry 269, Box 105, Records of the WMC, RG 211, NARA.

19   Samuel B. Hough to W. K. Hopkins, October 21, 1943, Folder: AR&SF RR-Back Pay, Box 1, Entry 196, Records of the WMC, RG 211, NARA.

20   W. H. Kirkbride to All Superintendents, September 14, 1943, Region XII Mexican Importation Committee 1943, Box 31, Series 269, Records of the WMC, RG 211, NARA.

21   José C. Gutiérrez to WMC, October 13, 1943, Folder: Mexican Workers, General Correspondence, 1943, Region XII, Box 37, Series 269, Records of the WMC, RG 211, NARA.

22   Similar accounts for requests to return to México can be found at WMC to PFE Plant Manager, August 1, 1945, Regional Central Files, Region XI, Box 106, Entry 269, Records of the WMC, RG 211, NARA. And in Mexican Track Workers General, July–December 1945, Box 2965, Series 269, Region XII, Records of the WMC, RG 211, NARA.

23   JWK. Hopkins to John P. Gifford, July 30, 1943, Folder: Mexican Nationals, Series 269, Records of the WMC, RG 211, NARA.

24   José C. Gutiérrez to WMC, October 13, 1943, Folder: Mexican Workers, General Correspondence, 1943, Region XII, Box 37, Series 269, Records of the WMC, RG 211, NARA.

25   Ernesto Galarza, "Personal and confidential memorandum on Mexican Contact Workers in the United States," Folder: México, Decimal File 1941–1949, Box 4821, General Records of the Depart of State, RG59, NARA, p. 5.

26   John D. Coates to Churchill Murray, July 9, 1945, Folder: New York Central, Entry 196, Box 6, Records of the WMC, RG 211, NARA.

27   Keith S. Rider to H. G. Pett, June 26, 1943, Divisional Office Files: "Gangs" Misc. Reports, 1943, Box 2964, Series 269, Region XII Regional/Central Files, 1942–1945, Records of the WMC, RG 211, NARA.

28   Mexican Importation Weekly Report Region 7, March 11, 1944, Folder: RRB Regional Reports, Box 8, Entry 191, Records of the WMC, RG 211, NARA.

29   John Gibson to Murray Latimer, October 9, 1945, General Subject Files, Box 16, Folder, Labor Relations, Selective Service System, General Records of the Department of Labor, RG 174, NARA.

30  E. H. Reneau, *Report of Meeting at San Francisco Consul's Office on March 13, 1945, March 14, 1945*. Folder: Mexican Track Workers Personal Injury, January 1945–June 1945, Box 2966, Series 269, Records of the WMC, RG 211, NARA.

31  William G. MacLean to Sidney O'Donoghue, August 12, 1944. Folder: Mexican Labor Decimal 850.4, Box 490, México Embassy, General Records, 1937–1949, Foreign Service Posts of the Department of State, RG 84, NARA.

32  George S. Messersmith to U.S. Secretary of State, July 16, 1942, Mexican Labor, México City Embassy, General Records, 1943, RG 84, NARA.

33  Anonymous to Honorable Secretary of Labor, July 14, 1945, Subject File of Secretary Lewis B. Schwellenbach 1945–48, Entry 26, Box 18, RG 174.

34  John J. Corson to W. E. Mitchell July 23, 1942, RRB 1942, Entry 191, Box 8, Records of the WMC, RG 211, NARA.

35  W. K. Hopkins to George E. Bodie, July 29, 1943, Folder: Mexican Nationals, Box 2901, Series 269, Records of the WMC, RG 211, NARA.

36  George W. Youngsdale to William A. Anglin, June 4, 1945, General Correspondence 1945–47, Entry 8, Box 17, Office of Labor War Food Administration, RG 224, NARA.

37  American Consulate Ciudad Juárez to Department of State, November 12, 1942, Mexico City Embassy, General Records, 1937–1949, Box 351, Entry 850.4, RG 84, NARA.

38  Cletus E. Daniel, *Chicano Workers and the Politics of Fairness: The FEPC in the Southwest, 1941–1945* (Austin: University of Texas Press, 1991), 155–56.

39  "Eliminating Employer Discrimination Hiring Practices," Folder: Eliminating Employer Discrimination Hiring Practices, Entry 110, Box 4, Records of the WMC, RG 211, NARA. American Consulate Ciudad Juárez to Department of State, November 12, 1942, México City Embassy, General Records, 1937–1949, Box 351, Entry 850.4, RG 84, NARA. Also see Daniel, *Chicano Workers*, 41–45, 75–76; and Emilio Zamora, *Claiming Rights and Righting Wrongs in Texas: Mexican Workers and Job Politics during World War II* (Arlington: Texas A&M University Press, 2009), 90.

40  Eleanor Roosevelt as quoted in *Washington Daily News,* June 1, 1945.

41  See *La prensa,* January 6, 1943; *El nacional,* May 18, 1944; *El universal,* December 31, 1945; and México City and American Embassy México City to Secretary of State September 29, 1945, Folder, México, Box 43, Entry 43, Records of the WMC, RG 211, NARA.

42  *Excelsior,* October 30, 1945.

43  *Washington Daily News,* June 12, 1945.

44  George Messersmith to U.S. State Department, July 30, 1945, Folder: México, Box 43, Entry 113, Records of the WMC, RG 211, NARA.

45  Julia J. Henderson, "Foreign Labor in the United States, 1942–1945" (PhD dissertation, University of Minnesota, 1946), 19.

46  Rafael de la Colima to Philip G. Burton, June 26, 1944, Exp. 73–0/243(72:73)/3 Embajada de México, Camacho Manuel Ávila (187), AGN.

47  Memorandum, February 26, 1945, 575.1/17, AGN.

48  Narrative Report, December 1945, Folder: AT&SF RR 1945, Box 1, Entry 196, Records of the WMC, RG 211, NARA.

49  James P. Blaisdell to W. K. Hopkins, September 4, 1943, Region XII Central Files, 1942–1945, Folder: "Various," Box 2967, Series 269, Records of the WMC, RG 211, NARA.

50　W. F. Northway to Claude L. Kemp, June 29, 1943, Region XII Central Files, 1942–1945, Folder: "Various," Box 2967, Series 269, Records of the WMC, RG 211, NARA.
51　Blaisdell to Hopkins.
52　José Luis Merino Fuentes to Churchill Murray, April 10, 1945, Folder: Northern Pacific RR, Box 6, Entry 196, Records of the WMC, RG 211, NARA.
53　Luis Fernández del Campo to Churchill Murray, January 2, 1946, Folder: Northern Pacific RR, Box 6, Entry 196, Records of the WMC, RG 211, NARA.
54　Denver, Entry 6, RG 224, NARA.
55　C. E. Herdt to H. W. Siddall, November 29, 1944, Folder: General Correspondence, Aug 1944, Box (Denver), NARA.
56　John J. Corson to W. L. Mitchell, July 23, 1942, "Difficulties Experienced in the Recruitment Program of Track Laborers for the Southern Pacific Railroad," Folder: RRB 1942, Box 8, Entry 191, Records of the WMC, RG 211, NARA.
57　George E. Bodle to Charles Paye, August 27, 1943, Box 38, Series 269, Region XII, Records of the WMC, RG 211, NARA.
58　Charles L. Hodge to WMC, January 5, 1945, Folder: Records of Bureau of Placement, Box 7, Records of the WMC, RG 211, NARA.
59　John Neily to Herbert S. Bursley, February 9, 1944. Classified Name File, Foreign Service Posts, Guadalajara Consulate, RG 84, NARA.
60　J. F. McGurk to John James Neily, March 5, 1942, Classified Name File, Foreign Service Posts, Guadalajara Consulate, RG 84; and Immigration, file, 56321/448, RG 85, NARA.
61　Gus T. Jones to R. A. Gibson, September 24, 1942. Post of the Department of Labor, México City Embassy, Folder: Mexican Labor, Box 352, RG 84, NARA.
62　Emil T. H. Bunje to Melvin S. Jacobus, September 11, 1943, Mexican Labor, México City Embassy, General Records, 1943, RG 84, NARA.
63　Ibid.

## Chapter 9. Split Families

1　"Monthly Labor Review," May 1944, Box 64, General Records of the Department of State, RG 219, NARA, p. 59.
2　Antonio L. Schmidt to A. J. Norton, October 4, 1943, Region XII Files, Folder: Mexican Workers, General Correspondence 1943, Box 37, Series 269, Records of WMC, RG 211, NARA.
3　Emory R. Worth to William K. Hopkins, July 22, 1943, Folder: Various, Box 2967, Series 269, Region XII, Central Files, 1942–1945, Records of WMC, RG 211, NARA.
4　Alston W. Sutton to Sam Kagel, January 10, 1945, Folder: Mexican Track Workers, General, July–December 1945, Box 2969, Series 269, Records of WMC, RG 211, NARA.
5　Gamio, *Hacia un México Nuevo*, 48.
6　*Southern Pacific Bulletin*, Pacific Lines, November 1944.
7　E. J. Travis to H. A. Whitlock, August 1, 1945, Folder: Region XII Central Files, 1942–1945, Records of WMC, RG 211, NARA. At other times, the solitude experienced by the young men far from their cultural environment had very tragic outcomes. At Davenport, Iowa, for example, bracero Juan Venegas Olivarez employed by the Chicago, Milwaukee, St. Paul and Pacific committed suicide by shooting himself after murdering a young woman; in WMC to Trabajo y Previsión Social, June 7,

1945, Folder: Daily File, June 1945, Entry 196, Box 3, Records of WMC, RG 211, NARA.

8   Henderson, "Foreign Labor in the United States," 5, 13.

9   "Historical Data in Connection with Employment of Mexican National Laborers Imported from Mexico," 45.

10  Robert L. Clark to J. F. Mc Gurk, January 6, 1944, Decimal File 1940–44, Box 3884, General Records of the Department of State, RG 59, NARA.

11  After the war the women's organization became the Bloque Nacional de Mujeres; see Alan Hynds, *Women in Mexico: A Past Unveiled* (Austin: University of Texas Press, 1999), 100–3.

12  A summary of war preparedness, including the participation of women in defense of México City, is found in: María Cristina Sánchez Fernández Mejorada, "El Distrito Federal Frente a la Segunda Guerra Mundial: Medidas e implicaciones," *Relaciones, Estudios de historia y sociedad* 22, no. 86 (Spring 2001): 249–92.

13  María Asunción Juárez to Manuel Ávila Camacho, January 28, 1946, 546.6/120, Camacho Manuel Ávila (187), AGN.

14  Churchill Murray to Luis Fernando del Campo, October 23, 1944, Folder: Daily File Oct 1944, Records of Bureau of Placement Records of Foreign Labor Section, Box 2, Records of WMC, RG 211, NARA.

15  Esperanza Fernández Bautista to Whom It May Concern, November 20, 1945, Folder, NPR, Entry 196, Box 6, Records of WMC, RG 211, NARA.

16  Churchill Murray to Luis Fernando del Campo, October 23, 1944, Folder: Daily File Oct 1944, Records of Bureau of Placement Records of Foreign Labor Section Box 2, Records of WMC, RG 211, NARA.

17  H. L. Carter to Director of Employment Claims, December 15, 1943, Folder: Northern Pacific RR, Box 6, Entry 196, Records of WMC, RG 211, NARA.

18  Ignacio García Téllez, "Las migraciones de braceros a los Estados Unidos de Norteamérica," *Boletín, Centro de Estudios de la Revolución Mexicana* (November 1983): 72.

19  William Royle to W. K. Hopkins, July 14, 1943, Folder: Various, Box 2967, Region XII, Regional Central Files, Records of WMC, RG 211, NARA.

20  Correspondence regarding this case can be found in Folder: AT&SF RR 1945, Box 1, Entry 196, Records of WMC, RG 211, NARA.

21  Josefa C. de Gómez to Secretaría de Relaciones Exteriores, August 10, 1943, 546.6/120, Relaciones Exteriores, Ávila Camacho, AGN.

22  Alfred T. Vollum to Wilson R. Buie, July 1, 1946, Folder: Mexican Labor, Box 38, Entry 8, RG 224, NARA.

23  The office was called Oficina Investigadora de la Situación de Mujeres y Menores Trabajadores. See Barbara A. Driscoll, "The Railroad Bracero Program of World War II," PhD dissertation, University of Notre Dame, 1980, p. 114.

24  Michael C. Meyer and William L. Sherman, *The Course of Mexican History*, 5th edition (New York: Oxford University Press, 1991), 634.

25  María Barragán to President Camacho, August 4, 1943, 546.6/120.4, Secretaría del Trabajo y Previsión Social, Manuel Ávila Camacho, AGN.

26  Taracena, *La vida en México bajo Ávila Camacho*, 225–28.

27  Ibid., 431–35.

28  Ibid., 431–34.

29  Ibid., 434.

30 Ibid., 224.

31 Ibid., 434.

32 B. C. Wallich to Mr. Knoke, June 5, 1946, 550/01/23/03, RG 82, NARA.

33 Carmen Gallegos González to Presidente Ávila Camacho, April 17, 1946, 546.6/120, Ávila Camacho, Secretaría del Trabajo y Previsión Social, AGN.

34 B. C. Wallich to Mr. Knoke, June 5, 1946, 550/0123/03, RG 82, NARA.

35 Lyndon L. Daly, "A History of the [United States] Railroad Mission in Mexico," (MS, Texas College of Arts and Industries, 1965), 78.

36 Wm. A. Whalen to Commissioner INS Philadelphia, September 23, 1942, Post of the Department of Labor, México City Embassy, Folder: Mexican Labor, Box 352, General Records of the Department of State, RG 84, NARA.

37 Messersmith to Larry Wells, August 21, 1942, Mexican Labor, México City Embassy, General Records, 1943, RG 84, NARA.

## Chapter 10. Victory and Going Home

1 *Monthly Labor Review*, June 1945, 97.

2 *Monthly Labor Review*, March 1945, 95.

3 T. F. Dixon to C. E. Denny, August 25, 1945, File 1389A-7 President's File 137Dg.4F, NPR President Files, MHS.

4 See Rural Industries and Migratory Labor Section, "Mexican Nationals Brought in for Railroad Track-Labor: A Temporary War-Emergency Measure 1943–1946," June 1946, Records of the Reports and Analysis Service, Entry 119, Box 3, Records of the WMC, RG 211, NARA.

5 Carlos Terrazas, August 31, 1945, file 5400, Box 20, N.P. Engineering WWII Equipment, 134.B.13.10F, NPR President Files, Minnesota Historical Society.

6 H. E. Stevens to F. M Wilson, November 28, 1945, Folder 1, President's Subject File 367–20, NPR President Files, MHS.

7 Record of Discussion at Meeting on Future of Mexican Railroad Labor Program, August 22, 1945, Folder: Mexican Track Labor Program 1943–46, Box 3, Entry 119, Records of the WMC, RG 211, NARA.

8 Ibid.

9 Ibid.

10 Ibid.

11 Ibid.

12 Letter from E. E. Milliman to James F. Brynes, August 15, 1945, *Brotherhood of Maintenance of Way Employees Journal*, no. 8 (1945): 9.

13 Record of Discussion, Records of the WMC, RG 211, NARA.

14 Ibid.

15 Ibid.

16 Ibid.

17 Ibid.

18 E. E. Milliman to Lewis B. Schwellenbach, October 23, 1945, Folder: Office of the Secretary Lewis B. Schwellenbach, 1945–1948, Box 18, Entry 26, Selective Service System, RG 174, NARA.

19 Record of Discussion, Records of the WMC, RG 211, NARA.

20 Rural Industries and Migratory Labor Section, Mexican Nationals Brought in for Railroad Track-Labor: A Temporary War-Emergency Measure 1943–1946, Re-

cords of the Reports and Analysis Service, Entry 119, Box 3, Records of the WMC, RG 211, NARA, p. 13.

21  Memorandum, September 13, 1945, U.S. Embassy México City, Folder: U.S. Embassy, Box 4, Entry 196, Records of the WMC, RG 211, NARA.

22  Rural Industries and Migratory Labor Section, Mexican Nationals Brought in for Railroad Track-Labor: A Temporary War-Emergency Measure 1943–1946, p. 13.

23  C. E. Denny to H. E. Stevens, September 22, 1945, Folder 1, President's Subject File 367–20, NPR President Files, MHS.

24  Churchill Murray to John D. Coates, October 3, 1945 Folder: Daily File, Box 3, Entry 196, Records of the WMC, RG 211, NARA.

25  Basilio D. y Núñez, Juan Urióstegui, and others, to Presidente, November 11, 1945, 546.6/120–1, Secretaría del Trabajo y Previsión Social, Ávila Camacho, AGN.

26  José Luis Herino Fuentes to Churchill Murray, April 2, 1945, 546.6/120–1, Relaciones Exteriores, Ávila Camacho, AGN.

27  John D. Coates to Churchill Murray, April 2, 1946, Folder: Claims of Mexican Nationals, Box 2, Entry 196, Records of the WMC, RG 211, NARA.

28  John D. Coates to Churchill Murray, February 5, 1946, Folder: General Correspondence, Aug, Entry 6, Box 13, Records of the WMC, RG 211, NARA.

29  Extracto, December 14, 1945, 546.6/120–1, Secretaría de Relaciones Exteriores, Ávila Camacho, AGN.

30  Espinoza de los Monteros to Presidente Camacho, November 11, 1945, 546.6/120–1, Secretaría del Trabajo y Previsión Social, Ávila Camacho.

31  Espinoza de los Monteros to Presidente Camacho, Nov., 12, 1945, 546.6/120–1, Secretaría del Trabajo y Previsión Social, Ávila Camacho, AGN.

32  Mexican Embassy, Memorandum, November 14, 1945, 546.6/120–1, Relaciones Exteriores, Ávila Camacho, AGN.

33  Ibid.

34  Memorándum Para Acuerdo Presidencial, November 21, 1945, 546.6/120–1, Secretaría del Trabajo y Previsión Social, Ávila Camacho, AGN.

35  James Patton to Lewis B. Schwellenbach, December 5, 1945, Folder: Mexican Railroad Workers, Box 3, Entry 62, Selective Service System, RG 174, NARA.

36  Philadelphia Council of the Railroad Workers of America to Lewis B. Schwellenbach, December 11, 1945, Folder: Mexican Railroad Workers, Box 3, Entry 62, Selective Service System, RG 174, NARA.

37  Edith T. Brener to L. B. Schwellenbach, December 7, 1945, Folder: Mexican Railroad Workers, Box 3, Entry 62, Selective Service System, RG 174, NARA.

38  Dorothy Pietzer to Secretary of Labor, December 6, 1945, Folder: Mexican Railroad Workers, Box 3, Entry 62, Selective Service System, RG 174, NARA.

39  Leslie S. Perry to Secretary of Labor, December 6, 1945, Folder: Mexican Railroad Workers, Box 3, Entry 62, Selective Service System, RG 174, NARA.

40  "Why All the Rush in Sending Mexicans Home," Railway Age, no. 26, (1945): 104.

41  "Historical Data in Connection with Employment of Mexican National Laborers Imported from Mexico," 2–43.

42  R. A. Shannon to O. Parrhysius, November 10, 1945, Chief of Special Agents, Files of Mexican Nationals Correspondence and Records, November 1945, Presidents' Subject File, 137.E.6. (F), NPR President Files, MHS.

43  Tetsuden Kashima, Judgment without Trial: Japanese American Imprisonment during World War II (Seattle: University of Washington Press, 2003), 115–16.

44  Howard A. Preston to William A. Anglin, July 30, 1945, Folder: "1945 Reports 1,"
    Records of the Office of Labor, General Correspondence, 1945–1947, Entry 8, Box
    17, RG 224, NARA.
45  C. E. Herdt to William G. MacLean, November 30, 1945, Folder: General Corre-
    spondence (1945–1947), Entry 8, Box 11, RG 224, NARA.
46  C. B. Doeabson to O. Parrhysius, December 8, 1945 Chief of Special Agents, Files
    of Mexican Nationals Correspondence and Records, November 1945, Presidents'
    Subject File, 137.E.6. (F); see also A.J. Dickerson to F. J. Gavin, November 5, 1945,
    NPR President Files, MHS.
47  G. C. Baker to A. H. Gass, November 17, 1944, Folder: General Correspondence
    August 1944, Box 13, Entry 6, RG 224, NARA.
48  Memorándum para el Sr. Presidente de la Republica, November 2, 1944,
    546.6/120, Secretaría del Trabajo y Previsión Social, Ávila Camacho, AGN.
49  Braceros Mexicanos to President, Telegram, January 5, 1946, 546.6/120, Secretaría
    del Trabajo y Previsión Social, Ávila Camacho, AGN.
50  George E. Bodle to Henry K. Anderson, August 10, 1943, Region XII, Folder: "Mexi-
    can Importation LM&U, 1943," Box 37, Series 269, Records of the WMC, RG 211,
    NARA.
51  Churchill Murray to John Dewey Coates, March 14, 1946, Records of the Bureau
    of Placement, Box 8, Entry 196, Records of the WMC, RG 211, NARA. Corruption
    thrived among labor contractors and foremen supervising agricultural braceros.
    At times the foremen entered false wages thereby pocketing some of the 10 per-
    cent due the men. The practice of paying the men with cash instead of checks
    made the braceros susceptible to unscrupulous crew leaders. William A. Anglin
    to Howard A. Preston, July 30, 1945, General Correspondence, 1945–47, Entry 8,
    Box 17, RG 224, NARA.
52  Railroad Retirement Board to Fay W. Hunter, January 26, 1945, Folder: Mexican
    Track Workers General July–December 1945, Box 269, Series 2965, Records of the
    WMC, RG 211, NARA, Region XII.
53  Frank E. Fleener to Regional Director Employment and Claims, December 28,
    1943, Folder: Atchison, Topeka, Santa Fe-Back Pay, Box 1, Entry 196, Records of
    the WMC, RG 211, NARA.
54  Luciano Espinoza Martínez to Churchill Murray, March 17, 1945, Folder: North-
    ern pacific RR, Entry 196, Box 6, Records of the WMC, RG 211, NARA.
55  Juan Ríos Balades to Whom the Matter Concerns, September 21, 1944, Folder:
    Mexican Track Workers, Box 2965, Divisional Office Files, Records of the WMC,
    RG 211, NARA.
56  Samuel B. Hough to A. W. Motley, September 30, 1943, Divisional Office Files,
    "Gangs" Misc. Reports, 1943, Box 2964, Series 269, Region XII Regional/Central
    Files, 1942–45, Records of the WMC, RG 211, NARA.
57  Silbino (Silvino) Rosas Gutiérrez to E. E. Mayo, December 11, 1945, Folder: Mexi-
    can Labor Decimal 850.4, Box 626, Foreign Service Posts of the Department of
    State, México General Records, 1937–1949, RG 84, NARA.
58  Herbert B. Murkey to Joe F. McGurk, February 19, 1943, Mexican Labor, Box 351,
    General Records, 1937–1949, RG 84, NARA.
59  William G. MacLean to Sidney E. O'Donoghue, July 1, 1945, Mexican Labor,
    México City General Records, Box 351, RG 84, NARA.
60  Sidney E. O'Donoghue to William MacLean, July 5, 1945, Mexican Labor, México
    City General Records, Box 351, RG 84, NARA.

61  Ibid.
62  Espiridión Ambriz Cruz to C. Jefe de esa Oficina, January 22, 1945. Folder: AT&SF-Back Pay, Box 1, Entry 196, Records of the WMC, RG 211, NARA.
63  Churchill Murray to Espiridión Ambriz Cruz, January 29, 1946, Folder: AT&SF-Back Pay, Box 1, Entry 196, Records of the WMC, RG 211, NARA..
64  *Monthly Review*, RRB, May 1944, Box 64, RG 219, NARA, p. 64.
65  Elizabeth C. Judson to F. N. Mortenson, July 3, 1945, Folder: 1945 Reports 1, Entry 8, Box 17, RG 224, NARA.
66  M. J. Byrnes to H. S. Steven, April 17, 1946, Folder 1, Presidents Subject File no. 367-20, NPR President Files, MHS.
67  Counsellor Office in Charge U.S. Consulate to J. F. Deasy, December 30, 1944, 850.4 Mexican Labor, Box 730, Foreign Service Posts of the Department of State, México City Embassy, General Records, RG 84, NARA.
68  Ernesto Galarza, "Personal and Confidential Memorandum on Mexican Contract Workers in the United States, August 28, 1944," Folder: México 4145-5-3145, Decimal File 1942–1949, Box 4821, General Records of the Department of State, RG 59, NARA, p. 7.
69  W. F. Northway to Claude L. Kemp, June 29, 1943, Folder: "Various," Box 2967, Series 269, Region XII Central Files, 1942–1945, Records of the WMC, RG 211, NARA; *Boletín del Archivo General de la Nación, México, Tercera Seis*, 4, no. 4 (October–December 1980), 32–33.
70  G. E. Leis to Banco del Ahorro Nacional, November 12, 1945, Folder: NP RR, Entry 196, Box 6, Records of the WMC, RG 211, NARA.
71  "Historical Data in Connection with Employment of Mexican National Laborers Imported from Mexico," 51.
72  U.S. Consulate to J. F. Deasy, December 30, 1944, 850.4 Mexican Labor, Box 730, Foreign Service Posts of the Department of State, México City Embassy, General Records, RG 84, NARA.
73  Rural Industries and Migratory Labor Section, "Mexican Nationals Brought in for Track Labor: A Temporary War-Emergency Measure 1943–1946," p. 14.
74  Chief of Special Agents-Files of Mexican Nationals Correspondence, January, 20-3-, 1946, NPR President Files, MHS.
75  Memorandum, October 19, 1945, 850.4 Mexican Labor, Box 730, Foreign Service Posts of the Department of State, México City Embassy, General Records, RG 84, NARA.
76  Vice President in Charge of Operations and General Manager SP 1947, "Historical Data in Connection with Employment of Mexican National Laborers Imported from Mexico," California State Railroad Museum Library, Sacramento, California, p. 53.
77  Ibid., 53–54.
78  Memorandum, October 19, 1945, 850.4 Mexican Labor, Box 730, Foreign Service Posts of the Department of State, México City Embassy, General Records, RG 84, NARA.
79  "Historical Data in Connection with Employment of Mexican National Laborers Imported from Mexico," 52.
80  Thomas M. Healy to Robert S. Mac Farlane, nd, President's Subject File no., 367-20-1, NPR President Files, MHS.
81  L. W. William to GNRR, April 17, 1957, President's Subject File 16187-A, NPR President Files, MHS.

82   F. M. Wilson to Herman Landon, October 4, 1945, 850.4 Mexican Labor, Box 730,
     Foreign Service Posts of the Department of State, México City Embassy, General
     Records, RG 84, NARA.
83   "Historical Data in Connection with Employment of Mexican National Laborers
     Imported from Mexico," 202.

## Chapter 11. Forgotten Railroad Soldiers

1   Churchill Murray to John Dewey Coates, August 14, 1945, Folder: Daily File Aug.,
    1945, Box 3, Entry 196, Records of the WMC, RG 211, NARA.
2   Churchill Murray to John Dewey Coates, August 14, 1945, Folder: Daily File Aug.,
    1945, Box 3, Entry 196, Records of the WMC, RG211, NARA.
3   Lizzie Collingham, *The Taste of War: World War II and the Battle for Food* (New
    York: Penguin Press, 2012), 469.
4   Sidney O'Donoghue to William G. Mac Lean, September 20, 1944, Foreign Office
    Posts of The Department of State, México City Embassy, General Records of the
    Department of State, 1939–1948, RG 84, NARA.
5   Department of State to George S. Messersmith, May 9, 1944 Folder: Mexican La-
    bor decimal 850.4, Box 488, Foreign Service Posts of Department of State, México
    General Records, 1937–1949, México General Records, 1937–1949, Decimal 850.4,
    General Records of the Department of State, RG 84, NARA.
6   Guadalupe Montoya Gonzales to D. S. Colby, December 7, 1948, NP 134.B.11.4 (f),
    WWII Employment, Chief of Labor Relations, NPR, MHS.
7   Herminio Ramírez to N.P. Railway Company, December 16, 1947, N.P, 134.B11.4 (f),
    WWII Employment, Chief of Labor Relations, NPR, MHS.
8   Northern Pacific Railway Company form letter NP, n.d., 134.B.11.4 (F), WWII Em-
    ployment, Chief of Labor Relations, NPR, MHS.
9   Secretaría de Hacienda y Crédito Publico to Banco del Ahorro Nacional, June
    1945, 546.1/120–4, Secretaría de Gobernación, Ávila Camacho, AGN.
10  Extracto, June 15, 1945, 546.1/120–4, Secretaría de Gobernación, Ávila Camacho,
    AGN.
11  Department of State to George S. Messersmith, May 9, 1944, Folder: Mexican
    Labor 850.4, Box 488, Foreign Service Posts of the Department of State, México
    General Records, 1937–1949, General Records of the Department of State, RG 84,
    NARA.
12  David Richard Lessard, "Agrarianism and Nationalism: Mexico and the Bracero
    Program, 1942–1947" (PhD dissertation, Tulane University, 1984), 187.
13  Ibid., 114.
14  Dispatch No. 771, April 26, 1948, Folder: Mexican Labor Railway Workers, 1948,
    Box 825, México City Embassy General Records, General Records of the Depart-
    ment of State, RG 84, NARA.
15  M. L. Stafford to William G. MacLean, August 8, 1947, Folder: 1947, 850.2–850–4
    Box 783, Foreign Service Post of the Department of State, México City Embassy,
    General Records of the Department of State, RG 84, NARA.
16  Catalina Montero de Salazar to War Food Administration, February 23, 1946,
    Folder: AT&SF Back Pay, Box 1, Entry 196, Records of the WMC, RG 211, NARA.
17  Mrs. Leonardo Reyna to American Consul, January 5, 1949, Folder: Mexican La-

bor Railroad Workers, 1948, Box 825, Foreign Service Posts of the Department of State, México City Embassy General Records, General Records of the Department of State, RG 84, NARA.

18  Railroad Retirement Board and Benefits for Mexican Railroad Workers under Agreement of April 29, 1943. December 18, 1943, Folder: General Department of State Records, Box 3884, General Records of the Department of State, RG 59, NARA.

19  Willard F. Barber, Memorandum of Conversation, March 22, 1950, Department of State, Folder: México General Records, 1941–1949, Box 122, General Records of the Department of State, RG 84, NARA.

20  P. J. Glaessner to Mr. Knoke, July 1946, "Annual Report of the Bank of Mexico," Folder: 550/01/23/03, RG 82, NARA.

21  Confidential Memorandum of Conversation, May 4, 1950, Department of State, Folder: México General Records, 1941–1949, Box 122, General Records of the Department of State, RG 84, NARA.

22  Horace H. Smith to Earl B. Wixcey, April 14, 1950, Department of State Records, 1950–1954, Box 4403, General Records of the Department of State, RG 59, NARA..

23  The agreement became known as the Mexican Non-Agricultural Workers: Termination of Agreement of April 29, 1943, and Refund of Deductions from Salaries under the Railroad Retirement Act, November 15, 1946.

24  Memorandum of Conversation, January 5, 1946, Foreign Posts of the Department of State, México City Embassy, General Records, 1937–1949, Box 729, Series 850.4 Mexican Labor, General Records of the Department of State, RG 84, NARA.

25  Paul J. Reveley to Secretary of State, August 1, 1946, México General Records, 1937–1949, Decimal 850.4 Mexican Labor Box 626, General Records of the Department of State, RG 84, NARA.

26  American Embassy, México City to the Department of State, Telegram, January 4, 1954, Folder: 811.06 (M)/3–2654, Box 4407, Department of State Records, General Records of the Department of State, RG 59, NARA.

27  Memorandum of Conversation, August 8, 1946, México General Records, 1937–1949, Decimal 850.4 Mexican Labor Box 626, General Records of the Department of State, RG 84, NARA.

28  Enrique Martínez to Gamboa, April 15, 2002, in the author's possession. See also Department of State Records, 1950–1954, Box 4403, General Records of the Department of State, RG 59, NARA. See Driscoll, *Tracks North*, 166.

29  Churchill Murray to John Dewey Coates, August 14, 1945, Folder: Daily File Aug. 1945, Box 3, Entry 196, Records of the WMC, RG 211, NARA.

30  Antonio Toledo Martínez to Presidente, February 29, 1944, 546.6/120, Secretaría del Trabajo y Previsión Social, Ávila Camacho, AGN. García Téllez, "La migración de braceros a los estados unidos de norte América," 69.

31  Antonio Toledo Martínez to Presidente, February 29, 1944, 546.6/120, Secretaría del Trabajo y Previsión Social, Ávila Camacho, AGN.

32  Manuel Gamio to Presidente Camacho, November 22, 1944, 546/120.33, Secretaría del Trabajo y Previsión Social, Ávila Camacho, AGN.

33  Barberton Chamber of Commerce to President of México, March 21, 1946, "Hands Across the Border," 546.6/120.6, Secretaría del Trabajo y Previsión Social, Ávila Camacho, AGN, pp. 1–6.

34  New York Central Railroad, news clipping, Foreign Office Posts of the Department of State, México City Embassy, General Records, 1939–1948, General Records of the Department of State, RG 84, NARA.

35  See Ernesto Galarza, *Strangers in Our Fields* (Washington, D.C.: Fund for the Republic, Joint United States–México Trade Union Committee, 1956).

36  "Historical Data in Connection with Employment of Mexican National Laborers Imported from Mexico," 67–68.

37  Vice President in Charge of Operations and General Manager SP 1947, "Historical Data in Connection with Employment of Mexican National Laborers Imported from Mexico," California State Railroad Museum Library, Sacramento, California, p. 68.

38  Office of the President to C. E. Denny, March 29, 1947, Folder 1: President's Subject File 367–20, NPR President Files, MHS.

39  Rural Industries and Migratory Labor Section, Mexican Nationals Brought in for Railroad Track-Labor: A Temporary War-Emergency Measure 1943–1946, Records of the Reports and Analysis Service, Entry 119, Box 3, Records of the WMC, RG 211, NARA, p. 12.

40  "Corrido de los trenes especiales," *El Mexicano* (January 1945), Records of the War Food Administration, RG 224, NARA, p.4, Washington, D.C., 1945.

41  Sidney E. O'Donoghue to Secretary of State, November 19, 1943, Mexican Labor, México City Embassy, General Records, 1943, General Records of the Department of State, RG 84, NARA.

42  F. Hunter to H. R. Harnish, March 30, 1945, Folder: Mexican track Workers General, July–December 1945, Box 2965, Records of the WMC, RG 211, NARA.

43  George I. Lewis to SP Company, February 14, 1945, Folder: Mexican Track Workers General, July–December 1945, Box 2965, Series 269, Records of the WMC, RG 211, NARA, Region XII.

44  F. W. Hunter to Sam Kagel, January 29, 1945, Folder: Mexican Track Workers General, July–December 1945, Box 2965, Series 269, Region XII, Records of the WMC, RG 211, NARA. The 1920 U.S. census record confirms Cardona's U.S. citizenship.

45  Ibid.

46  Ibid.

47  F. W. Bartles to H.E. Stevens, March 16, 1946, President's Subject File, No 367–20, Folder 1, NPR President Files, MHS.

48  W. W. Judson to C. E. Denny, April 24, 1947, President's Subject File, No 367-20, Folder 1, NPR President Files, MHS.

49  M. J. Byrne to H. E. Stevens, January 17, 1946, Folder 1, President's Subject File 367-20, NPR President Files, MHS.

50  Cady to White, September 1, 1950, Folder: 811.06 (M)/9-150, México City Embassy General Records, General Records of the Department of State, RG 84, NARA.

51  J. Elmer Monroe, *Railroad Men and Wages* (Washington, D.C.: Bureau of Railway Economics Association of American Railroads), 1947, 76.

52  M. J. Brynes to H. E. Stevens, February 7, 1946. President's Subject File no., 367-20-1, NPR President Files, MHS.

53  Joseph B. Eastman, Director, Office of Defense Transportation, Railroad Manpower Campaign, Fact Sheet, Railroad Recruitment Drive, Box 63, Series 33, Office of the Director, Division of Transport Personnel, 1942-19446, RG 219, NARA.

54  WMC to Dr. Joseph Spoto, September 17, 1945, Folder: Daily File September 45, Records of Foreign Labor File, Entry 195, Box 3, Records of the WMC, RG 211, NARA.

## Epilogue

1  The Binational Bracero Proa Alliance organized in 1998 such activist groups, among others, as the Binational Union of Braceros, to recover the workers' unpaid earnings. Decades earlier, during the 1940s, the National Alliance of Mexican Braceros in the United States (Alianza de Braceros Nacionales de México en Los Estados Unidos de Norteamérica) organized to work on behalf of braceros in México and the United States.

2  Bob Egelko, "Braceros Suit against U.S., Mexico Tossed Judge Says 1940s Case Not Covered by Law," *San Francisco Chronicle*, August 29, 2002. I drew from articles in various newspapers that carried this news when the court announced its decision on the bracero lawsuit.

3  México later offered compensation to all braceros employed from 1942 through 1964. See "Declaration of Stella María González Cicero, Head of the National Archives of the Federal Government of Mexico," Señorío Ramírez Cruz, Leocadio de la Rosa, Liborio Santiago Pérez, Felipe Nava, Ignacio Macías, and Rafael Nava, on behalf of themselves and all others similarly situated v. United States of America, et al., United District Court Northern District of California, 2002, pp. 16–17.

4  Ibid.

# Bibliography

## Manuscripts and Archival Sources

Ávila, Camacho Manuel (187). Archivo General de la Nación (AGN). México, D.F.

California Railroad Museum Library. Sacramento State Library. Sacramento, California.

Chinese Exclusion Files. Oregon District. Records of the District Courts of the U.S., 1839–1992. National Archives and Records Administration (NARA). Region 12. Seattle, Washington.

Final Accountability, Topaz Japanese American Relocation Center Digital Collection. Digital Collections. Utah State University Library. Logan, Utah.

Foreign Service Posts. *General Records of the Embassy in México City, Record* Group *84.* NARA. College Park, Maryland.

General Records of the Department of State. Record Group 59. NARA. College Park, Maryland.

Lawrence Cardoso Papers. American Heritage Collection. University of Wyoming. Laramie, Wyoming.

Mexican Heritage Project. Arizona Historical Society. Tucson, Arizona.

Northern Pacific Railway (NP), Chief of Labor Relations. Minnesota Historical Society (MHS). Saint Paul, Minnesota.

NP General Manager. MHS. Saint Paul, Minnesota.

NP President Files. MHS. Saint Paul, Minnesota.

Office of Defense Transportation. Record Group 219. NARA. College Park, Maryland.

Office of Labor War Food Administration. Record Group 224. NARA. College Park, Maryland.

Records of the Federal Reserve System. Record Group 82. NARA, College Park, Maryland.

Records of the U.S. Employment Service (USES). Record Group 183. NARA. College Park, Maryland.

Records of the War Manpower Commission (WMC). Record Group 211. NARA. College Park, Maryland.

Records of the WMC. Record Group 211. NARA. Region XII. San Bruno, California.

Secretaría del Trabajo y Previsión Social (210). AGN. México, D.F.

Selective Service System. Record Group 147. NARA. Region 11. Seattle, Washington.

Southern Pacific Railroad Museum Library. Sacramento State Library. Sacramento, California.

State of California. California Death Index, 1940–1997. Sacramento, California.

U.S. Bureau of the Census. Sixteenth Census of the United States, 1940. NARA. College Park, Maryland.

U.S. Congress. House of Representatives. Hearings before the Committee on Immigration and Naturalization. Immigration from Countries of the Western Hemisphere. 70th Congress, 1st session, February 21 to April 5, 1928.

U.S. Congress. House of Representatives. Hearings before the Committee on Immigration and Naturalization. Western Hemisphere Immigration. 71st Congress, 2nd session, January 28, 1930.

## Books

Barajas, Manuel. *The Xaripu Community. Across Borders: Labor Migration, Community, and Family.* Notre Dame: University of Notre Dame, 2009.

Calavita, Kitty. *Inside the State: The Bracero Program, Immigration, and the INS.* New York: Routledge, 1992.

Chan, Sucheng. *Asian Americans: An Interpretive History.* Boston: Twayne Publishers, 1991.

Cohen, Deborah. *Braceros.* Chapel Hill: University of North Carolina Press, 2011.

Collingham, Lizzie. *The Taste of War: World War II and the Battle for Food.* New York: Penguin Press, 2012.

Committee for the Protection of the Foreign Born. *Our Badge of Infamy: A Petition to the United Nations on the Treatment of the Mexican Immigrant.* New York: Committee for the Protection of the Foreign Born, 1959.

Daniel, Cletus E. *Chicano Workers and the Politics of Fairness: The FEPC in the Southwest, 1941–1945.* Austin: University of Texas Press, 1991.

Driscoll, Barbara A. *The Tracks North: The Railroad Bracero Program of World War II.* Austin: University of Texas Press, 1999.

Durand, Jorge. *Rostros y rastros: Entrevistas a trabajadores migrantes en Estados Unidos.* San Luis: Colegio de San Luis, 2002.

Edwards, Thomas G., and Carlos A. Schwantes. *Experiences in a Promised Land: Essays in Pacific Northwest History.* Seattle: University of Washington Press, 1986.

Farrington, S. Kip, Jr. *Railroads at War.* New York: Samuel Curl, 1944.

Fernández, Luis. *Los Braceros.* México City: Secretaria de Previsión Social y Trabajo, 1946.

Ficker, Sandra Kuntz, and Paolo Riguzzi. *Ferrocarriles y vida económica en México (1850–1950).* Austin: University of Texas Press, 1999.

Galarza, Ernesto. *Strangers in Our Fields.* Washington, D.C.: Fund for the Republic, Joint United States México Trade Union Committee, 1956.

Gamboa, Erasmo. *Mexican Labor and World War II: Braceros in the Pacific Northwest, 1942–1947.* Austin: University of Texas Press, 1990.

——, ed. *Voces Hispanas / Hispanic Voices of Idaho: Excerpts from the Idaho Hispanic Oral History Project.* Boise: Idaho Humanities Council, 1992.

Gamio, Manuel. *Hacia un México nuevo: Problemas sociales.* México City: Instituto Indigenista Nacional, 1935.

——. *Mexican Immigration to the United States: A Study of Human Migration and Adjustment.* New York: Dover Publications, Inc., 1971.

——. *Mexican Immigration to the United States.* Chicago: University of Chicago Press, 1930.

Goldfield, David, Carl Abbott, Virginia D. Anderson, Jo Ann E. Argensinger, Peter H. Argensinger, William L. Barney, and Robert M. Weir. *The American Journey.* Second edition. Upper Saddle River, New Jersey: Prentice Hall, 2000.

Gregory, Chester W. *Women in Defense Work during World War II: An Analysis of the Labor Problem and Women's Rights.* New York: Exposition Press, 1974.

Hertel, D. W. *History of the Brotherhood of Maintenance of Way Employees.* Washington, D.C.: Ransdell, 1955.

Hoffman, Abraham. *Unwanted Mexican Americans in the Great Depression: Repatriation Pressures, 1929–1939.* Tucson: University of Arizona Press, 1974.

Hofsommer, Don L. *The Southern Pacific, 1901–1985.* College Station: Texas A&M University Press, 1986.

Hynds, Alan. *Women in Mexico: A Past Unveiled.* Austin: University of Texas Press, 1999.

Jones, Harry E. *Railroad Wages and Labor Relations, 1900–1952.* New York: Bureau of Information of the Eastern Railways, 1953.

Jones, Robert C. *Mexican War Workers in the United States: The Mexico-United States Manpower Recruiting Program and Its Operation.* Washington, D.C.: Pan American Union, 1945.

Kashima, Tetsuden. *Judgment without Trial: Japanese American Imprisonment during World War II.* Seattle: University of Washington Press, 2003.

Labor Research Association. *Labor and the War: Labor Fact Book 6.* New York: International Publishers, 1943.

Majka, Linda C., and Theo J. Majka. *Farmworkers and the State.* Philadelphia: Temple University, 1982.

Martínez, Oscar J., ed. *U.S.-Mexico Borderlands: Historical and Contemporary Perspectives.* Wilmington: Scholarly Resources, 1996.

McCarl, Robert. *Latinos in Idaho Celebrando Cultura.* Boise: Idaho Humanities Council, 2003.

Meyer, Michael C., and William L. Sherman. *The Course of Mexican History.* Fifth edition. New York: Oxford University Press, 1991.

Mize, Ronald L., and Alicia C. S. Swords. *Consuming Mexican Labor: From the Bracero Program to NAFTA.* Ontario: University of Toronto Press, 2011.

Molina, Natalia. *How Race Is Made in America: Immigration, Citizenship, and the Historical Power of Racial Scripts.* Oakland: University of California Press, 2014.

Monroe, Elmer J. *Railroad Men and Wages.* Washington, D.C.: Bureau of Railway Economics Association of American Railroads, 1947.

Ngai, Mae M. *Impossible Subjects: Illegal Aliens and the Making of Modern America.* Princeton: Princeton University Press, 2004.

Northrup, Herbert R. *Organized Labor and the Negro.* New York: Harper and Brothers, 1944.

Ourada, Patricia K. *Migrant Workers in Idaho.* Boise: Boise State University, 1979.

Pelly, John J. "American Railroads in and After the War." In *Transportation: War and Postwar.* Edited by G. Lloyd Wilson. Philadelphia: Academy of Political Social Science, 1943.

Pérez, García Sebastián. *Rostros y rastros: Entrevistas a trabajadores migrantes en Estados Unidos.* San Luis Potosí: El Colegio de San Luis, 2002.

Pomeroy, Earl. *The Pacific Slope: A History of California, Oregon, Washington, Idaho, Utah, and Nevada.* Seattle: University of Washington Press, 1973.

Risher, Howard W., Jr. *The Negro in the Railroad Industry.* Philadelphia: University of Pennsylvania Press, 1971.

Rosas, Ana Elizabeth. *Abrazando el Espíritu: Bracero Families Confront the US-Mexico Border.* Oakland: University of California Press, 2014.

Rose, Joseph R. *American Wartime Transportation.* New York: Thomas Y. Crowell Company, 1953.

Schwantes, Carlos A. *Railroad Signatures across the Pacific Northwest.* Seattle: University of Washington Press, 1993.

Smith, Michael M. *The Mexicans in Oklahoma*. Norman: University of Oklahoma Press, 1980.

Stephen, Lynn. *Transborder Lives: Indigenous Oaxacans in Mexico, California, and Oregon*. Durham: Duke University Press, 2007.

Stan, Kevin. *Endangered Dreams: The Great Depression in California*. New York: Oxford University Press, 1996.

Taracena, Alfonso. *La vida en México bajo Ávila Camacho*. Mexico City: Editorial Jus, 1976.

Taylor, Paul S. *Mexican Labor in the United States: Bethlehem, Pennsylvania*. Berkeley: University of California Press, 1931.

Torres, Blanca. *Historia de la Revolución Mexicana, 1940–1952: México en la segunda guerra mundial*. México: El Colegio de México, 1979.

Vásquez, Carlos, and Manuel García y Griego, eds. *Mexican U.S. Relations Conflict and Convergence*. Los Angeles: University of California, 1983.

Whetten, Nathan L. *Rural Mexico*. Chicago: University of Chicago Press, 1948.

Whitney, A. F. *Railroad Rules: Wage Movement in the United States, 1944–45–46*. Cleveland: Brotherhood of Railroad Trainmen, 1946.

———. *Wartime Wages and Railroad Labor: A Report on the 1942–43 Wage Movement of the Transportation Brotherhoods*. Cleveland: Brotherhood of Railroad Trainmen, 1944.

Wyman, Mark. *Hobos Bindlestiffs, Fruit Tramps, and the Harvesting of the West*. New York: Hill and Wang, 2010.

Zamora, Emilio. *Claiming Rights and Righting Wrongs in Texas: Mexican Workers and Job Politics during World War II*. Arlington: Texas A&M University Press, 2009.

### Articles

Cuff, Robert D. "United States Mobilization and Railroad Transportation: Lessons in Coordination and Control, 1917–1945." *Journal of Military History* 53, no. 1 (January 1989).

Fernando, Saúl Alanís Enciso. "Nos vamos al norte: La emigración de San Luis Potosí a Estados Unidos entre 1920–1940." *Migraciones Internacionales, Tijuana: Colegio de la frontera norte* 2, no. 4 (July–December 2002).

Gabriel, W. Lasker. "Environmental Growth Factors and Selective Migration." *Human Biology* 24 no. 4 (1952): 262–89.

Gamboa, Erasmo. "Mexican American Railroaders in an American City: Pocatello, Idaho." In *Latinos in Idaho Celebrando Cultura*. Edited by Robert McCarl, 35–43. Boise: Idaho Humanities Council, 2003.

Gilmore, Ray, and Gladys W. Gilmore. "The Bracero Program in California." *Pacific Historical Review* 32, no. 1 (1963): 265–82.

Hediger, Ernest S. "The Impact of War on Mexico's Economy." *Foreign Policy Reports* 19 (June): 78–87.

Hewitt, William L. "Mexican Workers in Wyoming during World War II." *Annals of Wyoming* 54 (1982): 20–33.

Hu-DeHart, Evelyn. "Immigrants to a Developing Society: The Chinese in Northern Mexico." *Journal of Arizona History* 21 (Autumn 1980): 49–86.

Ichioka, Yuje. "Japanese Immigrant Labor Contractors and the Northern Pacific and

Great Northern Railroad Companies 1898–1907." *Labor History* 21 (Summer 1980): 325–29.

Landis, Paul H. "Rural Population Trends in Washington." *Washington State College of Agriculture Experimental Station Bulletin* (Pullman, Washington), no. 333 (July 1936).

Lasker, Gabriel Ward. "Environmental Growth and Selective Migration." *Human Biology: An International Record of Human Biology* 24, no. 4 (December 1952): 262–89.

Mathes, Michael. "The Two Californias during World War II." *California History Quarterly* 44, no. 4 (1965): 323–31.

Mercier, Laurie. "I Worked for the Railroad: Oral Histories of a Montana Railroader, 1910–1950." *Montana* 33, no. 3 (1983): 34–59.

Moreno, Luisa. "Caravans of Sorrow: Noncitizen Americans of the Southwest." In *Between Two Worlds: Mexican Immigrants in the United States*. Edited by David G. Gutierrez, 121–24. Wilmington: Scholarly Resources, 1996.

Parks, M. "A New Pattern in International Wartime Collaboration." *State Department Bulletin* (August 13, 1944): 160–65.

Pfeiffer, David A. "Riding the Rails up Paper Mountain: Researching Railroad Records in the National Archives." *Prologue* 29, no. 1 (1997): 1–3.

Potter, Michael F. "The History of Bedbug Management." *Thermal Remediation, Pest Control Technology* (August 2008): 1–8.

Reisler, Mark. "The Mexican Immigrant in the Chicago Area during the 1920s." *Journal of the Illinois State Historical Society* 66 (1973): 144–58.

Sánchez Fernández Mejorada, María Cristina. "El Distrito Federal Frente a la Segunda Guerra Mundial: Medidas e implicaciones." *Relaciones, estudios de historia y sociedad* 22, no. 86 (2001): 249–92.

Sherman, Janann, "'They Either Need These Women or They Do Not': Margret Chase and the Fight for Regular Status for Women in the Military." *Journal of Military History* 54, no. 1 (January 1990): 47–78.

"The Southern Pacific-Railroad Giant," *Look* 9, no. 26 (December 25, 1945): 23–27.

"Summer Brings the Mexican." *Commonwealth* 48 (July 2, 1948): 277.

Taylor, Paul S. "Increases of Mexican Labor in Certain Industries in the United States." *Monthly Labor Review* 32 (January 1931): 257–63.

Téllez, Ignacio García. "La migración de braceros a los Estados Unidos de Norte América." *Boletín centro de estudios de la Revolución Mexicana* (November 1983): 72.

Thompson, Gregory L. "The Interwar Response of the Southern Pacific Company and the Atchison, Topeka, and Santa Fe Railway to Passenger Road Competition." *Business and Economic History* 25, no. 1 (Fall 1996): 283–93.

Valentine, Frances Wadsworth. "Women's Emergency Farm Service on the Pacific Coast in 1943." *Bulletin of the Women's Bureau*, no. 204 (1945): 1–35.

## Dissertations and Other Unpublished Papers

Daly, Lyndon I. "A History of the [United States] Railroad Mission in Mexico." MS thesis. Texas College of Arts and Industries, 1965.

Driscoll, Barbara A. "The Railroad Bracero Program of World War II." PhD dissertation, University of Notre Dame, 1980.

Garcilazo, Jeffery Marcos, "Traqueros: Mexican Railroad Workers in the United States, 1830–1930." PhD dissertation. University of California, Santa Barbara, 1995.

Henderson, Julia J. "Foreign Labor in the United States, 1942–1945." PhD dissertation. University of Minnesota, 1946.

Lessard, David Richard. "Agrarianism and Nationalism: Mexico and the Bracero Program, 1942–1947." PhD dissertation. Tulane University, 1984.

Railroad Retirement Board. "Annual Reports for the Fiscal Year Ending June 1940–1945."

U.S. Immigration Commission. "Immigrants in Industries." Immigration Hearings, Reports of the Immigration Commission. Washington, D.C., 1911.

Vice President in Charge of Operations and General Manager, Southern Pacific 1947. "Historical Data in Connection with Employment of Mexican National Laborers Imported from Mexico." California State Museum. Pp. 1–65.

White, William Thomas. "A History of Railroad Workers in the Pacific Northwest, 1883–1934." PhD dissertation. University of Washington, 1980.

## Newspapers and Periodicals

*Brotherhood of Maintenance of Way Journal* [Detroit]
*Historia Mexicana* [México City]
*Railway Age*
*Railway Engineering and Maintenance*
*Southern Pacific Bulletin*

## Interviews

Arnulfo Alvarez. October 28, 2000. Pocatello, Idaho.
Eulalio Partida. March 6, 1997. Pasco, Washington.
Fernando Barba González. June 11, 2001. Pocatello, Idaho.
Frank Hernández. August 8, 2001. Tacoma, Washington.
Isidro Berones. April 8, 1997. Walla Walla, Washington.
Jesús Briones Flores. June 12, 2001. Pocatello, Idaho.
Juan R. Salinas. July 29, 1972. Toppenish, Washington.
Mike Rivera. June 12, 2001. Pocatello, Idaho.
Toribio Armijo. March 6, 1997. Pasco, Washington.
Vicky Sierra. June 11, 2001. Pocatello, Idaho.

# Index

accidents: work-related, 114–17, 121, 124, 153–54, 190; other causes, 120, 136

Addison-Miller Commissary, 131

African Americans, 16–17, 28–29, 57–59, 63, 138; "great migration" and movement of, 16–17, 63

Agricultural Credit Bank, 67

agriculture, expansion of production, 11, 44; in the Pacific Northwest, 3, 11, 50; production in Mexico, 42; and railroads, 4, 11, 23, 51

Alaska fishing industry, 21, 46

Alfaro, Esperanza Hernández de, 152

Alfaro, Gilberto T., 132

Alfaro Ramírez, Francisco, 152

Alianza de Braceros Nacionales de México en Los Estados Unidos de Norteamérica, 223n1

Almaraz, Enrique, 133

American Federation of Labor (AFL), 13, 16–17, 169

Amézquita, Manuel, 167

anti-Mexican sentiment, 22, 32, 41, 58–59, 138–42, 168; and violence, 41, 59, 61, 142

Asiatic Barred Zone Act, 46, 66

Association of American Railroads (AAR), 36, 52, 105, 163, 165

Association of Railway Executives, 17, 77

Asunción Juárez, María, 151

Atchison, Topeka and Santa Fe Railway (AT&SF), 52, 66, 89, 153–54, 161

Ávila, Consuela Méndez de, 151

Ávila, Jesús Enrique, 151

Ávila Camacho, Manuel, 39–40, 44, 65, 183, 187

Ávila Vera, G., 122

Aza, Eugenio, 142

back pay, 176, 181, 184–85, 198–200

Bahamians, 150, 201

Balades, Juan Ríos, 174

Baldwin Locomotive Works, 44, *fig. 13*

Baltimore and Ohio Railroad (B&O), 4, 162, 166

Banco de Crédito Agrícola, 67

Banco del Ahorro Nacional, 67, 72

banking, 172–73, 176; savings accounts, 172–75, 180–81, 199. *See also* wage deductions: for savings plan

Beltrán, León, 133

binational agreements, 4–5, 39–41, 47, 62, 68, 76, 113

Binational Bracero Proa Alliance, 223n1

Boland Agency, 24

bonds, departure, 69, 93, 106–07; forfeiture risk, 177–81, 184, 193, *fig. 12*

border crossings, 23, 73–74, 145, 171–72

Border Patrol, 46

Bracero Farm Workers Fund, 67

braceros: in agriculture, 47–48, 76–77, 167, 190, 192, 197; back pay, 176, 181, 184–85, 198–200; communication with family, 121, 145–46, 152; depart for U.S., 66, 72–74, 159, *fig. 6*; dismissals of, 122, 136–37, 148; forerunners of, 46–47; as ice pullers, 112, 143–44, 162, 166; identification of, 71–72, 178, *fig. 12*; from indigenous backgrounds, 109–10, 139, 188–89; leisure time, 68, 147–49; litigation, ix, 8, 116, 124, 138, 154, 190, 198–200, 223nn1,2,3; mentoring by previous immigrants, 107; and patriotism, 72–73, 181, 197; postwar detainment of, 164–67, 170–71; recruiting begins, 46–50; renewal of contracts, 8, 93, 152, 159, 161–62, 193, 199; retirement fund, 185–87; selection process, 70–72, 109–10; spokesmen/leaders, 77, 125; by state, 191*table*; unemployment, 183, 196

Bravo, Aquileo, 167

bribery and patronage, 43, 70–71, 127, 172, 218

Brotherhood of Maintenance of Way Employees (BMWE), 15, 29, 35, 63, 77, 106. *See also* discrimination: in unions

bus industry, 28, 33–34

Calavita, Kitty, 7

California Highway Commission, 26

California Shipbuilding Corporation, 40

Camacho, Manuel Ávila, 39–40, 44, 65, 183, 187

Ingram Content Group UK Ltd.
Milton Keynes UK
UKHW010646220323
418970UK00006B/357